Strategies in Reading A

Ethel Grodzins Romm

12.00

HARCOURT BRACE JOVANOVICH, PUBLISHERS

Orlando	New York	Chicago
San Diego	Atlanta	Dallas

ISBN 0-15-337118-8

Acknowledgments

For permission to reprint copyrighted material, grateful acknowledgment is made to the following sources:

Mary Evans Andrews: "Secret Stars" by Mary Evans Andrews, from *Cricket* Magazine, April 1980. Copyright (c) 1980 by Mary Evans Andrews.

Archie Comic Publications, Inc.: "Archie" cartoons from 11/11/75, 5/16/78, 4/26/79 and 11/11/80. (c) 1983 by Archie Comic Publications, Inc.

Isaac Asimov: "Santa Claus Gets a Coin" by Isaac Asimov from *Boys' Life* Magazine, December 1975. Copyright (c) 1975 by the Boy Scouts of America.

Berkshire Traveller Press: From *A Spy at Tyconderoga* by Calvin Fisher. Published by Berkshire Traveller Press. Copyright (c) 1975 by Calvin Fisher.

The Black Scholar Press: "Haiku" from *I've Been a Woman* by Sonia Sanchez.

Thomas A. Blumenfeld, M.D.: "Muscles and Weight Training" by Thomas A. Blumenfeld, from *Science World* Magazine. Copyright (c) 1982 by Thomas A. Blumenfeld.

Boy Scouts of America: Selections taken from *Boys' Life* Magazine: from "Skateboarding: Homemade Safety," November 1978 and "When the Music Stops — Fix It Yourself," December 1978 by Ken Fulton. Copyright (c) 1978 by Boy Scouts of America.

Curtis Brown, Ltd.: "Genevieve Trueheart, Man's Best Friend" from *Over the Horizon and Around the World in Fifteen Stories* by James MacNamee. Copyright (c) 1960 by James MacNamee.

Chicago Tribune: From "Is That You, Otis?" by Marianne Taylor from the *Chicago Tribune*, July 14, 1981. "One More Mountain" by Anne Keegan from the *Chicago Tribune*, July 10, 1981. Copyright (c) 1981 by Chicago Tribune.

Cobblestone Publishing, Inc.: "Clara Driscoll's Rescue Mission" by V. Kathryn Oler from *Cobblestone*, March 1982 issue: *Remember the Alamo! March 6, 1836.* Excerpt from "The Greatest Little Show on Earth" by Linda Andre from *Cobblestone*, August 1982 issue: *The Circus Comes to America.* Copyright © 1982 by Cobblestone Publishing, Inc., Peterborough, NH 03458.

Consumer Reports: From *Consumer Reports*, June 1981. Copyright 1981 by Consumers Union of United States, Inc., Mount Vernon, NY 10550.

Roger J. Crain: From "Super Sniffers of the Sea" by Roger J. Crain from *Cricket* Magazine, November 1980. Copyright (c) 1980 by Roger J. Crain.

Peggy Simson Curry and Boys' Life Magazine: "Trumpet in the Treetops" by Peggy Simson Curry from *Boys' Life* Magazine, April 1982.

John Curtin: "The General's Bugle Call" by John Curtin from *Boys' Life* Magazine, April 1979.

Delacorte Press/Seymour Lawrence: From *Tangles* by Marie-Louise Wallin, translated from the Swedish by Gerry Bothmer. Translation copyright (c) 1977 by Dell Publishing Co., Inc.

Dell Publishing Company, Inc.: "Soccer Before the Game" from *Secrets of the Super Athletes* by John Devaney. Copyright (c) 1982 by John Devaney, Cloverdale Press, Inc.

Dial Books for Young Readers, a Division of E.P. Dutton, Inc.: From *Edge of Two Worlds* by Weyman Jones. Copyright © 1968 by Weyman Jones. From *Roll of Thunder, Hear My Cry* by Mildred D. Taylor. Copyright © 1976 by Mildred D. Taylor.

Dodd, Mead & Company, Inc.: "Jenny" from *Sam Savitt's True Horse Stories* by Sam Savitt. Copyright (c) 1970 by Sam Savitt.

Doubleday & Company, Inc.: Excerpts from *The Story of My Life* by Helen Keller. Excerpt from *At Wit's End* by Erma Bombeck. Copyright (c) 1965, 1967 by Newsday, Inc. Excerpt from *How I Got to Be Perfect* by Jean Kerr. Copyright (c) 1957 by Jean Kerr.

Farrar, Straus and Giroux, Inc.: Excerpt from *A Swiftly Tilting Planet* by Madeline L'Engle. Copyright (c) 1978 by Crosswicks, Ltd.

Field Newspaper Syndicate: "Funky Winkerbean" cartoon by Tom Batiuk. (c) 1979 by Field Enterprises, Inc.

Larry Fox: From "Jim Plunkett . . . The Quarterback Who Didn't Drop Out" by Larry Fox from *Boys' Life* Magazine, October 1975.

The Benjamin Franklin Literary & Medical Society, Inc.: "Our Mysterious Past" by M. Regina Lepore from *Child Life* Magazine. Copyright (c) 1979 by The Saturday Evening Post Company, Indianapolis, Indi-

We wish to thank the following critical readers, who helped to evaluate materials for this book.

James Mills
Cleveland Public Schools
Cleveland, Ohio

Laurence J. Schulenberg
Council Bluffs School System
Council Bluffs, Iowa

Sharon Taylor
Central Middle School
Edgewater, Maryland

Contents

Chapter 1. Sentence Meaning

Chapter 2. Relationships

Chapter 3. Judgments

Chapter 4. Inferences

Chapter 5. Main Idea

Chapter 6. Dictionary

Chapter 7. Context

Chapter 8. Structure

Chapter 9. Word Origins

Chapter 10. Figurative Language

Chapter 11. Imagery

Chapter 12. Flexibility and Study Skills

Name _____

Chapter 1
Sentence Meaning

A sentence is a group of words expressing a complete thought. A sentence may be a statement, a question, or an order. In this chapter you will learn to understand the meaning of sentences that you read.

Lesson 1

Using Punctuation Marks as Clues to Meaning

Punctuation marks help you to read sentences. They tell you when to pause and when to stop. Three punctuation marks tell you to come to a full stop, since a sentence is ending. These are the period (**.**), the question mark (**?**), and the exclamation mark (**!**). For example:

Some swallows make their nests in barns**.**
Do you know where those birds have their nests**?**
Look out for the cat**!**

The period ends a sentence that is a statement. The question mark ends a sentence that asks a question. The exclamation mark ends a sentence that shows strong emotion or feeling. It also ends a sentence that gives a command. For example: Don't go**!**

The comma separates parts of a sentence. It tells you to take a slight pause before reading the rest of the sentence. For example:

Peter**,** Sally**,** and Michael live in the country.
When Hal visited Jane at her farm**,** he learned to ride a horse.

A dash (—) also tells you to take a slight pause before reading the rest of the sentence. For example:

Because her father was in the Army, she had lived in many places—Indiana, New Jersey, Ohio, Alaska, and Kansas.

A semicolon (;) separates two complete ideas that are closely related. It tells you to take a longer pause than you would for a comma. For example:

He liked the city**;** he loved the country.

Exercise. Read the following paragraphs from "Sneakers and the Swallows" by Louise K. Dooley. Then answer the questions that follow each paragraph. Write your answers in the blanks at the right.

(1)   I was sitting in the yard, rubbing our tomcat, Sneakers, behind the ears, when we were attacked. Three dark, shiny birds with forked tails began diving at us. They came so close that I could feel the breeze from their wings!

a. How many sentences are in paragraph 1? _____

b. In the first sentence of this paragraph, how many times should you pause slightly? _____

c. Which punctuation mark tells you that the last sentence expresses surprise? _____

(2)   I soon realized that these birds were the swallows that lived in our barn, and they weren't going after me. Their target was Sneakers! Did they think our lazy old tomcat would go after their babies in the barn? They didn't seem to be taking any chances. Right over his head they swooped, snapping their bills so fiercely that I jumped and Sneakers ran under the porch.

d. How many sentences are in paragraph 2? _____

e. Which sentence asks a question? (Write first, second, third, etc.) _____

f. In the last sentence of this paragraph, how many times should you pause slightly? _____

(3)   I was amazed that these small birds would come so close to a cat—and to me—but they weren't at all afraid. They were such good fliers that they had little to worry about; they could easily get away from the paws or jaws of a cat.

g. In the first sentence in paragraph 3, which punctuation mark tells you to pause slightly? _____

h. In the second sentence, which punctuation mark tells you to take a longer pause than you would for a comma? _____

(4)   Although barn swallows usually aren't so bold, they are known for being acrobats in the air. They have to fly well because they catch almost all of their food on the wing. They eat loads of flying insects—wasps, flies, beetles, flying ants, and bees. When our barn swallows aren't swooping after insects or skimming the surface of our pond for a quick drink, they often perch on the telephone wires near the road.

i. How many sentences are in paragraph 4? _____

j. When you read the third sentence, how many times should you pause slightly? _____

2

Name _____

Lesson 2

Using Quotation Marks

Opening (") and closing (") quotation marks set off the exact words a character says from the rest of the story. For example, notice the quotation marks around the exact words Laurie says in the sentence below.

Laurie looked in the mirror and said, "I will win!"

Laurie's exact words are: "I will win!"

Now read the next paragraph from "The Comeback" by Elizabeth Van Steenwyk.

Suddenly she caught her image in the mirror, then stood up and looked herself right in the eye. "Who are you kidding?" she asked. "And what makes you think you have a chance tonight?" She covered her eyes with her hands, and then said with determination, "I just have to win."

First Laurie asks, "Who are you kidding?" Then she asks, "And what makes you think you have a chance tonight?" Finally she says, "I just have to win."

Exercise 1. Read the following lettered items. Underline the exact words of the speaker in each item. Then write the name of the speaker in the blank at the right. If the item contains no quoted words—the exact words of a character—write *No* in the blank.

Speaker

a. "Hi, Laurie," Kathy said, suddenly bursting through the door. "Welcome back to the competition ranks. We've missed you these last six months."

a. _____

b. "I've missed being here," Laurie said.

b. _____

c. "How's the knee?" Kathy's face suddenly turned serious. "Is it going to slow you down? I mean, you had such a head of steam going for you. We really thought you'd be in the Seniors by now and then the Olympics."

c. _____

d. "I guess we'll find out tonight just where I stand." Laurie felt her confidence drain away.

d. _____

e. "We have some new competitions this year, Laurie," Kathy said, adjusting her bootlaces. "A girl from Connecticut named Jinny Jordan, who's really strong in everything—schools, freestyle, you name it."

e. _____

f. "I saw some of her figures this morning," Laurie said. "Unbelievable!"

f. _____

g. "Wait'll you see her freestyle program tonight," Kathy said. "She does four double axels and a triple toe loop at the end. Can you believe it?"

g. _____

h. Laurie thought about this and knew that she'd have to include a triple toe loop, too. She had hoped to leave it out because it put an additional strain on her knee, but now there was no choice. I'll have to try the triple and pray, she thought.

h. _____

i. "Is Jinny ahead in the scoring?" Laurie asked.

i. _____

j. "She's the one you have to beat this year," Kathy replied as she hurried out, slamming the door behind her.
(from "The Comeback" by Elizabeth Van Steenwyk)

j. _____

Exercise 2. Sometimes the speaker's exact words are quoted, or given, but the speaker is not identified. You can identify the speaker by noting the order in which the characters speak. In the selection below, first Greg speaks, and then Jimmy speaks. Read the selection. Then, for each lettered item, underline the exact words of the speaker. Write the name of the speaker in the blank at the right. If the item contains no quoted words, write *No* in the blank at the right.

a. "Lots of people came to this mountain leaving a world behind them," Greg said quietly. "They came to herd sheep—Irish people, Scottish people." He touched the trumpet in Jimmy's hand. "They brought their music with them and learned to enjoy a new world."

Speaker

a. _____

b. "Music?" Jimmy stared at him.

b. _____

c. "Sure. They had to have music to dance."

c. _____

d. "Dances—up here!"

d. _____

e. "They followed their old country custom of dancing on the green—fun dancing on green grass. But up here they had to put a tarp—tarpaulin—on the ground to cover rocks and stuff."

e. _____

f. "And played music in this faraway place?" There was a note of wonder in Jimmy's voice.

f. _____

g. "I'll say! Concertinas, accordions, flutes. They did deals like square dancing. Wives and girl friends loved tarp dancing on a moonlight night. I had a grandpa who did too."

g. _____

h. "One of my grandpas was Scottish," Jimmy said.

h. _____

4

i.   "Scotchmen played bagpipes at the tarp dances. But I don't
think they wore kilts up here."

i. _____

j.   Jimmy laughed, and Greg joined him. He felt close to Jimmy
for the first time. Maybe all the problems were over. Maybe things
would be different from now on.
(from "Trumpet in the Treetops" by Peggy Simson Curry)

j. _____

Lesson 3

Finding Core Parts

The core parts of the sentence contain its basic message. The
other parts of the sentence give additional information about the core
parts. Most sentences have at least two core parts. One part, the simple subject, answers the question "Who?" or "What?" The second
part, the simple predicate, or verb, answers the question "Did
what?" or "Does what?" For example, notice the two core parts in the
following sentences. The simple subject is underlined once. The
simple predicate is underlined twice.

Hal ran.

Later that evening Hal ran.

Later that evening Hal ran around the track.

Later that evening Hal ran around the track five times.

Anita exercises.

Every morning Anita exercises.

Every morning Anita exercises for an hour.

Every morning and every evening, Anita exercises for an

hour.

Some sentences have a third core part that completes the meaning of the simple predicate. For example:

Janet painted her room.

Who? *Janet.* Did what? *Painted.* Painted what? *Room.*

Mike mowed the lawn after school.

Who? *Mike.* Did what? *Mowed.* Mowed what? *Lawn.*

In the group of sentences on the next page, the simple subject is
underlined once, the simple predicate twice, and the word that completes the simple predicate three times.

Mr. Pearson <u>drank</u> the <u>cocoa</u>.

Mr. Pearson <u>drank</u> the steaming-hot <u>cocoa</u>.

Late that night Mr. Pearson <u>drank</u> the steaming-hot <u>cocoa</u>.

Late that night Mr. Pearson greedily <u>drank</u> the steaming-hot <u>cocoa</u>.

Exercise 1. Read each sentence below. Underline the simple subject once and the simple predicate twice.

a. The stuntman jumped from the roof of the building.

b. The spellbound crowd watched from the street.

c. This daring man fell onto a five-foot-thick styrofoam pad.

d. Because of his good timing, he landed safely on his shoulders and upper back.

e. The relieved crowd applauded wildly.

f. Then a stuntwoman appeared in the top-story window of the building across the street.

g. She climbed out of the window onto the ledge.

h. Inside the building a fire blazed.

i. After a few minutes the woman jumped eighty-five feet to the safety rig below.

j. The crowd sighed with relief.

Exercise 2. Read each sentence below. Underline the simple subject once, the simple predicate twice, and the word that completes the simple predicate three times.

a. A good pitcher has several different pitches.

b. Most batters like simple fastballs.

c. They really hate tricky curves.

d. A sinker fools the best batters.

e. Nowadays, few pitchers throw illegal spitballs.

f. During a game, the catcher orders many different pitches.

g. Many good pitchers throw excellent curves.

h. Sometimes the curve hits the person up at bat.

i. Wild baseballs hurt batters badly.

j. In nine innings, the pitcher's arm takes a beating.

6

Lesson 4

More Practice in Finding Core Parts

As you have learned, most sentences have at least two core parts, the simple subject and the simple predicate. The simple subject answers the question "Who?" or "What?" The simple predicate answers the question "Did what?" or "Does what?" For example, in the following sentences, the subject is underlined once and the predicate twice.

John Luther Jones came from Cayce, Kentucky.

Jones worked on the railroad.

The subject usually appears before the predicate, but sometimes may appear after the predicate. For example:

The *Cannonball* roared into the station.

Into the station roared the *Cannonball*.

Some sentences have a third core part that completes the meaning of the predicate. For example, in the following sentence, the subject is underlined once, the predicate twice, and the word that completes the meaning of the predicate three times.

Railroad tracks crisscrossed the country.

In some sentences, the simple predicate is made up of a verb plus one or more helping verbs. For example, look at the predicate, printed in **boldface,** in the following sentences.

The woman **was singing** about Casey Jones.
John Luther Jones **was called** Casey by his friends.
Many people **have heard** the song about Casey Jones.
Some people **will have heard** his story before.

Two common helping verbs are *to be* and *to have*. These verbs appear in the following forms:

am	be	have
is	being	has
are	been	had
was		
were		

Other common helping verbs are:

shall	can	should	may
will	could	would	might

Sometimes these helping verbs are separated from the main verb by another word. For example:

> We **may** never **know** the true story.

> **Have** you **heard** the song about Casey Jones?

Exercise 1. In each sentence below, the simple predicate is made up of a verb plus one or more helping verbs. Read each sentence below. Then write the predicate in the blank at the right.

Predicate

a. Casey Jones was working for the Illinois Central Railroad. _____

b. He had worked as a lightning slinger, or railroad telegrapher. _____

c. Now Casey was employed as an engineer. _____

d. On April 29, 1900, Casey had already done a full day's work. _____

e. He had hauled the *Cannonball* from Canton, Mississippi, to Memphis, Tennessee. _____

f. He was expecting a good night's sleep. _____

g. That same night, Casey was summoned as a replacement for a sick engineer. _____

h. Meanwhile, the *Cannonball* was being inspected. _____

i. The *Cannonball* should have left the station long ago. _____

j. Could Casey reach Canton on schedule? _____

Exercise 2. Each sentence below has two core parts. Underline the simple subject once and the simple predicate twice. In each sentence the simple predicate is made up of a verb plus one or more helping verbs.

a. The *Cannonball* was racing to Canton.

b. Its whistle was singing in the night.

c. However, disaster was brewing up the road.

d. Four freight cars were now sitting on the main line.

e. The northbound track could not be cleared.

Exercise 3. Each sentence below has three core parts. Underline the simple subject once, the simple predicate twice, and the word that completes the simple predicate three times. In each sentence the simple predicate is made up of a verb plus a helping verb.

a. Would Casey see the flagman's signal?

b. Could he stop the *Cannonball* in time?

c. Casey could greatly reduce the speed of the *Cannonball*.

d. He could not prevent the crash.

e. He did save everyone's life but his own.

Lesson 5

Understanding Modifiers

A modifier is a word that limits, or makes more definite, the meaning of another word. For example, read the sentences below:

> Alexander Calder was a **famous** sculptor. He created a **miniature** circus.

The word *famous* is a modifier. It tells you what kind of sculptor. The word *miniature* is a modifier. It tells you what kind of circus. (*Miniature* means "very small; tiny.")
Now read the next sentences:

> He **carefully** placed the **delicate** figure on top of the **tiny** horse.
> **Now his miniature** circus was done.

These sentences contain several modifiers. *Carefully* is a modifier. It tells you how he placed the figure. The modifier *delicate* tells you what kind of figure. The modifier *tiny* tells you what kind of horse. The modifier *now* tells you when his circus was completed. The modifier *his* tells you whose circus. The modifier *miniature* tells you what kind of circus.
Let's take out the modifiers. See how the information in these sentences is no longer precise, or exact.

> He placed the figure on top of the horse.
> Circus was done.

Why should you pay attention to modifiers when you read? They can be very important. If you miss the meaning of a modifier, you may miss the meaning of the sentence. For example, in the following two sentences, only the modifiers are different. Notice that the second sentence means the opposite of the first sentence.

> He worked **carefully.**
> He worked **carelessly.**

Exercise. Read the **boldface** sentences below from "The Greatest Little Show on Earth" by Linda Andre. As you read each sentence, pay special attention to the modifiers. Write your answer to each question that follows the boldface sentence in the blank at the right.

> **Calder was a sculptor who is remembered for making brightly colored mobiles.**

a. A *mobile* is a sculpture made with parts that move. Which two words tell you what kind of mobiles? _____

But back in 1926, long before he started working on his famous mobiles, Calder began making a wonderful toy circus.

b. Which modifier tells you what kind of mobiles? _____

c. Which modifier tells you whose mobiles? _____

d. The word *toy* modifies *circus*. Which modifier tells you what kind of toy circus? _____

Can you see him now as he opens a suitcase and takes out a miniature red-and-white striped tent?

e. The word *striped* modifies *tent*. Which words joined together by hyphens tell you the colors of the stripes? _____

f. Which modifier tells you the size of the tent? _____

Next come a few poles, ropes, and trapezes.

g. Which modifier tells you when these three things come? _____

h. Which modifier tells how many poles, ropes, and trapezes? _____

He rigs his highwire, pulling it just tight enough, and hangs a spotlight over the center ring.

i. Which modifier tells you whose highwire? _____

j. Which modifier tells you which ring? _____

Now he takes out the performers.

k. Which modifier tells you when he does this? _____

The ringmaster is only a few inches tall, but he wears a black top hat and a shiny star on his tuxedo.

l. Which modifier tells you the color of the top hat? _____

m. Which modifier tells you what kind of star? _____

n. Which modifier tells you whose tuxedo? _____

There are agile acrobats in Calder's Circus, as well as Japanese wrestlers, a sword swallower, a spear thrower, cowboys on bucking broncos, ragged clowns, glittering dancers, and even a little parachutist who sails down from the top of the tent.

o. Which modifier tells you what kind of acrobats? (This modifier means "nimble; able to move quickly and easily.") _____

p. Which modifier tells you what kind of wrestlers? _____

q. Which modifier tells you what kind of broncos? _____

r. Which modifier tells you what kind of clowns? _____

s. Which modifier tells you what kind of dancers? _____

t. Which modifier tells you the size of the parachutist? _____

Lesson 6

Understanding Pronoun Reference

Nouns are words that name persons, places, things, or ideas. For example, *Peter*, *girl*, *Seattle*, *country*, and *freedom* are nouns. **Pronouns are words used in place of nouns.** Some common pronouns are:

I, me, my, mine	we, us, our,	anybody
you, your, yours	ours	both
he, him, his	they, them, their	either
she, her, hers	myself	nobody
it, its	ourselves	none

Read the following two sentences.

Calder made a miniature, or tiny, circus. **It** received praise.

The pronoun *it* in the second sentence replaces the noun *circus*.
The following pronouns can also act as modifiers.

my	his	our
yours	hers	their
	its	whose

For example, read the sentence below.

Calder enjoyed making **his** circus.

The pronoun *his* acts as a modifier. It tells you whose circus.
When you read, it is important to understand to which word each pronoun refers. For example, read the comic strip below.

HAGAR THE HORRIBLE **by Dik Browne**

Naturally the soldier was confused. Hagar said, "When I raise my hand, you whack it with the ax!" The pronoun *it* seems to refer to *hand*. Therefore, the soldier whacks Hagar's hand. However, Hagar meant to tell the soldier to whack the rope.

Exercise. Read each paragraph below from "The Greatest Little Show on Earth" by Linda Andre. Pay special attention to the pronouns printed in **boldface.** Write the word or words to which each boldface pronoun refers in the blank at the right.

Calder worked on his circus for six years until he had 55 lively performers. **He** packed them into five suitcases and hauled them around, giving circus parties for his friends. Some of the guests sat right down on the floor so that **they** could see every move the little performers made. The guests came not only to watch the circus, but also to see Calder put on the show, for he was as much a performer as his tiny figures. As soon as the circus music started on the old phonograph, Calder got down on his hands and knees, blew the whistle for the ring-master, and made his circus come alive.

a. _____

b. _____

Calder roared for the lion and helped **him** leap out of his cage. He barked for the seals as **they** bounced their ball back and forth. He blew sawdust through the elephant's trunk and blew air into the clown's balloon nose until **it** popped. He wound up the belly dancer so that she could kick her legs and roll her body around, and he gave a little acrobat just the right kind of shove so that **he** could perform his handsprings.

c. _____

d. _____

e. _____

f. _____

Sometimes the performers made mistakes. When the trapeze artist missed and fell into the net while swinging from one trapeze to another, everyone in Calder's audience gasped and fell silent. All eyes were on her as the little lady got up to try again. Out **she** flew once more. She grabbed the second trapeze, then somersaulted in the air and latched onto another tiny lady hanging upside down on the other side of the tent. She did it! The audience cheered loudly.

g. _____

Calder had to pull the right string or push the right lever at precisely (exactly) the right moment if everything was to work successfully. Nobody knew for sure whether **he** could do it— not even Calder himself—but the suspense was part of the fun. If the spear thrower aimed at the glittering dancer by mistake, or if the aerialist plunged head over heels from the highwire, two wire men with big shoulders trundled (rolled) on with a stretcher and picked up the injured bodies.

h. _____

Calder had enormous fun with his toy circus. **He** played with it for many years until it became too fragile to handle. Then he gave **it** to the Whitney Museum of American Art in New York City where it remains today.

i. _____

j. _____

Name _____

Lesson 7

Reading Sentences in Poetry

Many poems are written to be read aloud with a certain rhythm. To help you catch and hold the rhythm, poets write their words in lines. Two or more lines may form a sentence. The sentences carry the meaning, but the lines carry the rhythm.

In English, people usually place the subject before the predicate and follow the predicate with the word that completes its meaning. (Remember: All sentences do not have a word that completes the predicate.) For example:

The tiger stalked the deer.

The deer ran.

Often poets end their lines with rhymes. In order to create rhymes, they may change the word order that people usually use.

Read the following stanzas from "How to Tell the Wild Animals" by Carolyn Wells. Some lines are not in natural word order.

> If ever you should go by chance
>   To jungles in the East;
> And if there should to you advance
>   A large and tawny beast,
> 5   If he roars at you as you're dyin'
> You'll know it is the Asian Lion.
>
> Or if some time when roaming round,
>   A noble wild beast greets you,
> With black stripes on a yellow ground,
> 10   Just notice if he eats you.
> This simple rule may help you learn
> The Bengal Tiger to discern.*
>
> If strolling forth, a beast you view,
>   Whose hide with spots is peppered,
> 15 As soon as it has lept on you,
>   You'll know it is the leopard.
> 'Twill do no good to roar with pain,
> He'll only lep and lep again.

Look again at lines 3-4.

> And if there should to you advance
>   A large and tawny beast,

Now let us rewrite these lines in natural word order. (Remember: This means that the subject comes before the predicate. If there is a

---

*discern (dĭ-sûrn') v.: detect; recognize.

word that completes the predicate, this word comes after the predicate.)

> And if a large and tawny beast should advance to you

Now look again at lines 13-14.

> If strolling forth, a beast you view,
> Whose hide with spots is peppered,

Let's rewrite these lines in natural word order.

> If strolling forth you view a beast
> Whose hide is peppered with spots

If you have trouble reading lines that are not in natural word order, try this strategy. Copy the lines on a piece of paper. Then rewrite them in natural word order. Once you understand the lines, go back to the poem and read them the way the poet wrote them.

Exercise. Rewrite the following sentences in natural word order. Write your answers on the blanks provided.

a. Drank the lion from the lake.

_____

b. Home they came that summer night.

_____

c. Sing they of the leopard's beauty.

_____

d. Brought they gifts of gold and silver.

_____

e. Ran the deer through the forest.

_____

f. Passengers on their backs the camels carried.

_____

g. Meat-eating animals you could see.

_____

h. From the forest came the wolves.

_____

i. The cry of the lion you should hear.

_____

j. The hunters you should separate from the prey.

_____

Lesson 8

Practice

While you read the following selection, pay special attention to the meaning of each sentence. Then complete the exercise that follows.

Santa Claus Gets a Coin
Isaac Asimov

Dad doesn't usually bring his work home with him, but it was the Christmas season, December 22, and it was spoiling everything. There's nothing like an unsolved problem to keep a detective from concentrating on enjoying the celebration.

"Can you imagine," he said that evening, "picking up one of those coins in a Santa Claus bucket? It was a youngster who threw it in, too."

We knew what he meant. The newspapers called it the Christmas Coin mystery. The museum began to miss coins just as the Christmas season started, and they were pretty valuable. It seemed like an inside job, but that meant a hundred people at least and there were no leads.

"A youngster?" I said.

"A kid about your age, Larry, and he goes to your junior high," Dad said. "He dropped one of those coins in a bucket with a Santa Claus ringing his bell over it. The Santa Claus saw it wasn't an American coin and since he had his stand near the museum, he thought it might be one of the stolen ones. Being honest, he turned it in. He could identify the kid, too. It was a neighborhood kid he'd seen often."

Mom looked very upset. "You mean the *child* was the thief?"

"No," said Dad. "But, you know, he had to be questioned and that upset his parents."

I said, "What happened, Dad? Where did the kid get the coin?"

Dad said, "A man in the museum asked him to drop it in the Santa Claus. Gave him a quarter."

I said, "Can the kid identify the man who gave him the coin?"

"No," said my father, shaking his head. "He didn't really look. You know how kids are." That annoyed me a little. I said, "No, Dad, I don't know how kids are."

Dad cleared his throat. "It was the fifth coin and the museum has been tightening its security. We don't know what system the thief used to dispose of the coins, but it must have been getting harder. This time he must have felt he'd be caught if he left the museum, so he got the kid to do it for him."

"And put it in the Santa Claus bucket?" I said. "That was stupid."

"He was in a hurry, maybe. It might have been the first place that occurred to him. Maybe he thought he could get it back later."

I ate my dessert and thought hard. Then I went to the dictionary. I came back and said, "Dad, is there a crèche near where the Santa Claus was standing? You know, a set of statues of the stable at Bethlehem and the Infant Jesus and the Virgin and Joseph and cows and donkeys."

"I know what a crèche is," said Dad, "so don't pretend you have to educate me. The answer is: No."

That was disappointing because I had hoped I would show up as a great detective. But then Mom said, "There's one south of the museum, just outside one of the churches. I see it when I'm shopping."

"How near the museum, Mom?"

"Less than a block away from the southern end, actually."

Dad said, "The Santa Claus got his coin near the northern end."

I said, "Could I speak to the kid myself, Dad? He might not mind talking to another kid and I'd like to ask him something."

Dad said, "Ask him *what*, Larry?"

But I shook my head. "You know how kids are, Dad. I just want to check it out, first."

"All right, then." I guess he was a little embarrassed at having made that crack about kids so he gave in. "But you go easy, son," he said. "Don't make it hard on the boy."

It was dark when we got there and the man who opened the door seemed unhappy when he saw Dad. He said, "Is something else wrong?"

"No," said Dad, "but my son wants to talk to yours if he's home."

He was and I recognized him and even knew his name. He wasn't a friend of mine, exactly, but I had seen him around the corridors. He was a class lower than I was.

We went aside to be private, and I said, "Jim, did that man say to drop the coin in the Santa Claus?"

"Yes, he did."

"Didn't he say, 'drop it in Santa Claus's bucket'?"

"No. He said, 'in the Santa Claus.' I remember because I thought maybe I should drop the coin in his pocket, but I decided he meant the bucket."

"Maybe he said something that *sounded* like Santa Claus. Was it *exactly* Santa Claus?"

Jim looked confused, then he smiled and said, "Oh, I remember. He didn't say Santa Claus. He said Kriss Kringle— but that's the same thing, isn't it?"

I could have shouted and jumped up and down but I managed to play it cool. "It's another name for Santa Claus, but it's a

16

different word. So he asked you to drop the coin in the Kriss Kringle. Not in the bucket, but in the Kriss Kringle?"

"Yes. He asked me if I knew where that was, and I said sure. Heck, I've seen that Santa Claus every day for a couple of weeks now."

"Thanks, Jim," I said.

Dad looked plenty puzzled but I wouldn't say a word till we found the crèche. I could still be all wrong. But once we got there, there was no doubt. The crèche had lights on it and there was a little slit near the Infant Jesus with a sign that said, "For the Poor this Holiday Season."

"There, Dad," I said, pointing. "The coins are in there, if it hasn't been opened yet."

Dad got the sexton of the church and he opened up the poor box. There were coins and bills in it—and also the four coins from the museum. They were going to open it on Christmas Day, you see, and I guess the thief knew that.

"You know, Dad," I said, afterward, "it didn't make sense to say 'in the Santa Claus' and I tried to think of anything else the man might have said, and I couldn't think of anything but Kriss Kringle. I looked that up in the dictionary and it comes from *Christkindl*, which in German is pronounced almost like Kriss Kringle. It means 'little Christchild.' That crèche was a good place to hide the coins if you knew it wasn't going to be opened till Christmas. I bet the thief planned to break it open the night before."

Dad said, "Good thinking, Larry. It doesn't help us get the man, but at least we have the coins back."

"Sure it helps you get the man, Dad. It's someone who was so excited, he meant to tell Jim to put the coin in the Christchild, but said it in German and told him to put it in the *Christkindl*. All you have to do is get someone in the museum who speaks German better than English. That ought to cut it down a lot."

It did. They caught the thief before Christmas Day and the museum gave Jimmy a $100 reward for remembering the word and $100 to the Santa Claus. That made it a good Christmas for them.

I wouldn't take a reward because I was just doing my job as detective, but it made it a good Christmas for me, too.

Exercise. Answer each of the questions below. Write your answers in the blanks at the right.

a. The paragraph below contains how many sentences?

Dad doesn't usually bring his work home with him, but it was the Christmas season, December 22, and it was spoiling everything. There's nothing like an unsolved problem to keep a detective from concentrating on enjoying the celebration.

b. Underline the exact words of the speaker in the sentences below. Then write the name of the speaker in the blank at the right.

"No," said my father, shaking his head. "He didn't really look. You know how kids are."

c. What is the subject of the following sentence?

The newspapers called it the Christmas Coin mystery.

d. What is the predicate, or verb, in the following sentence?

Dad cleared his throat.

e. What is the word that completes the predicate in the sentence in **d** above?

f. What is the predicate in the following sentence?

Being honest, he turned it in.

g. What is the word that completes the predicate in the following sentence?

The Santa Claus got his coin near the northern end.

h. In the following sentence, what word modifies *job*; that is, what word tells you what kind of job it seemed like?

It seemed like an inside job, but that meant a hundred people at least and there were no leads.

i. In the sentence in **h** above, what word modifies *leads*; that is, what word tells you how many leads there were?

j. In the following sentence, the pronoun *ones* takes the place of what noun?

The Santa Claus saw it wasn't an American coin and since he had his stand near the museum, he thought it might be one of the stolen **ones.**

Name _____

Chapter 2
Relationships

What is a relationship? A relationship is the way in which two or more things, events, or ideas are connected or joined. In this chapter you will study several relationship patterns. These are: time order, simple listing, spatial order, cause and effect, and comparison and contrast.

Lesson 1
Understanding Words That Signal Time Order

    Time order tells you when one event happens in relation to other events. It tells you the sequence of events. For example, in the comic strip below, Drabble is trying to teach Patrick how to mail a letter. He tells the events in their correct time order.

DRABBLE **by Fagan**

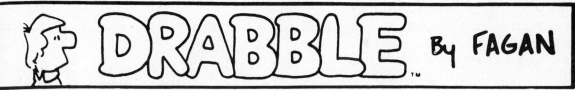

Some words signal a time order relationship. These words include:

after	earlier	meanwhile	then	whenever
as	finally	now	until	while
before	later	since	when	

In a time order relationship, events may be connected in three ways. (1) Two events may happen *at the same time*. (2) One event may happen *before* or *earlier than* the other. (3) One event may happen *after* or *later than* the other. Read the following sentence:

Seal *your envelope* **before** you mail it.

The word *before* signals time order. The action in the first part of the sentence, printed in *italics*, happens earlier than the action in the second part. This sentence can also be written:

Before you mail it, seal your letter.

Now read the next sentence.

She *wrote postcards* **while** she was on vacation.

The word *while* signals time order. She wrote the postcards at the same time that she was on vacation.

Read the next sentence.

She *found the unmailed postcards in the bag* **after** she came home from vacation.

The word *after* signals time order. The event in the first part of the sentence happened later than the event in the second part. This sentence can also be written: **After** she came home from vacation, she found the unmailed postcards in the bag.

Exercise. Read each sentence below. If the action or event in the first part of the sentence happens *before* that in the second part, write *B* in the blank at the right. If it happens *after*, write *A*. If both actions or events happen at the same time, write *S*.

a. *Clean your bike* **before** you put it away. _____

b. *Wipe the leather clean with soap and water;* **then** dry it. _____

c. *Anita cleaned her bike* **after** she rode it. _____

d. **After** *he finished his homework,* Lee rode his bike. _____

e. *Maria exercises* **while** she watches television. _____

f. *Leroy jogs* **before** he goes to school. _____

g. *Phyllis showered* **after** she played tennis. _____

h. **As** *she rode the bus to school,* Carla studied her social studies notes. _____

i. **Before** *you take a test,* get a good night's sleep. _____

j. **After** *he danced with Christina,* Peter danced with Randi. _____

Lesson 2

Understanding Time Order

Time order tells you when each event happened in relation to other events. Time order answers the question "When?" For example, in the following paragraph from *Tangles* by Marie-Louise Wallin, the events are arranged according to time order. The narrator tells you what she did first, what she did second, what she did third, and what she did last.

> We always followed the same schedule. First we brought up water from the well and carried it in to the horses. Then we shoveled hay from the loft through the trapdoor to the troughs down below. While the horses began their contented chewing we cleaned the stalls and covered them with straw, picked out hoofs, and brushed and groomed the horses. We filled the buckets with pellets and oats, and then our chores were finished, if the floor didn't happen to need a going-over with the broom.

Sometimes events are not told in their normal time order. For example, the paragraphs below are from "The Howard Hughes Biography" by Daniel Cohen. Howard Hughes was one of the wealthiest people in the United States. In 1971, Howard Hughes had not been seen in public for many years.

> In 1971 a major American publisher announced that it was going to publish Howard Hughes' life story. Of course Hughes had not written the book himself. The book had been written by a man named Clifford Irving. But Hughes was said to have given Irving all the facts and to have read the story. The news created a sensation.
>
> Irving was not a very well-known writer. But he had written a few other books. Why had Hughes picked him, of all people, to write his life story? Irving said it was because Hughes had read one of his other books and liked it. Then he had secretly got in touch with the writer. Since Hughes had strange ways of doing everything, the story seemed possible.
>
> The book Howard Hughes was said to have liked was called *Fake!* It was about an art forger Irving knew. That should have made someone suspicious. But at first no one was. The publisher gave Irving over $600,000. The payments were made out to H. R. Hughes. Irving said he would turn them over to Hughes.
>
> Once this news got around some people began to object. The Hughes Company said that the book was a fake. The company was going to court to try to stop it from being published.
>
> But Clifford Irving did not back down. He pointed out that the Hughes Company was not Howard Hughes. He hinted that

someone in the company was trying to stop the book for evil reasons. He said he was sure that soon Howard Hughes would tell the world that Irving's book was not a fake. Irving even took a lie detector test and passed it. Day after day newspapers and magazines were filled with stories of Clifford Irving and the Howard Hughes biography.

First, Clifford Irving wrote a book called *Fake!* Second, he wrote a book about Howard Hughes. Third, a publisher said it was going to publish Howard Hughes' life story. Fourth, the Hughes Company claimed the book was a fake. Finally, Clifford Irving took a lie detector test.

Exercise. Now continue reading "The Howard Hughes Biography" by Daniel Cohen. Then follow the directions at the end of the selection.

Finally Howard Hughes was heard from. He didn't appear in public, but he agreed to talk on the phone. A group of reporters who had known Hughes from the days before he began hiding, questioned the man on the phone. It may have been the strangest news conference ever held. And it was shown on television across the country.

The reporters all agreed that the man on the phone was Howard Hughes. The voice sounded like Hughes'. The man also knew things about Hughes that no one else could have known. And the real Howard Hughes said the book was a fake.

Irving kept saying that the book was not a hoax. He said Hughes had told him his life story. He didn't know why Hughes now said he hadn't. Irving said he was not even sure that the voice was really Hughes'. People stopped believing Irving. The publisher decided to stop the book. Irving was told to return the money that had been given to him.

Then it came out that the payment made to H. R. Hughes had been cashed in Europe. The person who had cashed it was not Howard Hughes, but a woman. The woman turned out to be Edith Irving, Clifford Irving's wife. She was using the name Helga R. Hughes. When she signed her name she just used the initials H. R. Hughes. The people at the bank gave her the money but they became suspicious.

Finally Irving told the truth. He had never met Howard Hughes. The whole thing had been a hoax from the beginning. He first got the idea when he did his book on art forgery. He saw how easy hoaxing was. Then he got an advance look at another book about Hughes. The book was by someone who had once worked for the multimillionaire. Irving used a lot of the facts from that book. He also used newspaper clippings. And he made up the rest.

Some people thought Clifford Irving's hoax was very funny. But the publisher didn't think so. Irving had already spent part of the money he had received. Clifford Irving, his wife and

Name _____

another writer who took part in the hoax were given short terms in jail.

They are all out of jail now. At last report Irving is writing novels and living in Mexico.

Directions. Arrange the events below in their proper time order. Write 1 by the event that happened first, 2 by the event that happened second, 3 by the event that happened third, 4 by the event that happened fourth, and 5 by the event that happened last.

_____ **a.** Clifford Irving's publisher decided to stop the book.

_____ **b.** Howard Hughes agreed to talk to a group of reporters on the telephone.

_____ **c.** Clifford and Edith Irving were sent to jail.

_____ **d.** Clifford Irving wrote a book about art forgery.

_____ **e.** People found out that in Europe Edith Irving had cashed the check written to H. R. Hughes.

Lesson 3

Understanding Simple Listing

A list is a collection of items, all of which fit into a particular category. For example, a list of *breeds of domestic cats* would include:

Abyssian
Siamese
Angora
Persian
Foreign White
Manx

A list of *breeds of dogs* would include:

Pointer
Retriever
Setter
Spaniel
Dalmatian
Dachshund
Collie
Chihauhau

In the comic strip below, Ditto decides to make a list.

HI & LOIS by Dik Browne

Ditto's list might look like this.

Things to Do
Take out the garbage
Write a paragraph for English
Complete exercises on p. 108 in math book
Decide on topic for science report
Call Jack about the party next Saturday
Help with the dishes
Watch *Spitfire* on television
Feed the cat

Exercise 1. Make two lists from the items below. Ten items will fit in the category called "Birds." The remaining ten items will fit in the category called "Stringed Instruments." (If you do not understand a word, look it up in the dictionary.)

violin	oriole	sparrow	harp	viola
nightingale	parrot	woodpecker	guitar	magpie
eagle	banjo	ukelele	owl	cello
wren	mandolin	skylark	double bass	lute

Birds	**Stringed Instruments**
_____	_____
_____	_____
_____	_____
_____	_____
_____	_____
_____	_____
_____	_____
_____	_____
_____	_____
_____	_____

Name _____

Exercise 2. Read each list below. One item does not fit in each list. Write this item in the blank at the right.

a. cow   turkey   rooster   hen   duck   _____

b. apple   pear   carrot   peach   apricot   _____

c. vanilla   chocolate   strawberry   rabbit   apricot   _____

d. surfing   chair   sailing   swimming   water skiing   _____

e. trees   diamonds   clubs   hearts   spades   _____

f. notebook   pencil   pen   paper   bear   _____

g. textbook   lantern   tent   sleeping bag   knapsack   _____

h. teaspoon   toe   tablespoon   knife   fork   _____

i. scarf   coat   box   gloves   cap   _____

j. saw   hammer   chisel   screwdriver   tomato   _____

Lesson 4

Understanding Spatial Order

Spatial order tells you where one object is in relation to other objects. For example, one object may be *in front of, in back of, above,* or *below* another. Spatial order answers the question "Where?" Read the sentence below.

The dog was under the table.

Where was the dog in relation to the table? The dog was *under* it.

In the following three paragraphs from "G. Trueheart, Man's Best Friend" by James McNamee, the words that help you see spatial order are printed in **boldface.**

This day, Tom knew that something was looking **at** him. He had the feeling. And there it was!

There it was, all eight feet of it, crouched **on** a rock, **above** him, a great golden cat, a cougar, a Vancouver Island panther! Its tail was twitching. Its eyes burned green, burned yellow, burned bright. Its ears were flat **against** its head.

Tom's feet stopped. His blood and all his other juices tinkled into ice, and for a moment the whole world seemed to disappear **behind** a white wall. A heavy animal brushed **against** him, and at the shock of that, Tom could see again. It was Genevieve. She had sat **down** and, to rest herself, was leaning **on** his leg.

Exercise. Genevieve Trueheart is a golden retriever who has grown up eating chocolates and other sweets. Instead of smelling like a dog, she smells like a candy store. Continue reading about Tom and Genevieve Trueheart's meeting with the cougar. Pay special attention to the spatial relation of one object to another. Then answer the questions that follow this selection from "G. Trueheart, Man's Best Friend" by James McNamee. Write your answers in full sentences.

(1)   The cougar's ears were still flat, its eyes burning as if lighted candles were in them. It was still crouched on the rock, still ready to spring.

(2)   Tom heard a thump, thump, thump, thump, thump, and he thought it was the sound of his heart, but it wasn't. It was Genevieve beating her tail against the gravel to show how happy she was to be sitting doing nothing. That made Tom mad. If she had been any kind of a dog she would have known about the cougar before Tom did. She should have smelled him. She should have been just out of reach of his claws and barking. She should have been giving Tom a chance to run away. That's what Rusty would have done. But no, not Genevieve; all she could do was bump her fat tail and look happy.

(3)   The cougar had come closer. Inch by inch, still in a crouch, it slid down the rock. Tom could see the movement in its legs. It was like a cat after a robin.

(4)   Tom felt sick, and cold, but his brain was working. I can't run, he thought, if I run he'll be on me. He'll rip Genevieve with one paw and me with the other. Tom thought, too, that if he had a match he could rip pages from one of his school books and set them on fire for he knew that cougars and tigers and leopards and lions were afraid of anything burning. He had no match because supposing his father had ever caught him with matches in his pocket during the dry season, then wow and wow and wow! Maybe, he thought, if I had a big stone I could stun him. He looked. There were sharp, flat pieces of granite at the side of the road where somebody had blasted.

(5)   The cougar jumped. It was in the air like a huge yellow bird. Tom had no trouble leaving. He ran to the side of the road and picked up a piece of granite.

(6)   Of course, when he moved, Genevieve Trueheart, who had been leaning against his leg, fell over. She hadn't seen anything. She lay there. She was happy. She looked like a sack of potatoes.

(7)   The cougar walked around Genevieve twice as if he didn't believe it. He couldn't tell what she was. He paid no attention to Tom Hamilton. He had seen people before. He had never seen anything like Genevieve. He stretched his neck out and sniffed. She must have smelled pretty good because he sat down beside her and licked one of his paws. He was getting ready for dinner. He was thinking, Boy, oh, boy! this is a picnic.

26

Name _____

Questions

a. In paragraph 1, where is the cougar in relation to the rock?

_____

b. In paragraph 2, Tom is angry with Genevieve because she is sitting doing nothing. Where does he think she should be in relation to the cougar?

_____

c. In paragraph 4, where are the sharp pieces of granite that Tom sees?

_____

d. In paragraph 5, where does Tom run when the cougar jumps?

_____

e. In paragraph 7, where does the cougar walk in relation to Genevieve?

_____

Lesson 5

Identifying Words That Signal Cause and Effect

A cause makes something happen. An effect is what happens. Many ideas and events are connected in a cause and effect relationship.

For example, look at the following two sentences:

> Nancy wanted to make the team. Nancy exercised every morning and watched her weight.

Let's connect these two sentences to show a cause and effect relationship.

> Because she wanted to make the team, Nancy exercised every morning and watched her weight.

Why did Nancy exercise every morning? She did this in order to make the team. The cause is *she wanted to make the team*. The effect is *she exercised every morning and watched her weight*.

Some words signal a cause and effect relationship. These words are:

accordingly	because	in order that	so that
as	consequently	since	therefore
as a result	for	so	thus

In the following sentences, the signal word is printed in **boldface,** the cause is underlined once, and the effect is underlined twice.

Since she had trained so hard, the coach decided to give her a chance.

She ran two miles a day **because** she wanted to get in shape.

She ran two miles a day; **as a result,** she developed strong leg muscles.

Because Nancy set the alarm for seven, she had plenty of time to shower and eat breakfast.

Nancy dressed warmly **so that** she would not freeze.

Exercise 1. Cause and effect plays an important part in the following selection, "Animals in the Rain" by Lee Stephenson. Read the selection carefully. Then follow the directions at the end of the selection.

What do animals do in the rain?

Large mammals such as elephants, horses, cows, and deer usually don't bother to get out of the rain except in a really bad storm. Deer may even *leave* the shelter of a forest in a heavy rain and move into a meadow. Why? Deer need to listen carefully for danger. But a hard rain in the forest makes so much noise that the deer can't hear if an enemy is sneaking up on them.

Medium-sized, furry mammals—raccoons, opossums, skunks, chipmunks, and foxes—usually take shelter from rain in their dens or burrows. When the animals are too far from home, they slip under any shelter they can find.

These animals are not so small that they'd drown in rainstorms, so why should they take cover? Probably because when their fur gets soaked it no longer keeps them warm. You may have noticed how cold you feel when your clothes are all wet. To get warm again you can put on dry clothes. But a furry animal can't, so it tries to keep its coat dry.

Most birds try to find shelter during a hard rain, often in a leafy tree. Since birds need to eat almost all day long, they hunt for food among the branches while waiting out the storm. Sometimes they even leave their shelter to find enough to eat. When the rain stops, they shake and fluff their feathers to stay warm and to dry off quickly.

Ducks and most other water birds have a special way to keep dry. They use their bills to spread waterproofing oil over their feathers. The oil comes from a gland at the base of their tails. Ducks don't mind a rainstorm unless it is very violent. They usually keep floating on open water but may tuck their heads next to their bodies and go to sleep.

Insect-eating birds, such as purple martins and chimney swifts, often fly toward a storm just before the rain begins. Many insects fly into the air ahead of an approaching storm. That makes them easy for birds to catch. Scientists aren't sure how the birds know the rain is coming. Maybe the birds can sense the sky getting darker, or the air becoming more humid, the wind blowing harder, or the temperature dropping. Some other animals may notice the same changes and take shelter from a storm.

Most insects also take cover in a rainstorm. You can imagine how heavy a raindrop would feel if you were the size of an ant! No wonder ants stay in their nests when it rains. If they are caught outside and cannot get home, they take shelter in the grass or under leaves or twigs.

During a flood, some ants that live on the North American prairie cling together in a big ball. This way they keep from getting separated from one another. The ball also becomes a kind of floating ant "raft," which turns over and over in the water. That way each ant gets a turn to breathe, so few of them drown.

Ants and other animals that live underground have more ways to protect themselves from drowning. They build their nests or burrows away from areas that flood often. Sometimes parts of their tunnels go below their nests. Rainwater collects in the lower parts instead of in the living areas.

Flying insects have a big problem when it rains. When their wings get wet they tear easily. Some flying insects hang onto the undersides of leaves in a storm. Raindrops or wind may shake the leaf, but the insects hold on very tightly and stay dry.

The bodies and wings of butterflies and moths are covered with scales and a very thin layer of wax. This covering stops rain from soaking their wings. A butterfly's wings stay dry for a while even when it falls into a lake or stream.

You may have heard that rain is good for fishing. It's true. Insects may be knocked into a lake or stream by wind or raindrops. This brings insect-eating fish such as bluegills to the surface where it's easier for people to catch them. The raindrops also break up the smooth surface of the water, which makes it harder for the fish to see the people fishing.

One kind of African animal does a kind of rain dance! During a very bad storm adult male chimpanzees sometimes gather in a clearing on the top of a hill. They sway back and forth, stamp their feet, and make loud noises. Female and young chimps watch from nearby trees. Suddenly the males charge down the hill—one by one or in small groups. On the way down some break off tree branches and swing them or throw them down the hill. No one is sure why they do this strange "dance."

The orangutan is a cousin of the chimpanzee, but no one has ever seen it dance. Like most animals, it takes shelter from rain. It may break off tree branches and use them as an umbrella. Or it may arrange them like a roof over a nest made quickly in a tree.

Next time it rains, you can see for yourself what animals do in the rain!

Directions. Circle the signal word in each of the sentences below. Then draw one line under the part of the sentence that is the cause. Draw two lines under the part of the sentence that is the effect.

a. Because they need to listen for danger, deer may leave a forest and move into a meadow during a heavy rainfall.

b. A raccoon takes shelter from the storm; as a result, its fur stays dry.

c. Since birds need to eat almost all day long, they may leave their shelters to hunt for food during a rainstorm.

d. Birds shake their feathers; thus, they dry off quickly.

e. A waterproofing oil covers the feathers of ducks; therefore, their feathers stay dry in the rain.

f. Because insects are very small, raindrops feel very heavy to them.

g. During a flood ants cling together so that they will not drown.

h. The wings of flying insects tear easily when wet; consequently, flying insects seek shelter from the rain.

i. Since the butterfly's body and wings are covered by a very thin layer of wax, it stays dry in the rain.

j. Fish have trouble seeing people fishing during a rainstorm because the raindrops break up the smooth surface of the water.

Exercise 2. Circle the signal word in each of the following sentences. Then underline the cause once and the effect twice.

a. Nancy didn't like team sports, so her gym teacher suggested she join the tennis club.

b. Because Nancy had several friends in the tennis club, she decided to join it.

c. She won her very first set; as a result, she was asked to join the tennis team.

d. She practiced her serve every day against the garage wall; consequently, she developed a very fast serve.

e. Since she had a fast serve, Nancy often won the first point.

Lesson 6

Understanding Cause and Effect

**Many ideas and events are connected in a cause and effect rela-
tionship. The cause is what makes something happen. The effect is
the result, or what happens.** For example, look at the comic strip
below.

CATHY by Cathy Guisewite

Why are there no pictures of Cathy? There are no pictures of
Cathy because she wouldn't let people take pictures of her.

Exercise. Read the following true story, "Jenny" by Sam Savitt.
Then, in complete sentences, answer each of the questions that follow it. Make sure each answer contains the word *because.*

This happened in upper New York state, around the year
1867, and I'll tell you the story just the way it was told to
me.

Dr. Kraft Payson Kimball lived in Burville, a small village
just outside of Watertown, New York, but his practice carried
him over a good part of the northwest corner of Jefferson

County. He made his rounds by horse and buggy most of the time, but whenever the roads were too muddy or snow covered, he rode a little brown mare named Jenny. The doctor told everyone she had Morgan and Arabian ancestry, but most of all she had a whole lot of good, everyday horse sense.

Now, men who spend many hours on horseback, like cowboys or cavalrymen or country doctors, have learned through necessity the knack of sleeping in the saddle. Doc Kimball was no exception. Many nights, after a long day of house calls, his good mare Jenny would carry him home while he slept in the saddle. She would plod along quietly, undisturbed by the things that spook most horses, and stop only when she arrived at the doctor's house.

This year the snow had lain deep all winter, and now, in April, with the addition of the constant spring rains, the roads became almost impassable. Jim McKay, who lived up near Saint Lawrence, had a tree fall on him, and when Jim's boy brought the news, Doc Kimball quickly saddled Jenny and rode out to the McKay place. He set two broken legs, and it was well after dark before he was ready to ride for home.

"You can't go out on a night like this, Doc," pleaded Mrs. McKay. "Stay over with us. You can head back in the morning with a good hot breakfast under your belt." But Doc Kimball wouldn't hear of it. He had some pretty sick patients down near Rutland. Besides, the rain had slowed down to a drizzle, and he could count on old Jenny to get him back home.

There were twelve miles to go. The doctor settled into the saddle and, with his head tucked into the upturned collar of his oilskin slicker, promptly dozed off.

He didn't know how long he'd slept, but he was startled awake suddenly when Jenny came to a halt. He found he was sitting on his horse beside the picket fence in front of his own house. The yellow light streaming through the open door fell across his stable boy Billy, who was holding Jenny's bridle and peering anxiously up into the doctor's face.

"Are you all right, Doc?" Billy's voice quavered.

"Of course I'm all right—why shouldn't I be?" the doctor answered. He slid to the ground and began unfastening his saddlebag.

"Which way did you come home?"

Billy's question was so intent and irregular that the doctor stopped what he was doing and looked searchingly at the boy.

"The way I always do," he answered softly. "Down Cumberland Road and across Brownville Bridge." He paused to sling the saddlebag across his shoulder.

"Why do you ask, Bill? You know darned well the route I take—it's the only one there is."

"But that's impossible, Doc." Billy's words came slowly and disbelievingly. "Brownville Bridge washed out over four hours ago!"

Next morning Dr. Kimball and Billy went down to the river crossing. Sure enough, the bridge was gone. Only one old rotten beam still spanned the swirling waters. But there in the mud, in the early light, they could see the hoofprints of old Jenny. The doctor and the boy traced them to the crumbling bank and stood in awe and amazement as their eyes unfolded the story of last night.

Old Jenny, in the stormy darkness, with the doctor asleep in the saddle, had crossed the single narrow beam to bring him safely home.

Questions

a. Why did Dr. Kimball often travel to the northwest corner of Jefferson County?

_____

_____

b. On this particular night, why did Dr. Kimball ride Jenny instead of traveling by horse and buggy?

_____

_____

c. Why did Dr. Kimball know how to sleep in the saddle?

_____

_____

d. Why were the roads almost impassable?

_____

_____

e. Why did Dr. Kimball ride out to the McKay place?

_____

_____

f. Why did Dr. Kimball refuse to spend the night at the McKay place?

_____

_____

g. Why did Dr. Kimball stop what he was doing to answer the stable boy's question?

_____

_____

h. Why did Billy ask Dr. Kimball which way he had come?

_____

i. The next day, why were Dr. Kimball and Billy amazed when they saw Jenny's hoofprints?

_____

_____

j. Why was Jenny's journey across the beam particularly difficult?

_____

_____

Lesson 7

Identifying Words That Signal Contrast

When you contrast two things, you show how they are different. For example, look at the photograph below. Let's contrast the size of the elephant with that of the mouse.

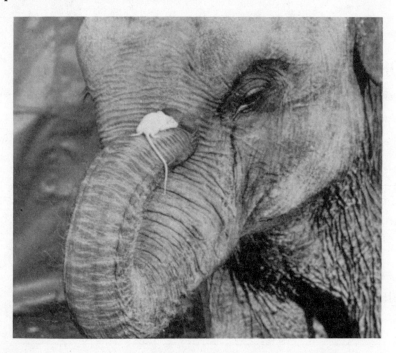

The elephant is very large, but the mouse is small.

Certain words signal a contrast relationship. For example:

although	on the other hand
but	whereas
however	while
instead	yet
nevertheless	

The sentence below contrasts the weight of the elephant with that of the mouse. The signal word is printed in boldface.

Raha the elephant weighs one ton, **whereas** Mighty Mary the mouse weighs only two ounces.

Exercise 1. Contrast plays an important role in the selection below, "Tricky Tracks" by Lynn Giroux Blum. Read this selection carefully. Then follow the directions at the end of the selection.

By "reading" tracks, you can discover exciting things about the animals that live near you. All it takes is practice.

It's easy to find tracks, whether you live in the country or the city. Look in snow-covered fields and forests or along the muddy banks of streams and ponds. Firm, moist sand at a beach and soft earth of almost any kind also make good places to look for tracks.

Wherever you live, the best place to start tracking is in your own backyard. The footprints that you will find most often probably are those made by dogs and cats. Can you tell which are which?

Both dog and cat prints show a center pad and four toes. But a dog's prints have claw marks. A cat's claws never show in its tracks.

When a cat walks, the tracks of its hind feet fall exactly on the tracks of its front feet. So its footprints look like those of an animal with only two legs. But a dog places its hind feet slightly ahead of the larger tracks made by its front feet.

The shape of a track can help you tell which animal made it. Cats and dogs walk on "tiptoes," as do bobcats, foxes, mink, and weasels. Only the center pads and toes show in their prints. Animals with hooves, such as horses, deer, moose, elk, cows, and sheep, are also "tiptoers." A hoof is like a toenail. These animals walk on the nails of just one or two toes! A deer's hooves make tracks that look like upside down hearts.

Some animals walk *flatfooted*. Bears, skunks, and porcupines place both heels and toes on the ground—just the way we do. Raccoons, beavers, and squirrels also walk on flat feet.

You can learn lots of things from an animal's tracks even if you can't name what animal made them. You can tell whether the animal was running, walking, hopping, looking for food, or trying to escape from another animal. You can even figure out whether the creature usually lives in trees or shrubs or on the ground.

Most mammals that live in trees hop or bound along when they're on the ground. (When hopping, their hind feet land *ahead* of their front feet.) If you look carefully at the prints made by the front feet, you will see they are side-by-side.

The front-feet tracks of hopping animals that live on the ground are different. They are usually found one in front of another. Rabbits and some mice make tracks this way.

Most birds that live in trees also hop along the ground. When sparrows and woodpeckers hop, for example, they leave tracks that are side-by-side in pairs.

Birds that spend most of their time on the ground leave prints that are one in front of the other. You might see the tracks of ground birds such as pheasants, quail, herons, and grouse. Robins and other thrushes both hop and walk, and their tracks often show it.

Being a wildlife detective is lots of fun. And it's one of the best ways to learn about the habits of wild animals. With practice, you'll discover as much from an animal's tracks as you can by watching the animal itself. Happy tracking!

Directions. Read each sentence below. In each sentence, circle the word that signals contrast.

a. Although reading tracks is easy, it takes practice.

b. A dog's prints show claw marks; however, a cat's prints never show claw marks.

c. Whereas a walking cat places its hind paws exactly where its front paws had been, a walking dog places its hind feet slightly ahead of its front feet.

d. Cats and dogs walk on tiptoe; on the other hand, bears walk on their heels and toes.

e. The front-feet prints of tree animals show their paws side-by-side, but those of ground animals show their paws one in front of the other.

Exercise 2. Reread the sentences in Exercise 1 to answer the questions below. Write your answers in the blanks at the right.

a. Exercise 1a says that reading tracks is easy. What idea is contrasted with this? _____

b. Imagine you see prints. They belong to either a dog or a cat. You notice claw marks. To which animal do they belong? _____

c. Imagine you see prints. They belong to either a walking dog or a walking cat. The hind feet are slightly ahead of the front feet. To which animal do they belong? _____

d. Imagine you see prints. They belong to either a cat or a bear. The prints show heels and toes. To which animal do they belong? _____

e. Imagine you are shown the front-feet prints of an animal. The paws are side-by-side. Does the animal live in the trees or on the ground? _____

36

Name _____

Lesson 8
Understanding Comparison and Contrast

When you compare things, you show how they are alike. When you contrast things, you show how they are different. The photograph below shows five calves. Let's compare the calves. Obviously, there are many ways in which these calves are alike. For example, they all have four legs, two ears, and two eyes. In addition, they all have a tuft of hair on their head.

Now let's contrast the calves. Their heights are different. Looking from left to right, the third calf is the shortest, the fourth is next in size, the second seems to be next in size, then the first, and the fifth calf is the tallest.

How else can we contrast them? We can show how the white spots on their foreheads are different. We can even show how the brown patches on their legs are different.

Exercise 1. The following selection from "Amigo Brothers" by Piri Thomas compares and contrasts two boys, Antonio Cruz and Felix Varga. Read this selection and then follow the directions at the end of the selection.

Antonio Cruz and Felix Varga were both seventeen years old. They were so together in friendship that they felt themselves to be brothers. They had known each other since childhood, growing up on the lower east side of Manhattan in the same tenement building on Fifth Street between Avenue A and Avenue B.

Antonio was fair, lean, and lanky, while Felix was dark, short, and husky. Antonio's hair was always falling over his eyes, while Felix wore his black hair in a natural Afro style.

Each youngster had a dream of someday becoming lightweight champion of the world. Every chance they had the boys worked out, sometimes at the Boys Club on 10th Street and Avenue A and sometimes at the pro's gym on 14th Street. Early morning sunrises would find them running along the East River Drive, wrapped in sweat shirts, short towels around their necks, and handkerchiefs Apache style around their foreheads.

While some youngsters were into street negatives, Antonio and Felix slept, ate, rapped, and dreamt positive. Between them, they had a collection of *Fight* magazines second to none, plus a scrapbook filled with torn tickets to every boxing match they had ever attended, and some clippings of their own. If asked a question about any given fighter, they would immediately zip out from their memory banks divisions, weights, records of fights, knock-outs, technical knock-outs, and draws or losses.

Each had fought many bouts representing their community and had won two gold-plated medals plus a silver and bronze medallion. The difference was in their style. Antonio's lean form and long reach made him the better boxer, while Felix's short and muscular frame made him the better slugger. Whenever they had met in the ring for sparring sessions, it had always been hot and heavy.

Now, after a series of elimination bouts, they had been informed that they were to meet each other in the division finals that were scheduled for the seventh of August, two weeks away—the winner to represent the Boys Club in the Golden Gloves Championship Tournament.

Directions. Read each of the sentences below. If the sentence shows how the two boys are alike, write *Compare* in the blank. If it shows how the two boys are different, write *Contrast*.

a. "Antonio Cruz and Felix Varga were both seventeen years old." _____

b. "Antonio was fair, lean, and lanky, while Felix was dark, short, and husky." _____

c. "Antonio's hair was always falling over his eyes, while Felix wore his black hair in a natural Afro style." _____

d. "Each youngster had a dream of someday becoming lightweight champion of the world." _____

e. "Antonio's lean form and long reach made him the better boxer, while Felix's short and muscular frame made him the better slugger." _____

Exercise 2. Read the following sentences. Write *Compare* in the blank at the right by each sentence that shows how the two boxers are alike. Write *Contrast* by each sentence that shows how the two boxers are different.

a. Mike and Jake were both heavyweights.   _____

b. Mike weighed 208 pounds, whereas Jake weighed 201.   _____

c. Both boxers were known for their lightning-quick lefts. _____

d. Mike ran every morning, just as Jake did.   _____

e. Mike ran five miles, while Jake ran seven miles.   _____

Lesson 9

Identifying Relationship Patterns

People, things, events, and ideas may be related in several different ways. These include time order, spatial order, cause and effect, and comparison and contrast.

A time order relationship answers the question "When?" It tells you when one event happened in relationship to another event. For example:

The crowd cheered when the batter hit a home run.

A spatial order relationship answers the question "Where?" It tells you where one object is in relationship to other objects. For example:

The ball sailed over the catcher's head.

A cause and effect relationship answers the question "Why?" The cause is what makes something happen. The effect is what happens. For example:

The manager increased the batter's salary because the batter had the highest batting average on the team.

A comparison and contrast relationship answers the questions "How are they alike?" and "How are they different?" A comparison shows how things are alike. A contrast shows how they are different. For example:

Both teams hoped to win tonight's game. The hometown team had won its last four games, but the visiting team had lost its last two games.

So far in this chapter we have been looking at these relationship patterns separately, but they are combined in most writing.

Exercise. Read the following selection, "How to Catch a Baseball" by Willie Mays. Then follow the directions at the end of the selection.

To my way of thinking, every ball in the air should be caught.

When a batter hits a fly ball, look at it from the moment it leaves the bat and don't take your eyes off it until it's squeezed in your glove. If you can't see the ball, you're not going to catch it. A good fielder tries to judge the height, speed, direction and distance of a fly ball. When he puts this all together correctly, he makes the catch.

CATCHING THE BALL

1. The glove or mitt is not a "ball catcher," but merely a tool to help you catch the ball. I suggest every youngster learn to catch a ball bare-handed before using a baseball glove. Practice catching a tennis ball with two hands. Once you master this, get the feel of squeezing the ball and knowing it is caught, you can start using a glove. Use the glove as an extension of your hand. Catch with two hands, and when the ball falls into the pocket of the glove, squeeze the gloved hand softly just as you did the tennis ball.

2. Don't be afraid of the ball. If you keep your eyes on it and keep it in front of you, it can't hurt you.

3. Get yourself in a comfortable position where you feel flexible and can move quickly. Most players do this by standing on the balls of their feet, with their feet apart and their knees flexed, with the upper part of their bodies bent slightly forward and their arms relaxed in front of them. I used to have my gloved hand sitting on my knee so it wouldn't get tired.

4. Be ready to move quickly to catch the ball. Concentrate by watching it all the time—from the pitcher's hand and off the hitter's bat. If the ball isn't hit to you, watch where it is hit and watch the throw from the fielder's arm to wherever he throws the ball. In this way, you're always prepared to handle the baseball.

FIELDING THE GROUND BALL TO THE OUTFIELD

1. Again, watch the ball off the hitter's bat so you know where the ball is going and where you have to go to get it.

2. Move aggressively toward the ball, keeping it in front of you, if possible.

3. Keep your head down and your eyes on the ball.

4. When reaching down to field it, flex your knees and lower your body. Do not bend over with your knees stiff.

5. Come up throwing to the right base. (By the time you get to the ball, you already should know where you want to throw it.)

CATCHING FLY BALLS
TO THE OUTFIELD

1. Watch the ball off the hitter's bat to determine where it is going, how high and how fast.

40

2. Move as quickly as you can to the spot where you feel the ball will come down.

3. Try to set yourself squarely facing the ball so you can catch it in front of you, if possible.

4. If the ball reaches you at a point below your belt, cup your hands into a kind of basket, palms up, hands close together, fingers pointing up.

5. If the ball reaches you at chest level or higher, the back of your hands should face your body for a ball chest high, and they should face your face for a ball above the chest. Your thumbs should be together, and your arms extended upward, with your palms cupped slightly.

Directions. In the blanks at the right, put T by any sentence that shows a time order relationship. Put S by any sentence that shows a spatial order relationship. Put CE by any sentence that shows a cause and effect relationship. Put CC by any sentence that shows a comparison and contrast relationship.

a. "When he puts this all together correctly, he makes the catch." _____

b. "The glove or mitt is not a 'ball catcher,' but merely a tool to help you catch the ball." _____

c. "Once you master this, get the feel of squeezing the ball and knowing it is caught, you can start using a glove." _____

d. "Move aggressively toward the ball, keeping it in front of you, if possible." _____

e. "Again, watch the ball off the hitter's bat so you know where the ball is going and where you have to go to get it." _____

Lesson 10

Practice

Pay special attention to relationships while you read the true story below. Then complete the exercise that follows the selection.

One More Mountain
Anne Keegan

It was a freak accident that took Sheila Holzworth's sight.

A wire retainer on her teeth—a kind of brace that wrapped around the back of her head—popped loose and ripped up into her blue eyes.

Sheila was only ten; but she could no longer see.

For the athletic young girl from Des Moines—one of six active children of a local doctor—the accident was a tragedy.

It did not stay a tragedy long. Neither the Holzworth family nor Sheila would let it.

Two years later, Sheila started running on her elementary school track team. She loved to run. She was fast. Being blind was not going to stop her.

When she got to high school she went out for the track team. Her specialty was the 100-meter dash. The coach accepted her. So did the other members of her team. But there were others, as there often are when handicapped people try to make inroads, who had a problem.

When she showed up for the first track meet, a track official came running down to her parents. "This girl," he told them, "cannot compete."

"Why?" asked her parents.

"Why, she's blind," said the official.

"So what?" said her parents. "She can still run."

Sheila did not give in either. She took her place in front of the starting block and announced, "I'm running." And she did.

At 19, Sheila was on her college varsity track team. With the aid of an electronic beeper, and wearing earphones, Sheila runs where her coach tells her to.

Running is not all Sheila Holzworth does. She rides her own horse. She canoes. She water-skis. She snow-skis.

And now, she has climbed a mountain. A very high mountain. On July 3, 1981, at 10:40 A.M., after a three-day climb, Sheila Holzworth struggled up to the 14,410-foot peak of Mt. Rainier in Paradise, Washington. She was the youngest one of her group to make it.

The group that conquered Mt. Rainier were all handicapped. Five blind and two deaf persons, an epileptic, and a Vietnam veteran with an artificial leg all climbed the mountain in honor of the International Year of Disabled Persons.

Like everyone else, they did it because the mountain was there.

But they also wanted to prove something to the world about handicapped people: that they can do plenty if given the chance. These nine got the chance. Eleven started out, but two did not make it to the summit.

Sheila decided last February to take the chance. From the day she said, yes, she'd give the mountain a try, she went into training. With her brother, Timmy, alongside her, egging her on, she ran two miles and swam half a mile every day.

"It was a new challenge," says Sheila. "I knew it would be hard to climb that mountain. But I also knew the self-satisfaction would be great. I wanted other people in the world to know handicapped people can do anything.

"When you go out to get a job, they see you are handicapped and they don't even bother to look and see if you are qualified. They just automatically say no. Hopefully, if we climbed this mountain, it would improve everybody's attitude toward the disabled."

Sheila worked out until a week before the climb. She then traveled to Aspen, Colorado, where the handicapped adventurers on the team all met. They took to each other immediately.

"We all knew we had to get along, and that we had to trust each other, if we were going to climb this mountain together," says Sheila.

"We had no doubts about each other—or doubts about whether we would make it. The only doubt we had was the weather."

The day the team of handicapped climbers—none of whom had ever done high-altitude climbing—met for the first time, they were told of the deaths of eleven climbers on Mt. Rainier in an ice fall.

It did not discourage them at all, says Sheila. In fact, it filled them with greater resolve. "We wanted to climb in honor of those eleven people."

From the first day, the deaf climbers were the blind climbers' eyes. The blind climbers learned sign language and became the deaf climbers' ears.

On Wednesday, July 1, the group, led by veteran mountaineer Jim Whittaker, began their ascent. Each climber carried a walkie-talkie. At any time they could be in instant communication with their leader, with another climber, or with the base camp and forest rangers down below.

Sheila, all of five feet three inches, began the climb with a 60-pound pack on her back.

"I wasn't afraid," says Sheila, who soon came to be known as the queen of one-liners in the group. "I couldn't see the bottom."

All day Wednesday they advanced up the mountain. They slept that first night at 10,000 feet. The second day, they made it to 11,000 feet on the Ingraham Flats. During the night, the wind blew their tents down.

Early the third morning, at 4:30 A.M., a voice crackled over the radio down at the base camp, announcing that the climbers were up and on their way.

"It was between 12,800 feet and 13,500 feet that was the hardest," says Sheila. "The altitude was getting to me. I could feel myself starting to get sick. I'd heard that people had literally crawled to get to the summit, and I thought, 'Baloney. I'm making it on my own two feet.' We were taking one step, and then taking two deep breaths. Then another step. I was getting sick when we stopped for lunch."

After a lunch of sugar, candy, and fruit drink, Sheila recovered. She hit the trail again. Finally, struggling up a mountain she could not see, she felt she was near the top. She could hear the wind, feel the gravity pull, feel the thin air.

Jim Whittaker made it first and let out a yell over the radio. Three minutes later, Sheila, tied by ropes to her guides, made it too.

"It was wonderful," says Sheila. "Jim hugged and kissed me and I started to cry, I was so happy.

"All the way up I kept saying, 'I know I'll make it'—and I did. We all were yelling, 'We made it, we made it.' Jim kept trying to stop me from jumping around so much, so I wouldn't fall off. We all held hands then. It was wonderful.

"We stayed up there two hours. We had an Indian medicine bag and threw the contents to the four winds—south, north, east, and west. We planted eagle feathers. We brought up three flags—the flag of the UN, the United States flag, and the flag for the International Year of Disabled Persons.

"Coming down was a lot harder. Coming up, I was on a thin trail and I could feel my footing. Coming down," says Sheila, "was like stepping into midair."

While coming down the team got a serious scare. Above them, an avalanche began. Terrified, the climbers ran and stumbled and fell to get out of the way. The avalanche stopped 100 feet from Sheila.

When the group got to base camp, they were exhausted, sunburned, and happy. But most of all, they were victorious.

"The key word is being given a chance," says Sheila. "All of us got a chance. If your own environment doesn't believe in you, you won't believe in yourself. I hope what we did will change the environment for disabled people."

The nine-member team of handicapped climbers went to Washington, D.C., to call on President Reagan. The President leaned down to Sheila and said, "Sheila, you are quite a gal."

He was right. For Sheila Holzworth, who lost her eyesight when she was only ten, has climbed more than just one mountain. In the last nine years, she has overcome a multitude of obstacles as big as mountains.

She has made it to the top.

Exercise. Refer to "One More Mountain" to answer the questions below. Write your answers on the blanks provided.

a. When Sheila was ten, a wire retainer on her teeth popped loose. What result did this have?

_____

b. Why did the track official tell Sheila's parents that she could not compete?

_____

c. What did Sheila do when the track official said this?

_____

d. Where did Sheila make her climb? (Be as specific as you can.)

_____

e. How was the group that climbed Mt. Rainier different from most mountain climbing groups?

_____

f. For what two reasons did this group climb Mt. Rainier?

_____

_____

_____

g. In February why did Sheila begin running two miles and swimming half a mile a day?

_____

h. Jim Whittaker was the first to make it to the top of the mountain. How much later did Sheila reach the top?

_____

i. An avalanche began when the group was coming down the mountain. Where did the avalanche stop in relation to Sheila?

_____

j. Make a list of five things this group did when they reached the top of the mountain.

(1) _____

(2) _____

(3) _____

(4) _____

(5) _____

Chapter 3
Judgments

You make judgments in order to choose wisely. In this chapter you will learn how to use reliable sources to judge information. You will see how to identify statements of fact and statements of opinion. You will practice forming valid opinions and drawing sound conclusions. In addition, you will learn to spot stereotypes and loaded words. Finally, you will practice identifying faulty reasoning.

Lesson 1

Identifying a Reliable Source

When you read information, try to determine whether or not the author is a reliable source. Ask yourself three questions:

1. Is the author qualified? Usually you can trust an author with training and experience in one field to give you accurate information about *this* field.

2. Is the author presenting the information fairly? Some authors try to be fair and present all the information truthfully. Others, however, may not tell you the whole story. They may stress only the good parts (or only the bad parts) in order to persuade you to do something that will benefit them.

3. Is the information accurate? If you disagree with the information in an article, check another source. You might check an encyclopedia, another book on the subject, or another expert in the field.

For example, imagine you and your parents are going to spend a weekend in New York City. Your parents tell you to choose a Broadway show to see. You remember reading an article about the show *Angels*. The article said that *Angels* was the best show to reach Broadway in years. It said that each number was a show stopper. The article was written by the producer.

Is the producer a reliable source of information? Let's look at our three questions.

Is the producer qualified? Obviously, the producer has training and experience in the field of theater. He has produced several successful plays and is respected in his field.

Is the producer presenting the information fairly? The producer may be presenting the information fairly. But keep in mind that he will benefit if the show is a success. Therefore, he may be exaggerating how good the play is in order to persuade you to see it. The producer is not disinterested. This means that he is not free from hope of personal gain. Therefore, he may not be a reliable source.

Is the information accurate? You can compare the information in this article with other articles about the show and reviews by critics. Also, you can compare it with information from people you know who have seen the show.

Look at the comic strip below. Hugo writes a notice that will help him sell his red cart. He stresses the good parts—three great wheels. He doesn't mention the drawback—one wheel missing.

TIGER by Bud Blake

Exercise 1. Read each quotation below. Then read the occupations that follow each quotation. Which occupation would give the writer the training and experience necessary to be a reliable source of information for this quotation? Put an X next to this occupation.

a. "That loud knocking sound means your fan belt is broken. You must not drive your car until the fan belt is fixed."

_____ drummer in a band

_____ painter

_____ auto mechanic

b. "With this ten-speed bike, you can easily do 25 miles an hour."

_____ movie maker

_____ electrician

_____ bicycle-racing champion

c. "Apply this medicine to the burn and it will ease the pain."

_____ nurse

_____ teacher

_____ dancer

d. *"Purrfection Cat Food* will give your cat all the vitamins and minerals it needs."

_____ veterinarian, or animal doctor

_____ movie star

_____ wrestler

e. "The *Voicewriter* is the best home computer on the market today."

_____ secretary

_____ computer engineer

_____ gardener

Exercise 2. Read the following statements. Each is followed by three sources. Put an *X* next to the most reliable source.

a. "Martha Susan is a natural actress. She is convincing and able to take on many different parts."

_____ director of a theater

_____ Martha Susan's aunt

_____ Martha Susan's business manager

b. "This bicycle is in excellent condition. You should buy it."

_____ owner of the bicycle

_____ your next-door neighbor

_____ bicycle mechanic

c. "Paradise Beach has mild temperatures every day. In summer, there is rarely a rainy day."

_____ friend who was there for a weekend last summer

_____ travel writer in local newspaper

_____ owner of hotel on Paradise Beach

d. "If used regularly, this soap will soften your skin."

_____ your dermatologist (skin specialist)

_____ your best friend

_____ the pitcher for your favorite baseball team

e. *"Tapping Feet* is the best dancing school in town. The teachers are enthusiastic and well trained.

_____ a five-year-old who is a student at Tapping Feet

_____ the National Association of Dance Schools

_____ the owner of Tapping Feet

Using Reliable Sources

There are three types of reliable sources. The first is a person with training and experience in the field. We call this person an expert. The second is an article or book written by an expert in the field. The third is a reference book, such as an encyclopedia or atlas. When you need accurate information about a subject, use a reliable source.

For example, imagine you are thinking about law enforcement as a career. You might talk to a police officer and ask for information. Also, you might read a library book about careers in law enforcement.

Imagine you are writing a report and need to know the population of Brazil. You could find this information in the latest edition of the almanac. Imagine you hear a news story about the Galápagos Islands. You want to find out where they are. You could find this information in a dictionary or in an atlas.

Exercise. Read each of the following items. Put an X in the blank by the most reliable source for information on each item.

a. Richard Oakes is thinking about working in a hospital. He needs information about careers in health.

_____ Richard's friend, clerk at East Avenue Drugstore

_____ Manny Gonzalas, student advisor, Health Careers, Orange County Community College

_____ the book *Painless Dieting*

b. Alice has saved her baby-sitting money to buy a bicycle. She needs accurate information about which bike to buy.

_____ television commercial

_____ article in a leading consumer magazine, "Which Is the Best Bike for You?"

_____ friend who owns a three-speed bike

c. For three days, Joe's puppy Crescent has had dull eyes and trouble breathing. She has been very quiet and slow moving. Joe needs accurate information about the dog's problem.

_____ *Little Foot Comes Home*, a television show about the adventures of a lost poodle

_____ a veterinarian

_____ Joe's best friend Mack, who has raised two cats since they were kittens

d. John Magoo has a very shady backyard. He wants to grow flowers in it. Although most flowers require a great deal of sun, a few don't. John needs accurate information about choosing the right plants for his yard.

_____ booklet published by the state university, *Growing Flowering Plants in the Shade*

_____ library book, *Flower Arrangement for Beginners*

_____ television show about flowering plants that grow in the desert

e. Janet Wainwright is writing a report on Benedict Arnold. She needs accurate information about his role in the Revolutionary War.

_____ the history textbook *Rise of the American Nation*

_____ friend whose ancestor fought in the Revolutionary War

_____ talk-show host who interviews famous people

f. Malcolm Reed is tracing his roots. He needs information about the marriage of his great-grandfather and great-grandmother. He knows they were married in Des Moines, Iowa. Fifteen years later they moved to Shreveport, Louisiana. Malcolm is now living in New Orleans, Louisiana.

_____ the minister of Malcolm's church

_____ Division of Records and Statistics, State Department of Health, Des Moines, Iowa

_____ Division of Public Health Statistics, State Department of Health, New Orleans, Louisiana

g. Patricia Nelson is preparing a report on the 1960 presidential election. She needs information about the family background of Richard Nixon and John F. Kennedy.

_____ article in the June 1960 issue of *American Heritage*, "Grandfathers of the Candidates"

_____ library book, *Tracing Your Civil War Ancestor*

_____ local supermarket owner who remembers well the Kennedy-Nixon debates

h. Luis Ortiz is planning a vacation in Nome, Alaska. He wants to find out the average temperature of Nome during the summer.

_____ library book, *Alaska During the 1890s*

_____ the latest almanac

_____ the dictionary

i. Peter McNee is a wrestler. He needs to lose seven pounds before the next match. He needs information about how to lose weight safely.

_____ commercial for diet aids by Hollywood star

_____ library book on losing weight safely by well-known medical doctor

_____ article on losing weight through crash diets

j. Michelle Robertson's sister is graduating from high school this year. She is planning to become a keypunch operator. She needs information about vocational schools.

_____ Uncle Phil, who was a keypunch operator fifteen years ago

_____ an advertisement for a keypunch school

_____ a pamphlet published this year by the state, _Guide to Choosing a Vocational School_

Lesson 3

Recognizing Statements of Fact and Statements of Opinion

A statement of fact contains information that can be proved true or false. It contains information about things that have happened in the past or are happening in the present. For example, here are two statements of fact:

> Benjamin Franklin flew his famous kite in 1752.
> Jayne is flying her kite in the park.

A statement of opinion expresses a personal belief or attitude. It contains information that cannot be proved true or false. For example, here are two statements of opinion.

> Kite flying is a thrilling sport.
> The most beautiful kites are shaped like tigers.

Statements that predict the future are statements of opinion, since you cannot prove whether the information they contain is true or false. For example:

> Kite flying will become even more popular in the future.

52

Exercise. Read the following selection, "Let's Fly a Kite" by Laura McFadden Yelsik. Then follow the directions at the end of the selection.

The first warm weather, blue skies, and gentle breezes of spring traditionally call to all kite lovers, "Let's fly a kite!"

Kiting, the sport of flying and making kites, has recently grown in popularity in the United States among adults as well as children. A National Kite Week has been established in May, and there are even kite shops where you can purchase kites of different types and sizes from all over the world.

Kites have entertained people of all ages for well over two thousand years. The actual inventor of the first kite, however, is unknown. While there are Chinese legends claiming that the first kite was invented by a Chinese general for use in war around 200 BC, early Greek and Egyptian history also refers to early uses of kites. Regardless of where kites may have made their first appearance, they now fascinate people all over the world. It is interesting to note that in many languages the words for kite and bird are similar.

Throughout history, kites have had many different uses. They have not always been used just for fun. The story of Benjamin Franklin's dangerous experiment with a kite in 1752 is a legend. He used a kite to discover that lightning is indeed static electricity.

Kites have helped scientists learn about weather. In Scotland in the eighteenth century, a series of kites with thermometers attached were sent skyward to record the temperature. Later scientists found that they could measure the wind velocity by attaching a wind meter to a kite and launching it. These early kites were the forerunners of the weather satellites we know today.

At the turn of the century, men experimented with kites, balloons, and gliders. The knowledge that they gained led to the invention of the airplane.

Kites aided the military in World War II. Target kites with pictures of enemy planes on them were used for gunnery practice. Soldiers, stranded in life rafts, sent kites soaring to guide search parties to them. The military sent cameras and radio equipment aloft, carried by kites.

Some of the more unusual roles kites have played include carrying the first line over the Niagara Gorge to begin the building of the suspension bridge near Niagara Falls.

One very creative English gentleman sported the first carriage powered by—that's right—a kite!

In parts of the Philippines, rice crops are watched over by kites in bird shapes—an attempt to scare off any unwanted pests.

Kites with advertising slogans printed on them sometimes attract attention in the sky. Some people even fish with kites instead of fishing poles. They attach their fishing line to the kite, fly it over the water to a likely spot, and drop the line. They claim the fish bite!

Several countries find kiting so popular that they hold kite festivals. In China, the Kite Flying Festival is celebrated on the ninth day of the ninth month. Kites of all sizes and shapes—dragons, fishes, birds, and butterflies—are seen flying.

Japan's Boys' Festival is held on the fifth day of May. A kite in the shape of the carp fish is flown by every boy in the household who hopes that he too will be as courageous as the carp.

The Festival of Spring in India finds kites being flown from the rooftops.

Now the United States holds a kite festival, too. National Kite Week, celebrated during May, is only a few years old, but it's growing in popularity. Many cities sponsor kite tournaments that include a variety of contests. Prizes are given for the highest-flying kites, longest-flying kites, largest kites, smallest kites, and best-constructed kites. If your city doesn't have a kite festival, organize your own with friends or ask if your school will sponsor one.

Directions. Read each statement below. Write *F* in the blank at the right by any statement of fact. Write *O* by any statement of opinion.

a. Benjamin Franklin was the wisest early American. _____

b. Benjamin Franklin discovered that lightning is really static electricity. _____

c. Eighteenth-century Scottish scientists used kites to record the temperature. _____

d. The best kite stores are found in large cities. _____

e. During World War II, soldiers used kites to help search parties find them. _____

f. Using kites with messages printed on them is a delightful advertising technique. _____

g. Kite festivals are held in China, Japan, and India. _____

h. In the United States, people celebrate National Kite Week in May. _____

i. As time goes on, this exciting festival will become more and more popular. _____

j. It is more fun to fly a kite alone than to fly it with a group of people. _____

Lesson 4

Understanding Mixed Statements of Fact and Opinion

A statement of fact contains information that can be proved true or false. For example, first look at the illustration below. Then look at the sentence following it.

Norman Rockwell called this picture *Triple Self-Portrait.*

This is a statement of fact. The information in this statement can be proved true or false.

A statement of opinion expresses a personal belief or attitude. For example, look at the statement below.

This self-portrait is very beautiful.

This is a statement of opinion. It contains information that cannot be proved true or false.

55

Some statements mix facts and opinions. They are called mixed statements of fact and opinion. Look at the following sentence.

Norman Rockwell was a popular illustrator **whose fame will last for many years.**

The first part of this sentence is a statement of fact. The second part, printed in **boldface,** is a statement of opinion. It predicts the future. Now look at the next mixed statement of fact and opinion.

His delightful pictures hang in museums, offices, and homes.

It is a fact that his pictures hang in museums, offices, and homes. It is an opinion that these pictures are delightful.

Exercise 1. Read the following selection, "Norman Rockwell: The Illustrator Everybody Knows" by Gloria May Stoddard. Then follow the directions at the end of the selection.

It was late December of 1907 in New York City. Students could hardly wait to decorate the classroom for Christmas. Miss Smith smiled and handed a box of colored chalk to a shy, skinny thirteen-year-old with big, round glasses and heavy corrective shoes. "You may draw on all the blackboards! Go to it!" she said.

Norman grinned and stumbled merrily to the front of the room. He could draw anything: horses, dogs, lions, birds, ships, automobiles, fire engines. But the Christmas display was special. What could he draw that would please everyone?

Ideas flashed through his mind. Then, with pure joy, he began drawing a Christmas scene with red and green and white chalk. But he erased it and started all over. He worked on and on, his tongue licking his upper lip as he concentrated.

At last the colorful murals were finished. Miss Smith and the students exclaimed with delight. Rockwell's favorite memory was of this eighth-grade teacher who had encouraged him in his drawing.

Unlike his older brother Jarvis, who was the best athlete in his school, Norman was the worst runner on the block. Because he could not compete in other ways, Norman concentrated on drawing. His father often read aloud from the many well-known stories of Charles Dickens. Norman would sketch the characters as his father read.

By the time he was in the eighth grade, Norman knew he wanted to go to art school. But he also knew that he would have to earn money for his tuition.

Norman was a choirboy in his church at Mamaroneck. His minister found him a job giving sketching lessons. He mowed lawns and raked leaves. During his first year in high school he had lessons every Wednesday and Saturday at the Chase School of Art in New York.

At sixteen he became a full-time art student. He studied at the National Academy School and later at the Art Students

League. To pay expenses, he worked as a waiter, actor, and poster painter. He illustrated stories for children's magazines. A teacher found him his first professional job as an illustrator for a set of books. Edward Cave, the editor of *Boys' Life*, asked Norman to illustrate several short stories and made him art director of the magazine.

Spurred on by a friend, Norman Rockwell sold his first cover picture to the famous *Saturday Evening Post* when he was twenty-two. He decided to be a full-time, free-lance artist.

Rockwell traveled and studied all over the world. He researched thoroughly. He painted Presidents, First Ladies, heads of state, and movie stars. He designed Boy Scout medals and three commemorative stamps; and he illustrated *Tom Sawyer*, *Huckleberry Finn*, and *Louisa May Alcott: America's Best Loved Writer*.

Above all else Norman loved people. So he painted pictures of lively youngsters and interesting adults in happy and humorous family situations. Each picture told a story and made the people smile and feel hopeful. His most popular *Post* cover, *Saying Grace*, shows a grandmother and her grandson blessing their Thanksgiving Day meal in a shabby railroad restaurant.

Because he firmly believed that all women, men, and children should love God and show kindness toward each other, he painted a picture called *The Golden Rule*. It won him the Interfaith Award of the National Conference of Christians and Jews.

He was a lifelong friend to all Boy Scouts. Every year for 40 years he painted a special picture for their official calendar. He was called "Mr. Scouting" and received the Silver Buffalo Award for distinguished service.

All his life Rockwell appreciated the beauty and strength of human character. He understood the spirit and soul of people of all ages. He said, "People somehow get out of your work just about what you put into it, and if you are interested in the characters that you draw, and understand and love them, why, the person who sees your picture is bound to feel the same way."

In 1943 Rockwell's studio in Arlington, Vermont, was destroyed by fire. His life's work was gone. But he didn't waste time brooding. He built a new studio and began all over again.

Norman Rockwell became rich and famous as the world's favorite illustrator. Yet he continued to use his talent even in his eighties. When he died at his home in Stockbridge, Massachusetts, an unfinished painting stood on his easel. Today his delightful pictures are in a new *Official Boy Scout Handbook* and in museums, offices, and homes all over America. They continue to bring joy to millions of people everywhere.

Directions. Read each mixed statement of fact and opinion below. Draw one line under the part of the sentence that is an opinion.

a. In eighth grade, Norman Rockwell decided to go to art school, which was the wisest decision anyone ever made.

b. Norman's minister, the best man in the world, found him a job giving sketching lessons.

c. Norman Rockwell illustrated stories for children's magazines, and these illustrations are extremely beautiful.

d. Rockwell painted Presidents, First Ladies, and heads of state, but his illustrations of American families are the most beautiful.

e. Some people like *Saying Grace,* but I think that *The Golden Rule* is his most moving picture.

Exercise 2. Read the mixed statements of fact and opinion below. Some words in each statement express an opinion. Write these words in the blank at the right.

a. When Norman finished his extraordinarily attractive murals, his teacher praised him.

_____

b. Since he was the most talented boy in the world, his teachers liked him.

_____

c. Norman's father often read aloud many stories by Charles Dickens—England's finest writer.

_____

d. Norman spent many hours sketching as his father read aloud in an extremely beautiful voice.

_____

e. Norman Rockwell became rich and famous because of his extremely delightful illustrations.

_____

Lesson 5

Forming Valid Opinions

A valid opinion is a judgment or belief supported by facts. People form valid opinions every day. For example, Janice decides that she will make a good veterinarian. She bases her opinion on facts. She has received good grades in science and mathematics for the last few years. She likes animals. When her cat was sick, she took care of it and helped it to get better.

Peter decides which bike is best for him. He reads a consumer report comparing three-speed bikes with ten-speed bikes. This report says that three-speed bikes cost less than ten-speed bikes. Usually, three-speed bikes are sturdier. They hold up better on poor roads. On the other hand, ten-speed bikes make riding up hills easier. They are lighter and they perform better than three-speed bikes in racing situations.

Peter has saved $150.00 to buy a bike. He lives in a flat area. There are few hills and certainly no mountains. He needs a bike to deliver newspapers in the city. On the basis of the facts, Peter decides that a three-speed bike would be the better choice for him.

Before you form an opinion, make sure you know the facts. In the comic strip below, Archie thinks the electronics store is offering a great deal on stereos. But Archie doesn't know the facts.

ARCHIE

Exercise 1. Read each opinion below. Then read the statements that follow each opinion. Write *Yes* by each statement that backs up the opinion. Write *No* by each statement that does not.

a. *Opinion:* Penny will win the public speaking contest.

_____ For the last three years, Penny has won every public speaking contest she has taken part in.

_____ Penny always wears very stylish clothes.

_____ The three other candidates have not won any other contests.

_____ Penny has worked hard to prepare for this contest.

b. *Opinion:* Ralph is the best candidate for school treasurer.

_____ Ralph is on the school football team.

_____ Ralph always receives good grades in mathematics.

_____ Ralph is known for his honesty.

_____ Ralph is my best friend.

c. *Opinion:* My younger sister Janet will like this book.

_____ Janet has enjoyed other books by this writer.

_____ My older brother Bob liked this book.

_____ This is a mystery, and Janet usually likes mysteries.

_____ The book did not cost very much.

d. *Opinion:* It will rain tomorrow.

_____ Tomorrow is Tuesday, and it always seems to rain on Tuesdays.

_____ We have planned a picnic for tomorrow.

_____ Today it rained to the west of us, and the weather front is moving from west to east.

_____ Satellite photographs show rain clouds moving in our direction.

Exercise 2. Read each opinion below. Then list two facts that would support each opinion.

a. Aretha will win the tennis match against Sally.

(1) _____

(2) _____

b. Peter will be the next class president.

(1) _____

(2) _____

c. Manuel will get his driver's license this year.

(1) _____

(2) _____

d. By June, Lynn will have enough money to buy the present.

(1) _____

(2) _____

Lesson 6

Drawing Conclusions Based on Facts

A sound conclusion is a judgment based on facts. For example, you draw sound conclusions every day. You walk up to a friend's house. You see several cars in the driveway. You hear music playing and people laughing. On the basis of these facts, you conclude that your friend is having a party.

Exercise. Read the following selection from "Secrets of the Alligators" by Sandy Huff. Then answer the questions that follow it.

Can mother alligators somehow predict the weather three months in advance? That's what a scientist in the Everglades is trying to find out.

Mother alligators make their nests during dry weather. The nests look like big messy piles of sticks and mud standing in the shallow, weedy Everglades. By the time the babies hatch three months later, the rains have started and the water is higher. But somehow the mother alligators have made their nests just high enough so the eggs stay dry until the babies hatch.

In years when little rain falls, the nests are fewer and lower than in years when there will be lots of rain. The scientist who is carefully measuring the nests is Marilyn Kushlan, a research biologist with the Everglades National Park Research Center.

Is it just coincidence, she wonders, or do the mother alligators have some way of knowing ahead of time how much rain will fall?

Kushlan has been studying alligators for the past five years. These animals are very important in the ecology of the Everglades. They dig deep holes for dens. In the dry season other animals find water in these gator holes, and fish live in them. Alligators act like plows when they swim, keeping channels open through the thick weeds that choke the waterways. They have also been called the "trash cans of the Everglades" because they eat the sick or dead animals. They keep the number of rattlesnakes down by eating rats, the snakes' main food.

Kushlan doesn't try to watch *all* the alligators that live in Everglades Park. Instead, she samples several study areas and carefully counts and watches the gators that live there.

Looking for Gators

Traveling through the soft mud and sharp sawgrass is difficult, so Kushlan uses an airboat, a flat-bottomed skiff with an airplane propeller that blows the boat over the shallow water. She always tries to drive in the same lanes to cut down on how much she disturbs the birds and animals that live there. For safety, she always takes a helper along on her trips. Sometimes, when she needs to look over her study areas quickly, she uses a helicopter and does her searching from the air.

Kushlan has to look hard because alligators are tricky to find. They are the same color as the brownish water, and when they hear her airboat coming, they don't run away—they sink! They can stay underwater a long time, too. Once she watched a big gator hold its breath for over two hours!

But alligators are nosey. Sometimes she goes to a pond where she knows a gator lives. She stops her motor and gets out her lunch. By the time she and her helper have eaten a sandwich, the gator has come up to look them over.

When she wants to catch a gator, Kushlan baits a snare with fish. The hungry gator has to put its head through a thick wire noose to reach the fish—and it's caught. Since many alligators look alike, she puts tags on their tails and toes before she lets them go. She has tagged over 1,000 alligators.

Alligators' Habits

To find out what alligators do all day, Kushlan puts radio collars on some of the larger alligators. By listening with earphones and a radio receiver for the signals, she can find the collared gators day or night. She found that female alligators usually stay near their home ponds, while males go as far as two miles from their dens.

Baby alligators stay close to their nest, where their mother watches over them. She chases away the birds, raccoons, and even bullfrogs that like to eat small alligators. As the babies get older, they drift away from their home pond and find other places to live.

For years people thought gators ate garfish, a long, armored fish. Kushlan decided the only way to know for sure was to see what the gators had in their stomachs.

First, Kushlan and her helper catch an alligator. They gently slide a tube down its throat and pour a little water down the tube to loosen up what's inside the gator's stomach. Then they hold the gator upside down over a bucket. Out comes the gator's last meal.

With their strong tails, hard claws, and sharp teeth, the gators fight fiercely, but Kushlan knows how to hold on tight. The largest alligator she ever sampled was an eight-footer!

While Kushlan wants to take more samples before she says for sure what gators eat, so far she has found fish, birds, crawfish, and snails in the stomachs of gators. She hasn't found any garfish. She *has* found rocks and bits of mangrove root, which alligators swallow to help grind up their food because gators don't chew their food when they eat.

Questions

a. You are studying alligators. You find there were far fewer alligator nests in 1982 than in 1983. The 1982 nests were much lower than the 1983 nests. What conclusion do you draw? Put an X next to your answer.

_____ (1) There was less rainfall in 1982 than in 1983.

_____ (2) There was less sunlight in 1982 than in 1983.

_____ (3) There was less food in 1982 than in 1983.

b. You are studying a certain area of the Everglades. You see no alligator holes. You notice only a few channels open through the thick weeds. A large number of rats live in the area. What conclusion do you draw?

_____ (1) Rats do not dig holes.

_____ (2) It has been an unusually rainy year.

_____ (3) Few alligators live in this section of the Ever-glades.

c. You observe a specific pond. You see an alligator, but the alligator also sees you. It sinks under the water. You watch the water until the alligator comes to the top again. The alligator doesn't come up for air until an hour and a half later. What conclusion do you draw?

_____ (1) An alligator can stay under water for over an hour.

_____ (2) An alligator cannot stay under water for an hour.

_____ (3) An alligator doesn't like staying under water.

d. You empty the stomachs of twenty alligators. You find birds, crawfish, and snails. You also find rocks and pieces of mangrove root. What conclusion do you draw?

_____ (1) Alligators eat garfish.

_____ (2) Alligators eat crawfish.

_____ (3) Alligators eat other alligators.

Lesson 7

Recognizing Stereotypes

A stereotype is an opinion about a group of people that does not allow for individual differences. A stereotype is not based on proof. Two common stereotypes are "All soldiers are strong men" and "All teenagers enjoy loud music and loud parties." A stereotype can cloud your judgment and prevent you from seeing the worth of an individual.

When you read a statement of opinion, watch out for words like *all, always, only,* and *never.* Often they signal a stereotype. For example, the following statement is a stereotype:

All kids hate spinach.

Be careful, though. The words *all, always, only,* and *never* are also used in statements of fact. For example:

All people who drive cars need a license.

In the comic strip on page 64, the queen holds an opinion that is a stereotype. She says, "Only important people have important (big) noses!" Then one of the least important people in the kingdom walks in—and he has a big nose.

Exercise 1. If the statement below is a stereotype, write *Yes* in the blank at the right. If the statement is not a stereotype, write *No*.

a. A good basketball player has to be at least seven feet tall. _____

b. All professors are forgetful. _____

c. Most dancers train hard and watch their weight. _____

d. Television is a wasteland; there are never any good programs on it. _____

e. Television programs can be educational as well as entertaining. _____

f. People who work in television are always glamorous and exciting. _____

g. Any politician who advertises on television is a good candidate. _____

h. Anyone who studies hard is boring. _____

i. Cramming is usually a poor way of studying for a test. _____

j. Elections for President are held every four years. _____

Exercise 2. Write *Yes* by any statement below that is a stereotype. Write *No* by any statement that is not a stereotype.

a. Athletes make poor students. _____

b. Several former Presidents of the United States were athletes when they were in school. _____

c. Football players are only interested in having a good time. _____

d. Soccer is not a good sport for girls. _____

e. Burt Reynolds once played football for the University of Oklahoma. _____

f. Men are better tennis players than women. _____

g. Billie Jean King once beat Bobby Riggs in a tennis match. _____

h. Hockey players are violent people. _____

i. The discipline you learn when you train for sports can help you with your school work. _____

j. Hank Aaron was a famous baseball player. _____

Lesson 8

Recognizing Loaded Words

Loaded words color, or slant, writing. They are charged with emotion and arouse strong feelings. Often, they express the writer's judgment of things.

Some loaded words arouse negative feelings. For example, think about the words *house* and *shack*. Both mean "a dwelling; a place where people live." *Shack*, though, also arouses negative feelings. It carries the meaning of crudely built and run down. Many people live in houses, but some people would be insulted to have their houses called "shacks."

Some loaded words create a positive impression. For example, think about the words *house* and *home*. Again, both mean a dwelling. *Home*, though, carries a positive meaning. It arouses good feelings about all the happy times we've had with our families. Even if we live in houses, we usually talk about our homes.

Exercise 1. Read each group of words below. Circle the word in each group that carries a negative meaning. You may use your dictionary to help you.

a. child,   youngster,   brat

b. unwise,   unthinking,   stupid

c. gossip,   talk,   chatter

d. surgeon,   sawbones,   doctor

e. gumshoe,   detective,   private eye

f. restaurant,   diner,   greasy spoon

g. curious,   nosey,   interested

h. beg,   ask,   request

i. mutt,   dog,   canine

j. lawyer,   mouthpiece,   counselor

Exercise 2. Read each group of words below. Circle the word in each group that carries a positive meaning. You may use your dictionary to help you.

a. store,   shop,   salon

b. petite,   short,   little

c. gaudy,   fancy,   luxurious

d. natural,   homely,   unpolished

e. show off,   flaunt,   dazzle

f. infant,   cherub,   baby

g. slender,   thin,   skinny

h. jokester,   wit,   wisecracker

i. pal,   companion,   acquaintance

j. old,   ancient,   antique

Exercise 3. For each word below, find a loaded word that has the same basic meaning. Use your dictionary to help you. Write your answers in the blanks.

a. cook _____   **f.** expensive _____

b. heavy _____   **g.** bold _____

c. thrifty _____   **h.** tall _____

d. serious _____   **i.** catch _____

e. inexpensive _____   **j.** studious _____

66

Lesson 9

Identifying Faulty Reasoning

Faulty reasoning is thinking that is not sound. Several traps can cloud your thinking and make your reasoning faulty.

First, a writer may disguise statements of opinion as statements of fact. For example, the writer may say:

> It's a fact that we shall discover life on other planets. Everyone knows that we will find that the Loch Ness monster exists.

Both of these are statements of opinions. Do not be fooled by the words "it's a fact" and "everyone knows."

Second, a writer may use evidence that doesn't fit or support the opinion or conclusion. For example, a writer may say,

> Science has not solved all the mysteries on Earth. It does not know why whales beach themselves and die. It cannot explain why spitting cobras are the only snakes that can spit their venom. It does not know why elephants suddenly go mad and attack everything in sight. Whether or not the creature called "Bigfoot" exists is a mystery. **Someday science will find that Bigfoot does exist.**

At the end of this paragraph, the writer states the opinion that science will find that Bigfoot does exist. The evidence the writer gives in this paragraph does not fit, or back up, this judgment.

Third, the writer may use name-calling or appeals to your emotions. For example, the writer may say,

> Only fools believe that the Loch Ness monster does not exist.

> All Americans who care about our future do not want other nations to get ahead of us. These good people will give to the Foundation for Scientific Advancement so that America will always be first.

These statements use name-calling and appeals to the emotions. No one wants to be considered a fool. Most people want to be considered good people and Americans who care about the future. People want America to be first.

Exercise 1. Write *F* by each statement of fact. Write *D* by each statement of opinion disguised as fact.

a. It's a fact that since 1945 over 100 planes and ships have disappeared in the area known as the Bermuda Triangle.

_____

b. Certainly we will find that these disappearances were caused by the supernatural.

_____

c. Everyone knows that scientists will find life on other planets. _____

d. Some stories suggest that UFOs have visited the Bermuda Triangle. _____

e. It's a fact that we will never know the truth about these spooky disappearances. _____

Exercise 2. In each of the following items, the opinion or conclusion is printed in **boldface**. If the evidence in the paragraph fits or supports the judgment, write *Yes* in the blank at the right. If the evidence does not, write *No*.

a. I believe that flying saucers have visited the Earth. My friend Jane believes this, too. Jane is the most popular girl in my class. She is invited to everyone's party, and she is the president of the drama club. Since I want to be popular, I follow Jane's example. She believes that flying saucers exist; therefore, I believe that they exist, too. _____

b. I believe that UFOs may exist. In the United States over 60,000 UFOs have been sighted since 1947. Some have been tracked by radar. Some have been sighted by trained observers. These observers include astronomers, radar operators, pilots, and astronauts. Although scientists have explained some of these sightings, by no means have they explained them all. _____

c. There really is a creature that lives in the waters of Loch Ness. I know this is true because I like believing in scary stories. Certainly I would be scared if I saw the monster. Imagine sitting in a boat on a sunny afternoon. Suddenly the monster surfaces. It attacks but you escape. What a thrilling adventure! What a story to tell your friends! Surely such a monster must exist! _____

d. The Abominable Snowman is alive and well and living in the Himalayas. I know this is so because I saw a movie about the Abominable Snowman. The movie starred two of my favorite actors—Jeannette Carroll and Lawrence Tanner. Carroll played the scientist searching for the Abominable Snowman. Tanner played the Abominable Snowman. The two met during an avalanche. The Abominable Snowman saved the scientist's life. They fell in love. Because of this, the scientist promised not to tell the world where to find the Snowman. The ending of the movie showed the scientist and the creature parting. It was so sad it made me cry. _____

Exercise 3. Read each statement below. If the statement contains name-calling or appeals to your emotions, write *Yes* in the blank at the right. If the statement does not, write *No*.

a. Only dull and unimaginative people would think that life exists nowhere else in the universe. _____

b. Do you want to be popular? Do you want people to laugh at your jokes and listen to your stories? Become the center of attention by joining SLOOP—the Society for Life on Other Planets. _____

c. All the people who reported seeing flying saucers were crazy. _____

d. Some scientists think that life may exist elsewhere in the universe. _____

e. Who knows what evil lurks in the woods? Protect yourself from the dark forces of nature with Shomugoo Powder. _____

Lesson 10

Practice

Use your judgment skills to read the selection below. Then complete the exercises that follow it.

Dinosaurs: Dead or Alive?
Dr. Roy P. Mackal

Could dinosaurs still survive somewhere? Most scientists don't think so. But a few do—and I'm one of them!

By the time you read this story, I will have returned to the heart of wild Africa. Why? To find out if a creature called *mokele-mbembe* (mō-kěl'lē mm-běm'bē) exists!

But let me backtrack. . . .

For over 200 years, tales have trickled in from an unexplored part of the Congo. Incredible tales! The natives of the area, called *pygmies* (pǐg'mēz), tell of strange encounters with giant, dinosaur-like reptiles.

They say these animals are huge, with small heads and long tails and necks. They wade in slow-moving rivers and dark-watered lakes. And they have been said to attack people—and kill them.

The first report of such a creature came in 1776. A French priest wrote of seeing weird footprints. They looked like those of an elephant, but they showed claw marks.

In the late 1800s, an explorer known as Trader Horn reported seeing similar footprints. He had also heard of a creature described by the natives as ". . . a huge monster, half elephant, half dragon."

Then an English hunter reported finding an eerie cave. On the walls were paintings of animals that looked a lot like dinosaurs.

From 1912 to 1938, four separate safaris set out. Each group searched for *mokele-mbembe*. But all four failed. The heat, swamps, disease, and hostile natives proved to be too much for them.

Well, the more I read about these mysterious animals, the more determined I became to find them. If there was even a slight chance that a dinosaur could still be alive, I had to go look for it.

A scientist friend of mine, James Powell, set out with me for Africa in 1980. But we had no idea how rough the going would be!

The swamps, rivers, and jungles of that part of the Congo are still pretty much uncharted. And they are incredibly dangerous. The only way to cross them is on foot or by air. Lacking wings, Jim and I set out on foot.

The smell of the swampy muck was horrible. The heat was over 90°F. (32°C) each day. It seemed that every living thing tried to bite us or suck our blood. We had only freeze-dried food, smoked meat, and a little fruit to eat. Finding drinking water was always a big problem. I was never so glad to see anything in my life as the village that was to be our base camp.

The first thing we did was start talking to everyone we could find. But most of the natives were afraid to talk about *mokele-mbembe*. They believed that to do so was to die.

Many of the pygmies said they had seen one of these animals. But most of the sightings happened a number of years ago. We would show them pictures of different kinds of dinosaurs. They always pointed to the brontosaurus and said, "*mokele-mbembe!*"

We combed the whole area and spoke with people of many different beliefs and customs. But they all told the same story: The animals had bodies the size of a hippo and long, snake-like tails and necks. Their feet were like those of an elephant, but with claws.

The animals' skin was said to be reddish-brown or gray, with no hair. Some of the creatures had rooster-like combs along the backs of their heads and necks.

Other natives told us that the animals sometimes came ashore at night. They would lumber up the banks and feed on a plant called the *molombo*. We were taken to places where the plants grew. They turned out to be long, climbing vines with pretty white flowers. The sap was sweet and the nut-like fruits were good to eat.

Then the pygmies showed us places along the rivers where the *mokele-mbembe* are said to have been seen. And they told us a frightening story about the "monsters":

About 20 years ago, two or three of these animals began coming to a lake where the pygmies liked to fish. The natives were terribly afraid. To stop the "monsters," the people cut down large trees and sharpened them into stakes. The stakes were driven into the river bottom near its entrance to the lake. But the fence didn't stop the *mokele-mbembe*.

One of the animals tried to break through. The pygmies speared it to death. They cut up the animal and ate the meat. Then, the story goes, all the people who ate *mokele-mbembe* died soon after!

70

The last time anyone reported seeing one of these animals was in 1979. The natives urged us to stay and perhaps see one for ourselves. But we were running out of food and supplies and could stay no longer.

My companions on the trip and I are sure that some strange animal is really out there. We want to find out what it is. One thing we do know for sure—it could be quite dangerous!

But this time we'll take along some very special equipment to help us. One machine will keep track of exactly where we are at all times. It tunes in on signals from a satellite circling the earth. This will help us make maps later on.

Another machine is a special kind of video tape recorder. It makes "movies" at night using light from the moon or stars. We'll set it up near the water where the animals might come ashore to eat.

A third machine is like the one being used to look for the Loch Ness monster. It bounces sound waves off large objects underwater. This gives us a rough picture of things we can't see with our eyes.

Is *mokele-mbembe* real? The dozens of people we talked to believe so. But we have to be very careful about just taking their word for it. So before I left Africa, I asked the natives to keep their eyes peeled for bones, skin, or droppings of these animals. Even a dead *mokele-mbembe* would be a fantastic find!

Mokele-mbembe could be a living dinosaur, or it could just look like one. My next trip may solve the mystery. Wish me luck!

Exercise 1. Answer each of the questions below. Write your answers on the blanks provided.

a. What is the author's profession?

_____

b. Does he have training and experience in the field he is writing about?

_____

c. Is the following a statement of fact or a statement of opinion: "The first report of such a creature came in 1776"?

_____

d. Is the following a statement of fact or a statement of opinion: "By the time you read this story, I will have returned to the heart of wild Africa"?

_____

e. The following is a mixed statement of fact and opinion: "They turned out to be long, climbing vines with pretty white flowers." Which word in this statement expresses an opinion?

_____

Exercise 2. On the basis of the evidence, Dr. Mackal concludes that some strange animal is really out there. List four facts on which he bases this conclusion.

a. _____

b. _____

c. _____

_____

d. _____

_____

Chapter 4
Inferences

We make many guesses, but some guesses turn out to be more accurate than others. These guesses are based on evidence. **Intelligent guesses based on evidence are called inferences.** In this chapter, you will learn how to make inferences when you read.

Lesson 1

Making Inferences Based on Evidence

An inference is an intelligent guess based on evidence. *To infer* means "to make an inference." You make inferences all the time. For example, on a rainy day you hear your brother walking up the front steps of the porch. You infer that his feet are wet. You base this inference on two facts. It is raining outside. Your brother has been walking in the rain. Therefore, before your brother even opens the door, you shout, "Wipe your feet!"

In the comic strip below, the woman infers that Mrs. Winslow has a dog. She bases her inference on facts—not just one paw print, but a doorful of paw prints.

MARMADUKE by Brad Anderson

Exercise. Each item below contains evidence that helps you make an inference. Read each item. Then put an X in the blank by the inference that best fits the evidence.

a. Lisa is packing for a vacation. She packs two bathing suits, a pair of flippers, an air tube, and goggles. What inference do you make about Lisa's plans for her vacation?

_____ She is planning to camp out every night.

_____ She is planning to go skydiving.

_____ She is planning to go snorkeling or skin diving.

_____ She is planning to spend a lot of time sunbathing.

b. You are visiting your cousin Myrna in Idaho. You do not know Myrna very well. You walk into her room. On her bed you see a silver baton, a short white skirt, a white jacket with orange trim, a hat with a bushy orange pompom, and high white boots. What inference do you make about Myrna?

_____ Myrna has a new outfit to wear to school.

_____ Myrna is a baton twirler.

_____ Myrna is trying out for the baseball team.

_____ Myrna sings in the school chorus.

c. Chris is ready to prepare dinner. Everything he needs for the main dish is on the kitchen counter. In the kitchen you see chopped meat, eggs, cream, chopped onion, bread crumbs, and spices on the counter. What inference do you make about the main dish?

_____ The main dish is tuna casserole.

_____ The main dish is spaghetti and meatballs.

_____ The main dish is roast chicken.

_____ The main dish is meatloaf.

d. You meet Mark, the new boy in school. You would like to get to know him better. You notice he is carrying four library books. They are *Worlds of Fantasy and Imagination*, *Science Fiction Tales for Young Adults*, *Visions of Tomorrow*, and *The People of the Golden Planet*. You make an inference about Mark's interests. Which topic do you decide to talk to him about?

_____ *Beyond Tomorrow*, a new science-fiction program

_____ *Jogging for Health*, a new exercise book

_____ *Introduction to Squash*, a course at the YMCA

_____ Mr. Higgins, your math teacher

e. You come home from school a little later than usual. You immediately notice that a window is broken. Your mother is talking to a boy you do not know. He is carrying a baseball bat and wearing a baseball cap. What inference do you make?

_____ The boy is asking your mother to donate money for the local baseball team.

_____ The boy has hit a baseball through your window.

_____ The boy is a new neighbor who has stopped in to introduce himself.

_____ The boy is selling tickets to the school football game.

Lesson 2

Making Inferences About Characters

Characters are the people in movies, plays, and stories. When you make an inference about a character, you make an intelligent guess about what this character is like or what this character is thinking or feeling. You base your inference on evidence. Evidence includes what the character does and what the character says. It also includes body language: Is the character smiling or frowning? Are the character's hands clenched or at rest?

For example, look at the photograph below. On the basis of the expression on the girl's face, you can infer that she is very happy.

Hugh Rogers, Monkmeyer

Often, authors plant clues that help you make inferences. For example, read the paragraph below.

Frank, a strong young man, walked up the driveway. As he entered the old house, his heart started to pound like a hammer. His mouth went dry, and his hand started to shake so that the beam from his flashlight was not steady. It took all his strength to keep his knees from buckling under him.

The author does not tell you directly that Frank becomes frightened when he enters the house. But you make this inference by paying attention to the clues—Frank's heart is pounding, his mouth is dry, his hand is shaking, and his knees are buckling.

Exercise. As you read the excerpt below from *Edge of Two Worlds* by Weyman Jones, pay special attention to clues that help you make inferences about Calvin. Then answer the questions that follow.

The only living things in the whole stretched-out and sun-burned world of Texas seemed to be Calvin and the yellow grasshoppers. He hadn't seen a jackrabbit since yesterday morning, and now not even a buzzard teetered in the empty sky. Just grasshoppers. They buzzed out from under every step he took, flailing their double wings, only to crash sprawled and scrambling in the white dust.

Calvin was tired, and beyond that. He was not walking anymore. Instead, he thought of his right foot, lifted it carefully past his left and put it down. Then he leaned on it, thought about his left foot, lifted that past his right and put it down. Between each step he paused to gather himself for the next.

He often fell. Sometimes he lay in the hot dirt a long time, watching the grasshoppers.

The lump on his head and the bruise on his side where he had been thrown against the wagon seat didn't hurt anymore. He didn't even feel his blistered feet and sunburned neck much now. When he hauled himself up to his knees and then staggered back to his feet, it was like moving underwater, pushing against something.

He wasn't hungry anymore either. Yesterday when he crossed a muddy creek, he caught three minnows and a tadpole with his hands. The minnows he ate raw, but the tadpole was so soft and squashy he couldn't put it in his mouth. After a few miles more he had decided that throwing the tadpole back had been silly. It was more like something to eat than grasshoppers.

But that was yesterday. Today he didn't care about anything.

Questions

a. Calvin is alone and seems to be lost. He's exhausted, but he puts one foot in front of the other, moving forward slowly. He often falls, but he gets up again. From this you can infer that Calvin is:

_____ mean and bad-tempered

_____ determined, doesn't give up easily

_____ clumsy, unable to do things right

b. Calvin has a lump on his head and a bruise on his side. His feet are blistered and his neck is sunburned. Yet whenever he falls, he staggers back onto his feet. From this you can infer that Calvin is:

_____ meek and uncomplaining

_____ stouthearted, able to bear up under pain

_____ cheerful and kind

c. Calvin is not carrying any food. Yet yesterday he caught three minnows and ate them raw. From this you can infer that Calvin is:

_____ resourceful, willing to do what is necessary to survive

_____ frightened, too scared to think straight

_____ lively, full of energy

d. The last paragraph says that today Calvin doesn't care about anything. From this you can infer that today Calvin is:

_____ utterly exhausted, at his breaking point

_____ glutted, full from a large meal of minnows

_____ serene, at peace with himself and the world

e. These paragraphs give you a good picture of what Calvin is like. Which group of words best describes Calvin?

_____ weak and cowardly

_____ playful and full of fun

_____ strong, usually full of resolve, and determined

Making Inferences About Motives

A motive is the reason a character does a certain thing or acts a certain way. When you make an inference about a character's motives, you make an intelligent guess about the reasons behind his or her actions. For example, read the following passage.

> Paul looked at his watch again. Eight more minutes before the bell. Mrs. Williams was calling the students in alphabetical order. That meant Janet Anderson and Bill Brunell would have to read their compositions before him. "Maybe the bell will ring before I'm called on," he thought.
>
> "Janet Anderson," the teacher said.
>
> "Oh, please, Janet, read slowly!" Paul thought. He looked at his composition. He knew it was good, but still . . .
>
> "Bill Brunell," the teacher called.
>
> Paul looked at his classmates. Although they were all his friends, Paul saw only a sea of unsmiling faces.
>
> "Oh, no," thought Paul. It's only eleven forty-five." Paul's hands began to sweat. He felt butterflies in the pit of his stomach. "Maybe I'll be sick," he thought.
>
> "Paul Smith," called the teacher.
>
> "I'm sorry," said Paul, "but I left my composition at home."

Why does Paul say that he left his composition at home? Perhaps he didn't write it. We know this isn't the answer because the passage tells us that he looked at his composition. Perhaps he thought his composition was not very good. Again, we know this isn't the answer because the passage tells us that he knew his composition was good.

Let's look at the details. When Paul looks at his classmates, he sees only a sea of unsmiling faces. His hands sweat and he gets butterflies in his stomach. Perhaps Paul gets nervous when he has to speak in public.

Exercise. The selection below is from *The Adventures of Tom Sawyer* by Mark Twain. Tom has to whitewash the fence, but he would rather be playing with his friends. Then along comes Ben Rogers, playing a steamboat game. Read this selection carefully. Then answer the questions that follow it.

> Tom went on whitewashing—paid no attention to the steamboat. Ben stared a moment and then said:
>
> "Hi-yi! *You're* up a stump, ain't you!"
>
> No answer. Tom surveyed his last touch with the eye of an artist, then he gave his brush another gentle sweep and surveyed the result, as before. Ben ranged up alongside of him. Tom's mouth watered for the apple, but he stuck to his work. Ben said:

"Hello, old chap, you got to work, hey?"

Tom wheeled suddenly and said:

"Why, it's you, Ben! I warn't noticing."

"Say—I'm going in a-swimming, I am. Don't you wish you could? But of course you'd druther work—wouldn't you? Course you would!"

Tom contemplated the boy a bit, and said:

"What do you call work?"

"Why, ain't that work?"

Tom resumed his whitewashing, and answered carelessly:

"Well, maybe it is, and maybe it ain't. All I know, is, it suits Tom Sawyer."

"Oh come, now, you don't mean to let on that you like it?"

The brush continued to move.

"Like it? Well, I don't see why I oughtn't to like it. Does a boy get a chance to whitewash a fence every day?"

That put the thing in a new light. Ben stopped nibbling his apple. Tom swept his brush daintily back and forth—stepped back to note the effect—added a touch here and there—criticized the effect again—Ben watching every move and getting more and more interested, more and more absorbed. Presently he said:

"Say, Tom, let me whitewash a little."

Tom considered, was about to consent; but he altered his mind:

"No—no—I reckon it wouldn't hardly do, Ben. You see, Aunt Polly's awful particular about this fence—right here on the street, you know—but if it was the back fence I wouldn't mind and she wouldn't. Yes, she's awful particular about this fence; it's got to be done very careful; I reckon there ain't one boy in a thousand, maybe two thousand, that can do it the way it's got to be done."

"No—is that so? Oh come, now—lemme just try. Only just a little—I'd let you, if you was me, Tom."

"Ben, I'd like to, honest; but Aunt Polly—well, Jim wanted to do it, but she wouldn't let him; Sid wanted to do it, and she wouldn't let Sid. Now don't you see how I'm fixed? If you was to tackle this fence and anything was to happen to it—"

"Oh, shucks, I'll be just as careful. Now lemme try. Say—I'll give you the core of my apple."

"Well, here—No, Ben, now don't. I'm afeard—"

"I'll give you all of it!"

Questions

a. Tom wants two things. First, he wants Ben to whitewash the fence for him. Why doesn't he simply ask Ben to do this?

b. Why does Tom pretend that he hasn't even noticed Ben?

_____

_____

c. Tom wants to convince Ben that he prefers whitewashing the fence to going swimming. To do this, he indicates that whitewashing isn't work, but fun. He says, "All I know, is, it suits Tom Sawyer." What else does Tom say to convince Ben that whitewashing is fun?

_____

_____

d. Finally, Ben begs, "Say, Tom, let _me_ whitewash a little." But remember, Tom wants two things from Ben. Why does Tom say no to Ben's request?

_____

Lesson 4

Making Inferences About Past and Present Events

When you make an inference about past events, you make an intelligent guess about what has happened in the past. For example, a friend knocks on your door. When you open the door, you see that she has a scraped knee and a cut above her eye. Her blue jeans are torn. Her bike, which is standing by the gate, is smashed. On the basis of this evidence, you infer that she had a bicycle accident.

When you make an inference about present events, you make an intelligent guess about what is happening now. For example, imagine you are sitting outside watching your cat, Crescent. Suddenly Crescent crouches and becomes very still. She focuses her eyes on a bird. On the basis of these actions, you infer that Crescent is getting ready to attack the bird.

Exercise. Read the five passages below. Three inferences about past or present events follow each passage. Choose the best inference you can make on the basis of the information in the passage. Put an X in the blank next to this inference.

a. You haven't seen your friend Marita for two months. You decide to bike over to her house. A big van is in front of her house. When Marita opens the door, you notice that the living room is filled with boxes. Marita's father and mother are in the kitchen emptying the cabinets. Marita says, "Oh, I'm so glad to see you. Come into my room. You can help me pack."
What do you think is happening?

_____ Marita's brother is going away to college.

_____ Marita's aunt is moving in with the family.

_____ Marita and her family are moving.

b. The school basketball team has been playing very well this year. Tonight's game will decide the championship. Everyone in school is excited and looking forward to winning. Unfortunately, you have to baby-sit. You will miss the game. But you will attend the party after the game. When you walk into the party that evening, you immediately notice how quiet everyone is. The happy mood of the afternoon has been replaced by gloom.
What do you think happened?

_____ Your school team lost the championship.

_____ Your school team tied for the championship.

_____ Your school team won the championship.

c. It is Tuesday morning during spring vacation. You decide to visit your aunt Maria. You reach her apartment, only to find that she is just leaving. Maria is dressed in a skirt and blouse and carrying a briefcase. She tells you to help yourself to some milk and cookies while you wait for her. She should be back in about two hours. Once inside her apartment, you pour yourself some milk and sit down at the kitchen table. You spot the newspaper, which is opened to the employment section. Several ads are circled. You decide to call your mother to let her know where you are. By the telephone, you notice the following message written on a pad: McKinley and Company—10:30—Tuesday.
What do you think is happening?

_____ Aunt Maria is shopping for a jacket to match her new skirt.

_____ Aunt Maria is at an interview at the local college.

_____ Aunt Maria is at a job interview.

d. Fred lives with his family in a large apartment in a big city. His bedroom window opens onto a busy avenue. Since it is the middle of winter, Fred keeps his window shut, but he can still hear the traffic noise from below. When Fred wakes up this morning, he knows immediately that something is different. Instead of traffic noise, there is silence below. Then, listening more carefully, Fred hears the sound of metal scraping against concrete.
What do you think happened?

_____ It snowed heavily during the night.

_____ Last night, the city banned traffic from this avenue.

_____ Fred's father put in extra-thick windows last night.

e. Nick has been nervous for three days. Last month he entered a writing contest. The contest officials will call the winner on Friday. As Friday grows nearer, Nick becomes more and more excited and nervous. On Friday, you are having lunch with Nick at his house. The phone rings. Nick races to the phone. After he answers it, he collapses in the chair. First a look of relief spreads across his face. This soon changes to a big grin.
What do you think has happened?

_____ Nick has won the contest.

_____ Nick has heard from an old friend.

_____ Nick has lost the contest.

Lesson 5

Making Inferences About Future Events

When you make an inference about a future event, you make an intelligent guess, based on evidence, about what will happen in the future. For example, read the following paragraph.

> The nurse smiles when Christopher walks into her office. She asks him to tell her what is wrong. Chris explains that he had a headache when he woke up this morning. Now he has a scratchy throat and he feels warm and sweaty. The nurse notices that Chris' eyes are watering and his face is flushed. She takes his temperature. It is 3 degrees above normal. Then she asks Chris if his parents are home today.

What do you think the nurse will do? On the basis of the evidence, you can infer that she will send him home.

Now look at the following comic strip. Nancy makes an inference about what will happen to her friend. On the basis of her knowledge of the two boys, she infers that her friend will be caught by the bully and the bully will hurt him. Therefore, she buys her friend a get-well card.

NANCY

Name _____

Exercise. Read the five paragraphs below. Three inferences about the future follow each passage. Choose the best inference you can make on the basis of the evidence in the paragraph. Put an X in the blank next to this inference.

a. Margie and Alice are as unlike as two sisters can be. Margie loves shopping, while Alice is bored by stores. Margie is the best-dressed student in her junior high school. Alice lives in jeans and sweat shirts. Although both girls have Saturday jobs, Margie spends all the money she earns on clothes and records. Alice, on the other hand, puts her earnings in the bank. Both girls would like to go to horseback-riding camp next summer. Their parents have given their permission on the condition that the girls save their own money to pay for the fees.
What do you think will happen next summer?

_____ Both girls will go to camp.

_____ Only Margie will go to camp.

_____ Only Alice will go to camp.

b. Caroline is thirteen. She would like to attend a professional modeling school when she turns fifteen. She has talked to some teachers at a modeling school. They have suggested that she begin a careful program of exercise and proper nutrition. Because of this suggestion, Caroline has asked her parents if she can enroll in the local Y. She is now taking regular exercise classes there. She has joined a class called "Improve Your Appearance Through Better Nutrition."
What do you think will happen when Caroline turns fifteen?

_____ Caroline will be accepted by the modeling school.

_____ Caroline will not be accepted by the modeling school.

_____ Caroline will become a television star.

c. At the beginning of this year, Carl was not doing well in math. Because of this, he spent extra time every night on his math homework. He also asked his sister Beverly, who is an A student in math, to help him. Mr. Johnson, the math teacher, teaches a special Saturday class for students who need extra help. Carl started attending these classes. Because of Carl's hard work, he received a passing grade in math at the end of the year. Carl felt good when both his math teacher and his parents praised him.
What do you think will happen next year?

_____ Carl will receive an A in math next year.

_____ Carl will decide to become a mathematician.

_____ Carl will work hard and pass his math course next year.

d. Lee receives a new bike for his thirteenth birthday. He leaves it out in the rain and in the snow. He never oils the chain. He forgets to clean the sprockets and axles. He fails to wipe oil slicks off the rubber tires.

What do you think will happen by Lee's fourteenth birthday?

_____ His bike will look as good as the day he received it.

_____ His bike will need repairs.

_____ His friend will buy the bike from him.

Lesson 6

Making Inferences About Time

When you make an inference about time, you make an intelligent guess about when events occur. One type of time you infer is the time of day. For example: Are the events occurring in the morning, the afternoon, the evening, or the night? Read the passage below from *Roll of Thunder, Hear My Cry* by Mildred D. Taylor.

> "Little Man, would you come on? You keep it up and you're gonna make us late."
>
> My youngest brother paid no attention to me. Grasping more firmly his newspaper-wrapped notebook and his tin-can lunch of cornbread and oil sausages, he continued to concentrate on the dusty road. He lagged several feet behind my other brothers, Stacey and Christopher-John, and me, attempting to keep the rusty Mississippi dust from swelling with each step and drifting back upon his shiny black shoes and the cuffs of his corduroy pants by lifting each foot high before setting it gently down again. Always meticulously* neat, six-year-old Little Man never allowed dirt or tears or stains to mar anything he owned. Today was no exception.
>
> "You keep it up and make us late for school, Mama's gonna wear you out," I threatened, pulling with exasperation† at the high collar of the Sunday dress Mama had made me wear for the first day of school—as if that event were something special.

When you read this passage, you probably inferred that the time is morning. You based your inference on evidence—the children are hurrying to school, and Little Man is carrying his lunch.

Another type of time you infer is the time of year. For example: Are the events occurring in the spring, the summer, the autumn, or the winter? When you read the passage above from *Roll of Thunder, Hear My Cry*, you probably inferred that the time is late summer or early autumn. You based your inference on evidence—it is the first day of school.

---

*meticulously (mə-tĭk′yə-ləs-lē) *adv.*: Extremely carefully.
†exasperation (ĕg-zăs′pə-rā′shən) *n.*: Annoyance; irritation.

Now look at the comic strip below. What time of year is it? It must be autumn because the leaves all fall from the trees when Nancy sneezes.

NANCY

© 1978 by United Feature Syndicate, Inc.

Another type of time you infer is the time period. For example: Are the events occurring in the present, the past, or the future? Now read the passage below from *A Spy at Tyconderoga* by Calvin Fisher.

> Twenty murderous British muskets stood upright in racks, each with a leather cartridge pouch hanging alongside. These muskets were the deadly Brown Bess of the British foot soldier and at the end of each barrel a long savage bayonet stuck out as sharp as a sword. Anger flared up inside him and flushed his face. His heart began to pound. He wanted to strike out at the British. There must be something he could do!

When you read this passage, you probably inferred that it took place in the past—the time of the Revolutionary War. You based your inference on evidence—British muskets, leather cartridge pouches, and the Brown Bess.

Exercise 1. Read the details below. Which details would you probably find in a story that takes place in the summer? Write *Yes* next to these. Which details would you probably not find? Write *No* next to these.

a. _____ children ice-skating outdoors

b. _____ flowers in bloom

c. _____ people swimming

d. _____ people wearing coats

e. _____ birds chirping

f. _____ beach balls

g. _____ skis and snowshoes

h. _____ mosquitoes

i. _____ suntan lotion

j. _____ iced tea and lemonade

Exercise 2. The passages below are from a short story called "Time in Thy Flight" by Ray Bradbury. Mr. Fields, a teacher from the future, takes his students on a field trip to the past. They visit the United States in 1928 to observe various customs and practices. Read each passage from this story and answer the questions that follow it.

They stood before the same house on the same street but on a soft summer evening. Fire wheels hissed, on front porches laughing children tossed things out that went bang!

"Don't run!" cried Mr. Fields. "It's not war, don't be afraid!"

But Janet's and Robert's and William's faces were pink, now blue, now white with fountains of soft fire.

"We're all right," said Janet, standing very still.

"Happily," announced Mr. Fields, "they prohibited fireworks a century ago, did away with the whole messy explosion."

Children did fairy dances, weaving their names and destinies on the dark summer air with white sparklers.

a. In the passage above, you learn directly that the season is summer. What special holiday do you think it is?

_____

b. Which details help you infer the holiday?

_____

October.
The Time Machine paused for the last time, an hour later in the month of burning leaves. People bustled into dim houses carrying pumpkins and corn shocks. Skeletons danced, bats flew, candles flamed, apples swung in empty doorways.

c. In the passage above, you learn directly that it is October. What holiday do you think it is?

_____

d. Which details help you infer the holiday?

_____

Exercise 3. The passage below is from the short story "The Gift" by Ray Bradbury. The parents are disappointed because they had to leave behind their son's Christmas gift. At the end of the story, though, they give him a far greater gift. Read the passage. Then answer the questions that follow it.

Tomorrow would be Christmas, and even while the three of them rode to the rocket port the mother and father were worried. It was the boy's first flight into space, his very first time in a rocket, and they wanted everything to be perfect. So when, at the custom's table, they were forced to leave behind his gift which exceeded the weight limit by no more than a few ounces and the little tree with the lovely white candles, they felt themselves deprived of the season and their love.

The boy was waiting for them in the Terminal room. Walking toward him, after their unsuccessful clash with the Interplanetary officials, the mother and father whispered to each other.

"What shall we do?"

"Nothing, nothing. What *can* we do?"

"Silly rules!"

"And he so wanted the tree!"

The siren gave a great howl and people pressed forward into the Mars Rocket. The mother and father walked at the very last, their small pale son between them, silent.

a. The time of this selection is Christmas Eve. Is the time period the present, the past, or the future?

_____

b. Which details help you infer the time period?

_____

Lesson 7

Making Inferences About Place

When you make an inference about place, you make an intelligent guess about where the events in a story occur. For example, imagine you are in the next room when your sister turns on the television. You can hear the program, but you can't see the picture. You hear a man's voice say, "But Mary, the doctor said it will be a few hours before your fever comes down. When Nurse Jenkins comes off her rounds, maybe she can make you more comfortable." On the basis of what you hear, you probably infer that the events are taking place in a hospital.

Now read the following paragraph from "Shark" by Zoltan Malocsay.

Bert forgot all about the abalone he was after, and he let himself rise slowly back to the surface. It was just a glimpse, a dark shape moving out of the gloom, but he knew it was a shark, knew before the outline got sharper, closer. He wondered if Lisa saw it too.

The author does not tell you directly that this event takes place in the ocean, but you probably had no trouble making this inference. You based your inference on details—the abalone, Bert's rising to the surface, and the shark.

Now look at the comic strip below.

FUNKY WINKERBEAN by Tom Batiuk

Probably Les is in a gym. He's holding on to a rope, but he's not hanging near a cliff or a mountain or a building. He has asked for wrestling mats, which are found in gyms. Also, he's wearing gym clothes.

Exercise 1. Read the details below. Which details help you infer that the events in a story are occurring in a large city? Write *Yes* next to these details. Write *No* next to those details that do not.

a. _____ buses

b. _____ skyscrapers

c. _____ horses

d. _____ cows

e. _____ concrete sidewalks

f. _____ crowded streets

g. _____ subways

h. _____ two airports

i. _____ many apartment buildings

j. _____ farms

Exercise 2. Read the passage below from *The Dangerous Game* by Milton Dank. Then answer the questions after each passage.

    Two days later the Germans entered the empty city in triumph. Rank after rank of gray-green-uniformed troops marched in a victory parade down the Champs-Élysées, their bands blaring at the head. Huge Nazi flags hung from the Eiffel Tower and the Chamber of Deputies to mark the conquest, and Charles trembled with anger at the sight of the swastika—that crooked black spider on a red background—that now floated above his beloved city. It was more than a patriot could stand; he had to do something. But what could one sixteen-year-old boy do against the mighty German Wehrmacht?

a. This story takes place during World War II. In what city do you think the events occur?

_____

b. Which details helped you make this inference?

_____

    Now Big Jim let him ride in the pickup to check fence lines, or they rode their horses to look for strays where the pickup couldn't go. But best of all Little Jim was allowed to ride his pony alone to look for strays.

    He had a good pony which Big Jim had trained well. When Little Jim had to get off to check a ravine or a place the pony couldn't go, all he had to do was drop the reins over the pony's head and the animal would wait patiently until he came back.

    Little Jim, on his pony, checked the hills and along the creek. He liked best to ride up on the Red Butte which was partly on Big Jim's ranch and partly on the neighboring ranch of Tom Russell.

    The butte was a high flat-topped hill that rose out of the level prairie as if some big hand under the ground had pushed it up. Little Jim's Grandpa told stories about how in the old days the young men of the tribe would go to the top of the butte and pray to the great *Wakantanka* for a spirit to guide them the rest of their lives.

    When Little Jim rode the narrow zig-zag trail up the side to the top of the butte, he knew he was riding over a path made by Indian braves of long ago. He'd get a scary, spooky feeling when he had to go to the top of the butte to look for cattle or horses which sometimes strayed there.

c. The events in the passage above, from *Jimmy Yellow Hawk* by Virginia Driving Hawk Sneve, take place in the United States. Do you think they occur in the Northeast, the Southeast, the Middle West, or the West?

_____

d. Which details helped you make this inference?

_____

Making Inferences About Exaggeration

Exaggeration makes something bigger than or greater than it really is. For example, you tell your friend, "I'm so hungry I could eat a cow." Certainly you could not eat a whole cow, but by exaggerating, you get your point across. It is important to notice which details are exaggerated. Read the paragraph below from "Pecos Bill Meets Paul Bunyan and Starts a New Ranch" by Leigh Peck.

> Then one day, imagine Pecos Bill's surprise and anger when he found someone else on his mountain! A hundred men were at work at the foot of the mountain putting up a big bunkhouse and a big cookhouse. They did not look like cowboys at all, and they did not have any cattle with them—except for one huge blue-colored ox. He was a hundred times bigger than any steer Pecos Bill had ever seen before, and he ate a whole wagonload of hay at one swallow!

The author makes the Blue Ox larger than life. He says that the Blue Ox was "a hundred times bigger than any steer Pecos Bill had ever seen before, and he ate a whole wagonload of hay at one swallow!"

Exercise. Continue reading this selection from "Pecos Bill Meets Paul Bunyan and Starts a New Ranch" by Leigh Peck. Then follow the directions at the end of it.

> Pecos Bill did not stop to think that he was only one man against a hundred men, and that the huge ox could kill a man by stepping on him. He rode right up to the camp and asked, "Who is in charge here?"
>
> "Paul Bunyan," answered one of the men.
>
> "I want to talk to him," said Pecos Bill.
>
> The man called, "Paul," and there walked out from among the trees the very biggest man in all the world—as big for a man as the Blue Ox was for a steer. Now Pecos Bill himself was a fine figure of a man, six feet two inches high, straight as an arrow and as strong and limber as a rawhide lariat. But this Paul Bunyan was so tall that his knee was higher than Pecos Bill's head! He had a long, dark beard. He wore flat-heeled, broad-toed boots, not like cowboy boots at all. He wore no chaps, and instead of a leather jacket he wore a queer woolen jacket of bright-colored plaid.
>
> But if Pecos Bill was startled, he did not show it. He asked very firmly, "What are you doing on my mountain?"
>
> "This is my mountain now," Paul Bunyan announced. "I've already settled on it."
>
> "That makes no difference. I laid claim to this land long ago," Pecos Bill argued.
>
> "Where's the law that says it's yours?" demanded Paul Bunyan.

"Here it is!" exclaimed Pecos Bill. "This is the law west of the Pecos," and he laid his hand on his pistol.

"That's not fair!" cried Paul Bunyan. "I'm not armed. In the North Woods, we don't fight with pistols. We fight with our bare fists or with our axes."

"Very well," agreed Pecos Bill. "I'll give you the choice of weapons. I have no axe, but I'll use my branding iron to hit with."

Now the branding iron that Pecos Bill carried that day was what is called a running iron. It was only a straight iron bar with a crook on the end of it. Cowboys heat the end of a running iron and draw letters on a steer's hide as you would draw with a piece of crayon on paper.

Pecos Bill heated the end of his branding iron on a blazing star that he had picked up the time the stars fell. He always carried it about with him in his saddlebag, so as to have a fire immediately whenever he needed one. Then the fight started.

Paul Bunyan hit at Pecos Bill so hard with his axe that he cut a huge gash in the earth. People call it the Grand Canyon of the Colorado River now.

Pecos Bill swung his red-hot iron, trying to hit Paul Bunyan, until the sands of the desert were scorched red-colored. That was the beginning of the Painted Desert out in Arizona.

Again Paul Bunyan tried to hit Pecos Bill and hit the ground instead. The queer rocks that are piled up in the Garden of the Gods in Colorado were split up by Paul Bunyan's axe in that fearful fight.

Pecos Bill's iron, instead of cooling off, got hotter and hotter, until the forests in New Mexico and Arizona were charred. These trees, burnt into stone by the heat from Pecos Bill's running iron, are called Petrified Forests now.

But neither man could get the better of the other. For the first and only time Pecos Bill had met his match. And it was the first and only time that Paul Bunyan's crew had seen a man that could stand up to him.

Finally they both paused to get their breath, and Paul Bunyan suggested, "Let's sit down and rest a minute."

"All right," agreed Pecos Bill, and they sat down on nearby rocks.

As they sat resting, Pecos Bill asked, "Stranger, why are you so anxious to take my land away from me? Isn't there plenty of other land in the West, that you could have just by laying claim to it?"

"Land!" exclaimed Paul Bunyan. "It's not the land that I want!"

"Then why are we fighting? What do you want?" inquired the surprised Pecos Bill.

"Why, the trees, of course," Paul Bunyan explained. "I'm no rancher. I have no use for land, any longer than it takes to get the timber off. I'll log the trees off that mountain, and then I'll be through with it. I'm a lumber man."

"Why didn't you say so at first?" exclaimed Pecos Bill. "You are more than welcome to the trees! I've been trying to find someway to get them off the land, so that the grass can grow and my cattle can graze here."

"They'll be off in a few weeks," promised Paul Bunyan, and the two men shook hands.

Pecos Bill and Paul Bunyan were good friends after that, each respecting the other for the fight that he had put up. Pecos Bill had his cowboys drive over a herd of nice fat young steers, to furnish beef for Paul Bunyan's loggers while they were clearing off the trees. When Paul Bunyan and his men were through, they left standing their bunkhouse and their cookhouse and the Blue Ox's barn, ready for Pecos Bill's outfit to move in.

Directions. Write *Yes* in the blank by each statement that contains exaggeration. Write *No* by each statement that does not.

a. "The man called, 'Paul,' and there walked out from among the trees the very biggest man in all the world—as big for a man as the Blue Ox was for a steer." _____

b. "But this Paul Bunyan was so tall that his knee was higher than Pecos Bill's head!" _____

c. "Cowboys heat the end of a running iron and draw letters on a steer's hide . . ." _____

d. "Paul Bunyan hit at Pecos Bill so hard with his axe that he cut a huge gash in the earth. People call it the Grand Canyon of the Colorado River now." _____

e. "Pecos Bill swung his red-hot iron, trying to hit Paul Bunyan, until the sands of the desert were scorched red-colored. That was the beginning of the Painted Desert out in Arizona." _____

f. "Again Paul Bunyan tried to hit Pecos Bill and hit the ground instead." _____

g. "Pecos Bill's iron, instead of cooling off, got hotter and hotter, until the forests in New Mexico and Arizona were charred. These trees, burnt into stone by the heat from Pecos Bill's running iron, are called Petrified Forests now." _____

h. "But neither man could get the better of the other. For the first and only time Pecos Bill had met his match. And it was the first and only time that Paul Bunyan's crew had seen a man that could stand up to him." _____

i. "Pecos Bill and Paul Bunyan were good friends after that, each respecting the other for the fight that he had put up." _____

j. "When Paul Bunyan and his men were through, they left standing their bunkhouse and their cookhouse and the Blue Ox's barn, ready for Pecos Bill's outfit to move in." _____

Lesson 9

Making Inferences About Realistic and Fantastic Details

Realistic details are drawn from life. For example, a young woman beginning her first job is a realistic detail. **Fantastic details are unreal or highly unusual and difficult to explain.** For example, a young woman beginning her first job as a ghost catcher is a fantastic detail.

Read the following passage from "To Starch a Ghost" by Andrew Benedict. The person who tells this story is named Sue.

> Grown-ups are so strange. I mean, how can you ever understand them? For one thing, they worry so much. They worry about the stock market and the lawn and the price of building materials—Dad is an architect—and Europe and Asia and Africa and the world situation and just everything.
>
> They even worry about ghosts! I just discovered that this week. How old-fashioned can you get? Why, worrying about ghosts is prehistoric! But I suppose it's a symptom of getting old.
>
> The other evening I was studying my math and Mom was making a braided rug out of old nylon stockings. All of a sudden Dad rushed in, looking pale, his eyes big and his hair practically on end.
>
> At first Mom was sure he'd been in an accident. But it wasn't that. After Dad had had a cup of strong coffee to calm him down, he was able to tell us what had happened.
>
> "By George, Mary!" he said—Mary is Mom—"Harry Gerber has a haunted house on his hands. I just came from the place with him. It's absolutely crawling with ghosts. He's so upset, he almost wrecked us getting back to town. I don't blame him! We saw some of the ghosts and—"

Dad's being an architect, Sue's studying math, and Mom's making a braided rug are all realistic details. Worrying about ghosts, buying a haunted house, and seeing ghosts are all fantastic details.

Exercise. Continue reading this selection from "To Starch a Ghost" by Andrew Benedict. Then follow the directions at the end of it.

> At that point Dad needed some more coffee. Of course, I was all ears. I'll just put down the simple details as Dad told them to us.
>
> As I said, Dad is an architect, and Mr. Gerber, the big real estate man—he's very fat and also he owns a lot of real estate—had hired him for a job.

On the edge of town there is a grand old mansion, built to imitate an English castle. It's made of stone and timber and has about fifty rooms. It was put up way back when, by a very rich man named Mr. Ferguson. After Mrs. Ferguson, who lived to be ninety-nine, lost Mr. Ferguson, she stayed right on living in the big house in spite of high taxes and the cost of help these days.

But when finally Mrs. Ferguson went, too, the old house stayed empty for a long time. Dad said it was a shame, because they don't build houses like that any more. But nobody wanted it, the taxes were so high. Then Dad had an idea. It could be remodeled into a retirement home for elderly people who like nice surroundings.

Dad persuaded Mr. Gerber to buy Ferguson's Castle, as the house is called by just everybody, and hire him to remodel it. They were out looking the property over, lingered until after dark, and suddenly had a terrible shock when a positive parade of phantoms started appearing.

To quote Dad, he and Mr. Gerber got out of there fast. Now, and I'm quoting him again—grown-ups use such prehistoric language—the fat was in the fire. Mr. Gerber blamed Dad for ever getting him into the deal. In fact, Mr. Gerber was coming over soon to see what ideas Dad had for despooking Ferguson's Castle, and if Dad didn't have any, Mr. Gerber was going to get nasty.

Dad was drinking his third cup of coffee when Mr. Gerber burst in. I mean he really did. Just stormed in and threw his hat on the floor and shouted.

"Carter, you've ruined me! You got me to invest two hundred thousand dollars in a hotel for haunts, and I hold you personally responsible!"

His manners were simply terrible. But then, what can you expect of the older generation these days?

Dad gave Mr. Gerber some coffee, and by and by they were able to talk without anybody shouting.

"I've done some fast checking, Carter," Mr. Gerber said. "I've learned where those ghosts in Ferguson's Castle came from. Every single one of them is imported."

"Imported?" Mom asked. "What do you mean?"

"The Fergusons were great travelers," Mr. Gerber sighed. "And Mrs. Ferguson was psychic. She could get in touch with spirits. See them. Talk to them. Naturally, being a lady, she never made it public. I learned about this from a daughter of her former maid."

"Go on," Dad urged him. "Do I understand that Mrs. Ferguson, in her travels abroad, used to meet up with ghosts and bring them back home with her?"

"That's exactly what she did. She and her husband wanted a collection that would be unique, something no one, no matter how rich, could match. So they collected ghosts. They didn't stop until they had one for every room in the place, including the main entrance hall. That Thing that chased us out of there is an authentic Japanese dragon ghost from the fifth century, and we were right—it *was* breathing fire at us!"

He shuddered so hard that in order not to spill his coffee he had to drink it all. Then he said in a hollow voice:

"Do you understand, Carter? Every single room in that confounded place is haunted!"

I thought it was a wonderful idea myself. Mr. and Mrs. Ferguson must have been very unusual grown-ups to think of collecting ghosts.

Directions. In the blank at the right, put *F* by each detail that is fantastic. Put *R* by each detail that is realistic.

a. Mr. Gerber hired Dad to help him remodel an old mansion. _____

b. The mansion has about fifty rooms. _____

c. Each room has a ghost. _____

d. When Dad and Mr. Gerber look at the property, they see a parade of ghosts. _____

e. Mr. Gerber has terrible manners. _____

f. All the ghosts in the mansion are imported. _____

g. The Fergusons traveled around the world. _____

h. Mrs. Ferguson used to talk with the spirit world. _____

i. Mr. and Mrs. Ferguson wanted to collect something unique. _____

j. The Fergusons brought a fifth-century dragon back with them from Japan. _____

Lesson 10

Making Inferences About Tone

Tone is the author's attitude or feeling toward what he or she has written or said. For example, the tone of a selection may be humorous or it may be serious. The tone may be solemn or it may be light-hearted. When you read, you can infer the author's tone by looking carefully at the author's choice of words and details, and by determining the author's purpose. For example, read the paragraph below from "Dogs That Have Known Me" by Jean Kerr.

I never meant to say anything about this, but the fact is that I have never met a dog that didn't have it in for me. You take Kelly, for instance. He's a wire-haired fox terrier and he's had us for three years now. I wouldn't say that he was terribly handsome but he does have a very nice smile. What he *doesn't* have is any sense of fitness. All the other dogs in the neighborhood spend their afternoons yapping at each other's heels or chasing cats. Kelly spends his whole day, every day, chasing swans on the millpond. I don't actually worry because he will never catch one. For one thing, he can't swim. Instead of settling for a simple dog-paddle like everybody else, he has to show off and try some complicated overhand stroke, with the result that he always sinks and has to be fished out. Naturally, people talk, and I never take him for a walk that somebody doesn't point him out and say, "There's that crazy dog that chases swans."

Jean Kerr includes several unusual, or outlandish, details. First, she tells you that she has "never met a dog that didn't have it in for (her)." Second, she indicates that this dog has owned her, rather than that she has owned the dog. Third, she likes the dog's smile. Fourth, she tells you that the dog spends its day chasing swans. And finally, she explains that the dog is a failure at this activity. He always tries "some complicated overhand stroke, with the result that he always sinks and has to be fished out."

Obviously, Jean Kerr's purpose is to amuse you. Therefore, you can infer that her tone is humorous.

Now read the following passage from "Our Poisonous Snakes" by George Laycock.

All who roam the outdoors should recognize poisonous snakes. North America's poisonous snakes are coral snakes and pit vipers. Pit vipers include copperheads, cottonmouth water moccasins, and rattlesnakes. All have small openings between their eyes and nostrils. These are heat sensing organs to locate prey.

Most poisonous snake bites do not cause death. But all are dangerous and require a doctor's care at once. The best advice is to stay alert and use common sense.

In snake country, wear long trousers and high boots. Watch where you walk or sit. Don't put your hands onto rocky ledges or logs where you can't see, or step over logs without first looking on the other side.

Snakes stay out of the way of people if they can, but are likely to strike if they are touched or surprised. They do not have to be coiled to bite. Poisonous snakes are part of the balance of nature, and there is usually no reason for killing one.

George Laycock's purpose is to inform. He gives you several details that create an accurate picture of poisonous snakes. Therefore, you can infer that his tone is serious.

Exercise. Read each passage below. Then decide whether the author's purpose is to inform or to amuse you. Finally decide whether the author's tone is serious or humorous.

Cats are, of course, no good. They're chiselers and panhandlers, sharpers and shameless flatterers. They're as full of schemes and plans, plots and counterplots, wiles and guiles, as any confidence man. They can read your character better than a $50-an-hour psychiatrist. They know to a milligram how much of the old oil to pour on to break you down. They are definitely smarter than I am, which is one reason why I love 'em.

Cat haters will try to floor you with the old argument, "If cats are so smart, why can't they do tricks, the way dogs do?" It isn't that cats can't do tricks; it's that they won't. They're far too hep to stand up and beg for food when they know in advance you'll give it to them anyway. And as for rolling over or playing dead, or "speaking," what's in it for Kitty that isn't already hers? (from "My Boss the Cat" by Paul Gallico)

a. What is the author's purpose? _____

b. What is the tone? _____

The Arctic fox is a mammal of the far north. He trots along the seashore in winter, searching for food among the jumbled piles of ice. Once in a while he finds a dead whale that has washed onto the icy beach. Sometimes he finds a dead fish or bird. All of these are food for the fox.

Cold doesn't bother the little Arctic fox. His winter coat is very thick and warm. Even when the temperature falls far below zero, he is well protected. (from "Arctic Fox" by George W. Frame)

c. What is the author's purpose? _____

d. What is the tone? _____

The black widow spider has a rather nasty reputation: her bite is deadly, and she is notorious for killing and eating her mate. But what most people don't know is that she is also very shy, has terrible eyesight, and attacks only to catch her food or to protect herself or her eggs.

Like most animals, she is dangerous when provoked, so it is important that you do not play with her web or try to touch her. But if you watch her from a safe distance and treat her with caution and respect, this sinister member of the spider world might prove very interesting to you. (from "A Dangerous Lady" by Katherine B. Hauth)

e. What is the author's purpose? _____

f. What is the tone? _____

The piranha is well-equipped to be a deadly predator. Its sharp, pointed teeth snap together like a steel trap. Strong bony plates on its head protect the fish as it smacks against the body of its prey.

The piranha has a very keen sense of smell. When a wounded animal goes into the water, the fish can smell its blood from far away. Soon piranhas race toward the smell from all directions. Sometimes they get so excited that they start a "feeding frenzy." When this happens, piranhas will gobble up anything they can grab—even each other. (from "Piranhas!" by Lynne Martin)

g. What is the author's purpose? _____

h. What is the tone? _____

When the dogs in the city talked among themselves, the conversation always drifted to the suburbs.

It was the dream of every canine to someday live out where every dog had his own tree, where bad breath had been conquered, and where fleas had to register at the city limits and carry their I.D.'s at all times.

The suburban dog had it made. Owners pampered them to death with dietary dog food, dental appointments, knitted stoles to take off the evening chill, dog beds shaped like hearts, doggie bar nibbles, and car seats.

I personally felt I could live a fulfilled life without a live-in lawn fertilizer, but my husband convinced me the children would grow up to steal hubcaps without the security and affection of a dog.

In a weak moment, we bought Arlo. (from "The Pampered Dog" by Erma Bombeck)

i. What is the author's purpose? _____

j. What is the tone? _____

Lesson 11

Practice

While you read the following selection, pay special attention to clues that help you make inferences. Then complete the exercise at the end of the selection.

Helpless Hero
Sandra Fenichel Asher

Michael Patrick O'Rourke, champion ice skater of Larson junior high, had taken a really spectacular fall. Now, one week later, he lay propped up in his bed, his broken hip wrapped in what felt like six tons of plaster. One week was gone. There were several more to go, then crutches, then just taking it easy. There would probably be no summer job, no swimming, no ball. Once an all-around athlete, Mike now felt more like a helpless blob.

His parents had even had a phone installed next to his bed in case he needed to call them at work.

"I'm not *that* helpless!" he had protested. But after staying alone in the house all day, he admitted he felt better with the phone there, even though he hadn't used it yet.

To pass the time, Mike read and kept up with his schoolwork. From his bed, he could see out the window. But about the only thing that moved on his street was old Mrs. Malone, and she certainly didn't move much.

Mike already had her daily schedule memorized. At 8:30 a.m., she came outside, picked up her newspaper and carton of milk, and went back in. At 10 a.m., she came out, dressed in her navy blue coat and bright red beret and walked two blocks to the shopping center. At 11:00, she returned, carrying a small bag of groceries.

At 2:30 p.m., she came out again, got her mail, and went back in. That was it, except for her small parade of visitors. In healthier days, Mike had been one of the most frequent visitors at the neat little white frame house across from his. Its tiny garden had seemed to burst with colorful blossoms from early spring to late fall.

Mike's friendship with Mrs. Malone had started with Mike's mother suggesting he stop over each day after school to see if their elderly neighbor needed any help. Mike soon discovered that, although she was probably more than 70 years old, Mrs. Malone was a long way from being helpless. What she couldn't do physically, she made up for with her lively imagination.

"Well, hello," she chirped, when Mike first went over to introduce himself, "I'm Mrs. Malone, and I'm Irish."

"So am I!" said Mike. "Well, half-Irish. But I've never been to Ireland. Neither have my parents. They were born in the United States, too."

"Well, Michael Patrick O'Rourke," said Mrs. Malone, serving him some home-baked cookies, "you start saving your pennies, and I'll save mine, and we'll go over there together. I'll take you to my old home near Shannon, a garden spot that would put Eden itself to shame."

And so began a series of fascinating descriptions of "over there," mixed up with so many folktales and leprechauns that Mike was never sure what was real and what wasn't. He was sure, though, that he wanted to see Ireland, so he really did begin saving his allowance and whatever he could earn at odd jobs. Now that he had lots of time to think, his favorite daydreams were about historic Dublin, where his ancestors had lived, and, of course, Mrs. Malone's beloved Shannon.

In fact, he was in the midst of just such a daydream today, one week after his accident, when he saw Mrs. Malone slip on her front step while getting her newspaper. She certainly seemed to land hard, but she got up all right and went inside, so Mike forgot about it for the moment.

But later, as he ate the lunch his mother had left on his night table, Mike suddenly realized Mrs. Malone hadn't made her 10 a.m. shopping trip.

Maybe she's having leftovers tonight, he thought, although he really couldn't imagine Mrs. Malone eating leftovers. She was always cooking or baking something. And she went to the grocery every day but Sunday. Mike was beginning to feel very uneasy.

Promptly at 2:30 the mailman came. Mike watched him drop letters in Mrs. Malone's mailbox and waited for her to pop out of the door. An hour later, the letters were still untouched in the mailbox.

Mike began to worry in earnest now. He fidgeted with his pillow and blanket, feeling more helpless than ever. Just then, one of Mrs. Malone's elderly friends drove up the snow-covered street. Mike watched him ring the bell.

Thank goodness, sighed Mike, somebody will see that she's OK.

But his relief was short-lived. When Mrs. Malone didn't answer the bell, her visitor drove away, assuming she had gone out. What could have happened to her? And what could he do?

Suddenly he remembered the phone.

"Operator," he said, "please give me the police."

"Sergeant, my name is Michael Patrick O'Rourke, and I think my neighbor is in trouble." Then he told his story, beginning with Mrs. Malone's fall on the steps that morning and ending with her failure to answer the doorbell.

"We'll take care of it," said Sergeant Gregg. "Thank you for calling."

Mike hung up the receiver and fell back on his pillow, exhausted. The next thing he knew, his mother was rushing into his room shouting, "Mike, are you all right?"

"Sure," he mumbled, still half-asleep. "What's the matter?"

"We saw an ambulance across the street as we drove up. Dad went over to Mrs. Malone's, and I ran up here to check on you!"

Just then, Mike's father came in. "It was for Mrs. Malone," he said. "Seems she fell this morning and broke her hip!"

Now Mike was wide awake. "Is she OK?" he asked, anxiously.

"About as OK as you are," smiled his father.

They got the rest of the story from a reporter who came later that evening to take Mike's picture.

"I just took Mrs. Malone's picture at the hospital," he said. "Quite a lady. After she fell this morning she managed to get to her sofa before fainting from the pain. When she came to, she knew she had better not move, so she just waited and prayed. She really wasn't frightened until her friend rang the doorbell and then went away."

Name _____

"That's when I got really scared, too," said Mike.

"I can see why," said the reporter. "What if everyone thought she had gone out of town or something? But the police broke in her door because of your call."

"Wow, I guess I'm not so helpless after all," laughed Mike. "Broke down a door by remote control!"

That quote appeared under his picture in the paper, with the headline "Hip Hero Helps Hip Grandma."

But Mike liked the quote under Mrs. Malone's picture best. She had said, "Some might say I have the luck of the Irish, but I'd say Mike has the *pluck* of the Irish!"

Exercise. Answer each of the questions below.

a. Mike has memorized Mrs. Malone's weekday schedule. At 8:30 each morning, Mrs. Malone picks up her newspaper. What happens when she picks up her newspaper this morning?

b. Although Mike sees this happen, he infers that Mrs. Malone is not hurt. On what evidence does he base this inference?

c. What does Mrs. Malone usually do each morning at 10:00?

d. What happens at 10:00 this morning?

e. How does Mike explain this?

f. What does Mrs. Malone usually do every afternoon at 2:30?

g. What happens at 2:30 this afternoon?

h. What happens when one of Mrs. Malone's friends comes to visit her?

i. What inference does Mike then make?

j. Why does Mike call the police?

Chapter 5
Main Idea

What is a main idea of a piece of writing? The main idea is the most important idea. It is the main point that the author wants to make. Sometimes the main idea is stated. Sometimes it is implied, or suggested. In this chapter, you will learn several strategies for finding the main idea.

Lesson 1
Identifying Topics

The subject of a paragraph is called the topic. The topic is what the paragraph is about. Usually, the topic is stated in one word or in a very few words. For example, read the paragraph below from "Ice Cream" by the editors of *Consumer Reports*.

> Years ago, ice cream was a special treat. It was children chasing after the ringing bells of an ice-cream truck on a summer evening. It was a boy and girl sharing a banana split and holding hands in an ice-cream parlor. It was the whole family cranking out a homemade batch, just for the fun of it.

The topic of this paragraph is *ice cream*. Notice that the word *ice cream* appears in the first sentence. The pronoun *it*, which stands for the word *ice cream*, begins every other sentence.

Read the next paragraph from "A Dangerous Lady" by Katherine B. Hauth.

> The black widow's poison is more powerful than a rattlesnake's, and she has more than enough venom to kill the small creatures such as crickets or grasshoppers she eats for dinner. It's also enough poison to make a grown person very sick, and is especially dangerous for children or elderly people. But even though her venom is potentially fatal, very few people have ever died from the black widow's bite. And now there are serums to counteract the effects of the spider's poison. If you are ever bitten by a black widow spider, call a doctor immediately. But most important, be careful and know how to identify her.

In this paragraph the word *poison* and its synonym *venom* appear five times. The paragraph, though, is not about just any poison, but a special kind of poison—the black widow spider's poison. Therefore, the topic of this paragraph is *the black widow spider's poison*.

Exercise. Read each paragraph below. Then write the topic of each paragraph in the blanks provided. Remember: The topic may be expressed as one word or a group of words. The topic is not a complete sentence.

a.   Kudzu is a plant whose vines grow so fast some people call it "the mile-a-minute plant." Others joke that when you plant kudzu, jump back quickly; it grows so rapidly that if it catches you, you'll never get away. (from "Mile-a-Minute Vine" by George Laycock)

Topic: _____

b.   Raspberries grow wild over most of the northern hemisphere. The tasty fruits grow on prickly canes that are two to six feet tall. The berries come in red, yellow, or black. The canes live for two years, bearing a few fruits the first year and dozens the second year. Dead canes should be cleared out of the thicket to allow room for new canes. New canes start either from the seeds in raspberries or from the roots of the plants. The ones that come up from the roots are called *suckers* or *clones*. (from "Nature's Medicines" by Lois Wickstrom)

Topic: _____

c.   In early April of 1865, Abraham Lincoln woke up from a disturbing dream. He described to his wife what he had seen in the dream: the Capitol Building was draped in mourning with black crepe, and a coffin lay beneath the dome of the great rotunda. On April 14, Lincoln was shot at Ford's theater by John Wilkes Booth, and within three days the Capitol Building was draped with the black crepe of mourning, and Lincoln's body lay in state beneath the rotunda dome. (from "Dreams at Work" by Diane Ratkowski)

Topic: _____

d.   My father was a master storyteller. He could tell a fine old story that made me hold my sides with rolling laughter and sent happy tears down my cheeks, or a story of stark reality that made me shiver and be grateful for my own warm, secure surroundings. He could tell stories of beauty and grace, stories of gentle dreams, and paint them as vividly as any picture with splashes of character and dialogue. His memory detailed every event of ten or forty years or more before, just as if it had happened yesterday. (from *Roll of Thunder, Hear My Cry* by Mildred D. Taylor)

Topic: _____

104

e. With the arrival of automatic bank tellers that greet customers by name with pleasant beeps and bright green letters, the concept of "talking" machines is not an unfamiliar one. The automatic teller's "Good morning, Charles. Please select a transaction," appears on a screen in front of the customer. With little thought, Charles punches back an answer to the machine's "personalized" request. (from "Is That You, Otis?" by Marianne Taylor)

Topic: _____

Lesson 2

Distinguishing Between the Topic and the Main Idea

The subject of a paragraph is called the topic. Usually, the topic is stated in one word, or in a very few words. For example, the topic of a paragraph may be *ballooning* or *choosing a bicycle*.

The main idea of a paragraph is the most important idea a paragraph gives about the topic. The main idea is usually stated as a complete sentence. For example, the main idea of a paragraph about *ballooning* might be: *Ballooning demands skill as well as courage.* The main idea of a paragraph about *choosing a bicycle* might be: *You should follow three steps when choosing a bicycle.*

The topic of the following paragraph, from "Super Sniffers of the Sea" by Roger J. Crain, is *how scientists work*. The main idea is: *Scientists work by asking questions that lead to new questions.*

> Have you ever asked a question and found that the answer you got led you to ask yet another question? Scientists do this all the time. They'll devise an experiment to answer one question, and the answer will suggest another question, and its answer will lead to still another question—on and on and on. That's why science is so interesting; there's always another puzzle to solve.

Exercise. Read each paragraph below. Then answer the questions that follow each paragraph.

a. Imagine a wind that can't be seen, heard, or felt. Now picture it traveling immense distances faster than the speed of sound. Does this seem like science fiction to you? It isn't. Such a wind really does exist. It's called the solar wind, and

scientists are just beginning to understand this amazing phe-
nomenon. (from "Wind from the Sun" by Sue Kneale)

(1) The topic of paragraph a is:

_____ wind

_____ solar wind

_____ scientists

(2) The main idea of paragraph a is:

_____ It is hard to imagine a wind that cannot be seen.

_____ Scientists do not understand everything.

_____ Scientists are just beginning to understand solar wind.

b.   All of us, at one time or another, have been afraid of
something. Perhaps the fear was of an animal, a person, the
dark, or a nightmare we had. Not everyone feels frightened
in exactly the same way, or for exactly the same reasons. But
everyone feels fear. Fear is a perfectly normal reaction for
people of all ages. (from "Overcoming Fears" by Arlene S.
Uslander)

(3) The topic of paragraph b is:

_____ reactions

_____ people

_____ fear

(4) The main idea of paragraph b is:

_____ Everyone has experienced fear.

_____ Some people become afraid after a nightmare.

_____ Some people are afraid of the dark.

c.   Viewing an eclipse can be dangerous. The concentrated
sun rays can damage the eye retina. *Never look directly at
the sun during an eclipse*, even through smoked glass, dark
photo film, or heavy sunglasses. Instead, project the image of
the eclipse onto another surface for safe viewing. (from "Nature's Own Blackout" by Edward G. Martin)

(5) The topic of paragraph c is:

_____ viewing an eclipse

_____ sun rays

_____ sight

(6) The main idea of paragraph c is:

_____ You should wear sunglasses during an eclipse.

_____ You should look at an eclipse through smoked glass.

_____ Looking at an eclipse can be dangerous.

Name _____

d. There is an old saying that goes "I don't believe in ghosts, but I'm scared stiff of them." Most people think of ghosts, fairies, and Santa Claus as only imaginary. Yet there have been many eerie happenings in dwellings around the world that cannot be explained scientifically. In some people's minds these eerie happenings can only be explained by the presence of a ghost. (from "Is There a Ghost in the House?" by Cheryl Joy Trulen)

(7) The topic of paragraph d is:

_____ old sayings

_____ Santa Claus

_____ ghosts

(8) The main idea of paragraph d is:

_____ Some people believe that ghosts exist.

_____ Some people believe that Santa Claus exists.

_____ Some people believe that ghosts do not exist.

e. Mention Yellowstone and people immediately think of geysers, those natural springs that shoot their jets of hot water high into the air. There is a very good reason for this. At least two-thirds of the world's known geysers and hot springs are located within the boundaries of the park. A walk through Mammoth Hot Springs, the Norris Geyser Basin, or the Fountain Paint Pots Nature Trail (be sure to stay on the boardwalk) will take you past a gurgling, bubbling, hissing display of geothermal wonders. (Geothermal means anything having to do with the heat found deep inside the earth.) (from "The Wonders of Yellowstone" by Eric A. Kimmel)

(9) The topic of paragraph e is:

_____ Yellowstone's geysers and hot springs

_____ walks

_____ Norris Geyser Basin

(10) The main idea of paragraph e is:

_____ Yellowstone is known for its geysers and hot springs.

_____ There are geysers in Norris Geyser Basin.

_____ Stay on the boardwalk when you hike Fountain Paint Pots Nature Trail.

Finding the Topic Sentence of a Paragraph

The topic sentence tells the main idea of the paragraph. Often, the topic sentence appears at the beginning of the paragraph. However, it may appear near the middle of the paragraph or at the end of the paragraph. The other sentences in the paragraph add information about the main idea.

In the paragraph below, the first sentence is the topic sentence. The other sentences add information about the main idea expressed in the topic sentence.

> **Hurricane Allen did a great deal of damage to the Caribbean Islands.** It produced high tides that wrecked houses and beachfront buildings. It killed 81 people, all from the islands. In addition, it destroyed crops throughout the region.

In the next paragraph, the topic sentence, printed in **boldface,** appears near the middle.

> How do you know a storm is approaching? What sign tells you to prepare? **A barometer is an instrument that helps you predict a storm.** The barometer measures atmospheric pressure. The mercury in the column of the barometer rises when the atmospheric pressure rises. The mercury falls when the atmospheric pressure falls. When the mercury falls, you know that a severe storm is approaching.

In the next paragraph, the topic sentence appears at the end.

> The sky over San Juan was overcast. A powerful wind was coming out of the east. The barometer was falling. Then the rain began to fall. **These signs indicated that the hurricane was headed for Puerto Rico.**

Exercise. Read each of the following paragraphs carefully. Draw a line under the topic sentence in each paragraph.

a.   The role of a grandmother has never been really defined. Some sit in rockers, some sky dive, some have careers. Others clean ovens. Some have white hair. Others wear wigs. Some see their grandchildren once a day (and it's not enough). Others, once a year (and that's too much). (from *At Wit's End* by Erma Bombeck)

b.   Spotting a UFO can be fun and exciting. People get their pictures in the paper. Reporters and investigators interview them. Friends and neighbors ask a lot of questions, pay a lot of attention. And maybe, if the UFO is particularly interesting or different, the one who spotted it is invited to be on television talk shows or to lecture to groups around the country. There's a buzz of activity around the person who spots a UFO . . . and it's terrific to be in on the action. There can be money as well. (from *UFO Encounters* by Rita Golden Gelman and Marcia Seligson)

c.   Who invented bread? And how did folks get along without it before it was invented? Actually, people have eaten bread in one form or another throughout history. Prehistoric hunters and gatherers liked nuts and seeds, and these foods added important nutrients to their diets. But nuts and seeds can be very hard to chew and digest, so people ground the nuts and seeds, moistened them to make dough cakes, and baked these cakes on hot rocks in the sun. Eventually, when people started cooking with fire, these cakes were baked on hot coals. Finally, about 4,000 years ago, people in the Middle East started making ovens in which to bake their bread. At about the same time, yeast, which causes bread to rise, was discovered. Yeast made the bread light, tasty, and more digestible. Bread, already an important food, became even more wholesome. (from "What's a Sandwich Without Bread?" by Karen Schlenker)

d.   Fifty years ago the future of air travel seemed to be in airships. No airplane then built could carry so many passengers so far. Airships were developed from balloons, by adding engines to make them go and changing their shapes so they could move through the air more easily. They came to look like giant whales swimming in the sky. (from "Lighter Than Air" by Jack Myers)

e.   In 206 B.C., Chinese Emperor Tsin-Shi had a "magic mirror" in his palace. When someone stood before this mirror, the image was reversed, but the person's organs and bones were visible. Was this "magic mirror" really an X-ray machine? (from "Our Mysterious Past" by M. Regina Lepore)

Finding the Implied Main Idea

The main idea is the most important idea about the topic. Sometimes the main idea is stated directly in the topic sentence. Many times, though, the main idea is implied, or suggested. You have to read closely, add up all the details, and state the main idea in your own words.

In the following paragraph, from *Child of the Owl* by Laurence Yep, Casey Young studies the charm worn by her Paw Paw, her Chinese grandmother.

> Up to then, I had thought of Chinese art as a bunch of vases and snuff bottles with a lot of gentlemen and ladies sitting in a garden drinking tea; and if they were really whooping it up, they'd even be smiling. But the charm looked more like Mexican Indian stuff. It was like someone had taken a full, frontal view of an owl and slit it down the middle and spread the parts out across the charm. And every little part had come to life and was playing a violent game with the other parts: an eyebrow was more than an eyebrow, it was also a little scaled dragon that was trying to swallow up the eyes which weren't just eyeballs—they were also miniature snakes swallowing their own bodies before the dragon could get them. But it was the smiling beak that caught my attention—it seemed at any moment ready to crawl off the charm and down over my arm. The smiling beak, sinuous* and twisting, was a tiger, dangerously playful as it stretched its paws and tail ever so slightly upwards across the broad feathered cheeks (that also looked like fields of what I thought was grain but which Paw-Paw said were rice plants) toward the snake eyeballs.

In this paragraph, Casey learns something about Chinese art. What does she learn? Let's look at the details. Casey says that she had thought Chinese art wasn't lively. In other words, she had thought it was boring. Then she studied the Chinese owl charm. Every part of the charm seemed to be alive and active. In fact, she says the charm seemed so alive that the owl's beak, which is in the shape of a tiger, appeared "ready to crawl off the charm."

The main idea is: *Casey learns that Chinese art can be lively and exciting.*

---

*sinuous (sĭn′yōo-əs) *adj.*: Curving or winding.

Exercise. Read each of the paragraphs below. Then put an X next to the statement that best expresses the main idea.

    a.   Julie shivered more from excitement than from the freezing weather as she moved up the snowy mountainside in the chair lift. Finally, Danny had noticed her and asked her to ski with him. She didn't mind that he had waited until pretty late in the afternoon to do it. At least they'd get one run in before the lifts stopped today. Then tomorrow they could ski from daybreak to dark. (from "Terror on Tanglewood" by Elizabeth Van Steenwyk)

_____ Julie was freezing as she moved up the snowy mountain.

_____ Julie was excited that Danny had asked her to ski with him.

_____ Julie went up the mountain in a ski lift.

b.   One April day, four tourists were walking on the beach at Rhodes, Greece, when they suddenly heard a wild yell from above. They looked up and to their horror saw a man jump from the roof of a seaside hotel. A high hedge blocked their view of the ground, but they ran toward the spot where the man must have fallen—and were shocked to hear clapping and calls of "bravo . . . good show." Beyond the hedge, smiling and unhurt, stood the man they thought had committed suicide. He was an athlete named Martin Grace, and he had been practicing a stunt for *Escape to Athena*, a World War II adventure movie being filmed in Rhodes at that time. (from "Secret Stars" by Mary Evans Andrews)

_____ Tourists ran to the spot where the man had fallen.

_____ A man jumped from the roof of a hotel in Rhodes, Greece.

_____ Martin Grace was performing a stunt when he jumped from the roof.

c.   When I was in junior high school, I read about a newspaper writer of the late 1800s named Nellie Bly. The stories that she wrote told about things that needed to be changed and convinced people to change them. Once Nellie Bly took a dare to go around the world in eighty days. She made the trip in seventy-two days, which was very fast in the days before the airplane. Nellie Bly led an exciting life, and I decided I wanted to be like her when I grew up. (from "Photojournalist: Reporter with a Camera" by Lauren Stockbower)

_____ Nellie Bly wrote stories about things that needed to be changed.

_____ When Lauren Stockbower, the author of this paragraph, was in junior high school, she read about Nellie Bly and decided she wanted to be like her.

_____ Nellie Bly traveled around the world in seventy-two days.

d.   To what use does a kangaroo put its great heavy tail? It leans back and props itself on it, as a man does on a shooting stick. Many lizards use their tails that way too. The original monster lizards, almost certainly, swung their tails as weapons, in a carry-over from the tail-swinging technique of fish. And today? Is it true that a crocodile uses its tail as a weapon? Yes. It can knock a man over with one wallop. Do any warm-blooded animals do the same sort of thing? Yes again. Take an ant bear.* It thwacks with its tail as powerfully as a bear with its forepaw. (from "Animals' Tails" by Alan Devoe)

_____ The kangaroo uses its tail as a prop.

_____ The crocodile can knock over a person with its tail.

_____ Some animals use their tails as props and some as weapons.

Lesson 5

Using the Formula "Who?" "Did What?" "Why?"

The three questions "Who?" "Did what?" and "Why?" are sometimes helpful for finding the main idea of a paragraph that is long or that seems difficult to understand. For example, read the opening paragraph from the autobiography *The Lady and Her Tiger* by Pat Derby, a wild animal trainer.

It has to begin with elephants. I was born in love with all elephants: not for a reason that I know, not because of any of their individual qualities—wisdom, kindness, power, grace, patience, loyalty—but for what they are altogether, for their entire elephantness. When I was a little girl in Sussex, I must have driven my father crazy, begging him eternally to take me to see the elephants at a circus or a carnival or a zoo sometimes halfway across England. We almost always got there, somehow. My father always knew how it was between elephants and me.

Use the three questions to find the main idea of this paragraph.
Who: Pat Derby
Did what? As a little girl, Pat Derby went to see every elephant she could.
Why? Elephants were very important to her.
Main Idea: *As a little girl, Pat Derby went to see every elephant she could because elephants were important to her.*

---

*ant bear: A large anteater.

Name _____

Exercise. Read each of the paragraphs below from *The Lady and Her Tiger* by Pat Derby. Then answer the questions that follow each paragraph. Finally, write a statement expressing the main idea of the paragraph.

   a.   The trouble was that I hated circuses, and carnivals, and zoos. I hated the way their keepers and trainers treated the elephants—the other animals too, but the elephants most of all. Elephants bring out a fury in many men as no other creature does: a rage to dominate and to hurt.

Who? _____

Did what? _____

Why? _____

Main Idea: _____

_____

   b.   My father eventually learned to take me to visit the elephants a day or so early, while the show was still setting up, with the elephants hauling on great cables and guy ropes, dragging tent poles into position, and carrying crates of equipment on their backs from this place to that. It was usually easy enough to find someone who would take a five-pound note to let the two of us trail him around the lot all day, keeping more or less out of his way and out of trouble. We'd talk with the grips and roustabouts and share their lunches, and even help shift or shovel where we were allowed. My father was a red-haired, green-eyed man who stood almost six feet six inches tall, and if he hadn't been teaching Shakespeare at Cambridge, he would have had a very good time working in a carnival.

Who? _____

Did what? _____

Why? _____

Main Idea: _____

_____

   c.   But what I came for was to be with the elephants. How much of their vast, gentle presence I was able to enjoy each time depended on my own quickness, on my father's diversionary actions, and on the occasional tolerance of an elephant man. One way or another, there would always come at least one moment when I would be standing alone in that shadow that was home, between those scratchy, gunnysack-feeling legs, while a trunk touched my face with a cold, sticky daintiness to see who I was, and as far over me as the ceiling of my parents' bedroom, a heart like an oven roared and flamed. I was never afraid. I breathed the elephants in, as they breathed me in, and I disappeared into their rumbling tenderness—so much so that I could never understand how my father knew where to find me, nor how he could see me at all when he came looking.

Who? _____

Did what? _____

Why? _____

Main Idea: _____

d.   To this day, when I crawl away from a stupid, humiliating, useless afternoon spent juggling bills, lying to creditors, and scrounging money from strange Hollywood people to pay for chicken necks and horsemeat, I can still cleanse myself by standing close to an elephant, leaning between her forelegs with the heat of her heart over me. Her name is Neena. She's fifteen years old, which is like being a fifteen-year-old girl. There are moments when it seems to me that it was an elephant who got me into this strange and arduous thing I do, and that it's only Neena who keeps me from getting into my car and driving away from all of it forever. *There's no other reason but that crazy elephant, who wouldn't understand.*

Who? _____

Did what? _____

Why? _____

Main Idea: _____

Lesson 6

Finding Supporting Details

Supporting details are facts or ideas that back up the main idea of a paragraph. For example, read the following paragraph.

One of the most interesting ways to collect stamps is to save first-day covers. Since they are envelopes mailed on the day the stamp is first issued, they can become valuable. They have fascinating postmarks because they are mailed from the place the new stamp comes from or honors. Some first-day covers also have artwork that gives information about the stamp.

The main idea of this paragraph is: One of the most interesting ways to collect stamps is to save first-day covers. The rest of the paragraph supports this claim or idea. The first supporting detail is: Since they are envelopes mailed on the day the stamp is first issued, they can become valuable. The second supporting detail is: They have fascinating postmarks because they are mailed from the place the new stamp comes from or honors. The third supporting detail is: Some first-day covers also have artwork that gives information about the stamp.

Exercise 1. The first-day cover below honors Pablo Picasso. Read the statements about Picasso that appear below the cover. These statements are not in the order in which they would appear in a paragraph. Write *M.I.* by the statement that expresses the main idea. Write *S.D.* by each statement that contains a supporting detail.

_____ **a.** Pablo Picasso's painting *Guernica** is widely praised.

_____ **b.** Picasso's early paintings, which were realistic, or lifelike, show his mastery of technique.

_____ **c.** Picasso's portrait of Gertrude Stein is one of his most famous works.

_____ **d.** Many people consider Pablo Picasso one of the greatest modern painters.

_____ **e.** Picasso's cubist paintings influenced other artists.

***Guernica** (gĕr-nē′kä) n.: A town destroyed during the Spanish Civil War.

Joseph Stella:
The Brooklyn Bridge:
Variation on an Old Theme,
1939. Whitney Museum of
American Art

Exercise 2. The painting above is by Frank Stella. Read the statements below. These statements are not in the order in which they would appear in a paragraph. Write *M.I.* by the statement that expresses the main idea. Write *S.D.* by each statement that contains a supporting detail.

_____ **a.** Some photographers, like Edward Steichen, photographed the Brooklyn Bridge.

_____ **b.** Some playwrights, like Arthur Miller, wrote plays in which the Brooklyn Bridge was important.

_____ **c.** Some poets, like Hart Crane, wrote poems about the Brooklyn Bridge.

_____ **d.** The beauty of the Brooklyn Bridge has inspired many artists.

_____ **e.** Some painters, like Frank Stella, painted pictures of the Brooklyn Bridge.

116

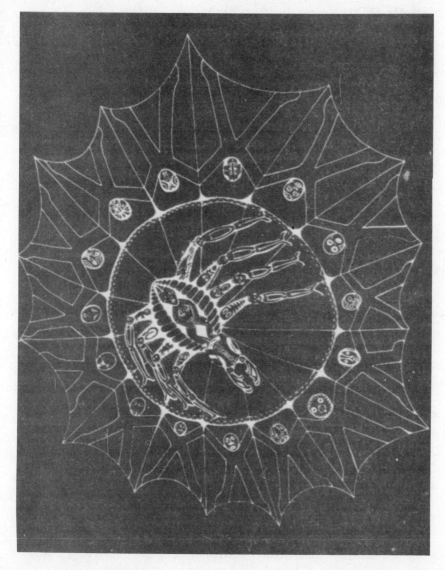

Joseph Geran: *Anansi*, 1971.
Private Collection

Exercise 3. The pen-and-ink drawing above is by the artist Joseph Geran. Read the statements below. These statements are not in the order in which they would appear in a paragraph. Write *M.I.* by the statement that expresses the main idea. Write *S.D.* by each statement that contains a supporting detail.

_____ **a.** The main figure is, of course, Anansi the Spiderman.

_____ **b.** Anansi is a folk hero of the Ashanti people.

_____ **c.** In Geran's drawing, Anansi is encircled by his web.

_____ **d.** In his pen-and-ink drawing, *Anansi*, Joseph Geran draws upon his African heritage.

_____ **e.** If you look closely, you will see that each section of his web is made up of a stick figure wearing an African mask.

Ordering the Importance of Ideas

When you order the importance of ideas, you decide which idea is the most important and which ideas are less important. For example, here are three statements about Chris.

1. Chris throws an amazing curve ball.

2. Chris' fastball is envied by most players.

3. Chris is an excellent baseball player.

The most important idea is that Chris is an excellent baseball player. The two other ideas are less important. They help explain why Chris is an excellent baseball player.

Exercise. Read the selection below, from "Jim Plunkett . . . the Quarterback Who Didn't Drop Out," by Larry Fox. Jim Plunkett was one of football's most popular stars. Then follow the directions at the end of the selection.

Jim Plunkett had known success through most of his football career, but he also had been forced to cope with adversity.* The combination had forged an indomitable† will within his heavily muscled, 6-foot-2, 210-pound body with an arm that former Jet coach Weeb Ewbank said "could throw a football like a javelin."

Plunkett was born Dec. 5, 1947 in Santa Clara, Calif.; he has two older sisters. His parents, of Mexican descent, had met at a school for the blind in New Mexico. His mother was totally blind; his father, "legally blind"—he could see the picture if he put his face up close to the TV screen, for instance. The Plunketts moved often from one small rented home to another in the poorer sections of San Jose, where Jim's father operated a newsstand.

Jim's father died several years ago and Jim remains very close to his mother. He points out firmly, "We never thought of our mother as being handicapped. She just couldn't see."

After Jim completed his high-school career as quarterback for an undefeated championship team, he had scholarship offers from schools all over the nation. But he told all the recruiters he intended to stay near home and his parents. Eventually he accepted a scholarship from Stanford, in nearby Palo Alto, Calif.

However, that summer during a preschool physical exam, doctors discovered a lump in Jim's neck near the thyroid gland. Tests confirmed that surgery would be required. Jim feared he

---

*adversity (ăd-vûr′sə-tē) n.: Hardship; misfortune.
†indomitable (ĭn-dŏm′ə-tə-bəl) adj.: Strong; not able to be defeated.

might never play football again, but the operation was relatively minor.

Within weeks, Jim was trying to play football again with the Stanford freshmen, but he was in too much of a hurry. He played poorly and was equally ineffective during spring practice. Still, he was totally unprepared when Coach John Ralston told him that if he wanted to play with the varsity that fall he should consider switching to defensive end or linebacker.

Tears came to Plunkett's eyes. "Don't make up your mind on me right now. Wait until fall," he pleaded. "In the meantime, tell me what I have to do to make myself a college quarterback."

The answer, of course, was hard work. That summer Plunkett threw hundreds of passes a day to a former high-school teammate. As fall approached, he felt his skills returning. There was no more talk of Plunkett playing defense, but Stanford had plenty of quarterbacks and so they decided to "red shirt" Jim. He would practice all year, but play in no games, and thus retain three full seasons of varsity eligibility. By the next spring, there was no question that Jim Plunkett was Stanford's quarterback of the future.

Stanford had long been one of the Pacific Eight Conference's weaker teams but in Jim's first two years they rolled to a combined 13-5-2 record and Plunkett was recognized as one of the nation's leading passers. At this point, Jim faced a critical decision. Because he had been red-shirted, he could make himself eligible for the NFL draft that January. But, despite the tremendous economic pressures at home, he decided to remain in school.

"Coach Ralston, all of our coaches, and my teammates have been building something at Stanford," Plunkett explained. "If I were to leave now, I would always have the feeling that I let them down. Besides, we are always telling kids today not to drop out, to finish school, to set targets and to work for them. What would they think if I were to drop out now for professional football?" (Today, Plunkett's main off-field activity involves seeking increased educational opportunities for Mexican-Americans, among others.)

The decision, made for idealistic reasons, paid off in a practical way for Plunkett. He set dozens of school and national passing records, Stanford won the Pac-Eight championship with an 8-3 record and, for the first time in years, played in the Rose Bowl, where Plunkett capped his college career by upsetting undefeated Ohio State.

He made every all-America team and was named winner of the Heisman Trophy as the best college football player in the land. That January, the Patriots made Plunkett the first draft choice in professional football.

Directions. Below are four groups of statements about Jim Plunkett. For each group, write *M* next to the statement that expresses the most important idea. Write *L* next to the statements that express the less important ideas.

a. _____ Jim Plunkett's mother was totally blind, and his father was legally blind.

_____ Jim Plunkett has known difficulty or hardship.

_____ Jim Plunkett's parents were poor.

b. _____ Jim Plunkett is not easily defeated.

_____ After a thyroid operation, Jim Plunkett had to work very hard to regain his skill.

_____ Jim Plunkett was back playing football within weeks after an operation on his thyroid.

c. _____ After his father died, Jim Plunkett took care of his mother.

_____ Jim Plunkett is devoted to his family.

_____ Although Jim Plunkett received scholarships from all over the country, he decided to stay near home.

d. _____ Jim Plunkett won the Pac-Eight championship.

_____ Jim Plunkett won the Heisman Trophy for best college football player.

_____ Jim Plunkett has had a successful football career.

Lesson 8

Understanding Paragraphs as Signals

A new paragraph signals a change. Sometimes the new paragraph moves you from the description in the story to the words spoken by one character. Other times the new paragraph moves the story to a different time, to a different place, to a different event, or to a different character.

For example, read the paragraphs that follow from "The King Who Ate Chaff,*" a Burmese tale by Harold Courlander.

(1)   Once a king went for a walk through the outskirts of his city. As he didn't want to be recognized by his subjects, he disguised himself as a common merchant and took only a single servant with him. He looked on with interest at all the things that ordinary people were doing, and at last he turned back toward home. At that moment he saw an old

---

*chaff (chăf) n.: The husks of grain.

"The King Who Ate Chaff: A Burmese Tale" from *The Tiger's Whisker and Other Tales From Asia and the Pacific* by Harold Courlander. Copyright © 1959 by Harold Courlander.

woman winnowing* rice. The chaff that the woman threw away smelled very sweet to the king, and suddenly he had an overpowering desire to eat some of it. He walked on a few steps, and then ordered his servant to go back and bring him some chaff to eat.

(2)   The servant was shocked. He protested that it was a disgraceful thing for a great king to eat chaff, which was food fit only for cows and pigs. But the king told him not to give advice, and spoke angrily. So the servant brought him the chaff, and the king ate it eagerly, as though he had never tasted anything so good. When he was through, he spoke sternly to his servant, saying: "If you say the slightest word to anyone about this affair, you will lose your head."

The first paragraph introduces the story. It mainly tells about the king. The second paragraph moves the story to the servant.

---

*winnowing (wĭn′ō-ĭng) v.: Separating the chaff from the grain.

Exercise 1. Continue reading "The King Who Ate Chaff." Then answer the questions that follow it.

(3)   After they had returned to the king's house, the servant was overcome with an irresistible urge to tell someone what he had seen. He couldn't sleep for thinking about it. He lost his appetite. He did everything he could think of to help him forget. Nothing helped. "If I could even whisper it to someone I would feel better," he thought. But he didn't dare to say a word.

(4)   Two or three days passed. The servant became ill and haggard from lack of sleep, and worst of all the itch to tell his secret still tortured him. At last, unable to bear it any longer, he rushed out of the house to a grove of trees where he could whisper the words without anyone hearing him. But there was a woodcutter nearby, so he got in a boat and rowed himself out to the middle of the river. He saw fishermen there, so he fled back to the shore and went to the cemetery, but once there he thought the gravediggers might overhear him. At last he went out to the forest, and putting his head into the hollow of a big tree, he whispered fervently:* "The great king eats chaff! The great king eats chaff! The great king eats chaff!" After that he felt better and went home.

(5)   Many months later, the great palace drum, which announced the hours, cracked and broke, and the royal drum makers went into the forest and cut down a tree for a

---

*fervently (fûr′vənt-lē) adv.: With a lot of emotion.

new drum. It happened that the tree they chose was the very one into which the servant had whispered his terrible secret.

(6)   In a few weeks the new drum was ready. It was a beautiful drum. Everyone looked at it and admired it. It was installed with pomp and ceremony on its stone platform. The king and his court and visitors from the city and the countryside stood and watched.

(7)   At the height of the ceremony the drum was beaten for the first time. The people were amazed, because the drum did not say "boom, boom" as the old drum had. Instead, it said: "The great king eats chaff! The great king eats chaff! The great king eats chaff!"

Questions

a. Paragraph 3 signals a change in time. Look at the first word in this paragraph. Do the events in paragraph 3 happen earlier or later than the events in paragraph 2?

_____

b. Paragraph 4 also signals a change in time. When do the events in paragraph 4 happen in relation to the events in paragraph 3?

_____

c. Paragraph 5 signals another change in time. When do the events in paragraph 5 happen in relation to the events in paragraph 4?

_____

d. Which words in paragraph 6 tell you that the events in this paragraph happen after the events in paragraph 5?

_____

e. When do the events in paragraph 7 occur?

_____

Exercise 2. Read the following Chinese folk tale, "The Spear and Shield of Huan-Tan," by Harold Courlander. Then answer the questions that follow it.

(1)   Once in the old days there was a weapons maker named Huan-Tan, a man who never overlooked any kind of argument that would help to sell his spears and shields. For Huan-Tan, no remark was too extravagant when he praised the qualities of the weapons he made.

(2)   One day Huan-Tan was standing in his shop, calling to the crowd of people that surged back and forth in the street. He waved one of his spears in the air and cried out: "If there are soldiers among you, here is the spear you are looking for! The hardest steel that was ever forged! The sharpest edge that ever was honed! A shaft that is light as the wind! This spear has a will of its own! It cannot be blunted; its edge can never be dulled! And, soldiers, listen to this: The spear I hold in my hand will go through any armor that was ever made! It will go through the toughest metal that is known to man!"

"The Spear and Shield of Huan-Tan" from *The Tiger's Whisker and Other Tales From Asia and the Pacific* by Harold Courlander. Copyright © 1959 by Harold Courlander.

(3)   Some of the passers-by stopped to listen as Huan-Tan paid this tribute to his spear. One of them said: "It isn't a spear that I'm looking for, but a shield."

(4)   Hearing this, Huan-Tan put down the spear and took up one of his new shields. "My friend," he said, "this is the shield you are looking for! The hardest steel that is known to man! Look at that polished surface! There is no blade in the world that can dent it or scratch it! Where is the spear that can penetrate this shield? Nowhere, my friend, because it has never been made!"

(5)   The man to whom Huan-Tan was directing this speech was thoughtful. "Yes, yes," he said, "a wonderful thing. Here you have a shield that can't be penetrated by any spear in existence. And there beside you is a spear that can penetrate anything. Now, how about giving us a demonstration? Why don't you try your wonderful spear against your wonderful shield and let us see what happens?"

(6)   The enthusiastic weapons maker looked at the shield in his hand, then at the spear leaning against the wall. His eyes went from one to the other, back and forth, and he was unable to utter a word.

(7)   Suddenly he cupped his hand to his ear, saying: "Hark!" He appeared to listen intently for a moment. Then he laid down the shield and said: "It is my wife calling again." And Huan-Tan disappeared into the darkness of the back room of his shop.

(8)   A great roar of laughter went up outside, and then the spectators drifted away.

Questions

a. Paragraph 1 introduces the story. Paragraph 2 focuses on Huan-Tan. Paragraph 3 changes the focus to whom?   _____

b. Paragraph 4 changes the focus to which speaker?   _____

c. Does paragraph 5 change the focus to another time, another place, or another speaker?   _____

d. Paragraph 6 changes the focus to which character?   _____

e. In paragraph 7 Huan-Tan speaks and then disappears. Paragraph 8 changes the focus to the spectators. However, it is not their words that rise up, but their what?   _____

Understanding Paragraphs with Conflicting Main Ideas

The main idea of a paragraph is the most important idea about the topic. Two paragraphs may be about the same topic. But the main idea of each may be completely different.

For example, the topic of both paragraphs below is cats.

> Cats make wonderful pets. If their people treat them well, cats show much tenderness toward them. Often, they run to the door to greet their people and cuddle up close to their people during the night. In addition, cats are adaptable. They can keep themselves company for hours while still delighting in their owners' company. They take great pleasure in chasing a piece of paper across the floor and in hiding in grocery bags. Watching a cat play with a ball of yarn can provide you with hours of entertainment.
>
> Cats make terrible pets. They are aloof and avoid people. They are not loyal to their masters. Cats will not retrieve a ball or bring the paper to you. They will not run in the woods with you nor hunt by your side. When cats play, they play by themselves, not with their owners.

The main idea of the first paragraph is: Cats make wonderful pets. The details in this paragraph support this main idea. The main idea of the second paragraph is just the opposite. It is: Cats make terrible pets. The details in this paragraph support this main idea.

Exercise. Below are ten topic sentences that could be used to begin a paragraph. For each topic sentence, write three statements containing details that support the main idea.

a. The best advice for traveling is "See America first."

(1) _____

(2) _____

(3) _____

b. The best advice for traveling is "Visit foreign countries."

(1) _____

(2) _____

(3) _____

c. A beach vacation is your best choice for a summer vacation.

(1) _____

(2) _____

(3) _____

d. A mountain vacation is your best choice for a summer vacation.

   (1) _____

   (2) _____

   (3) _____

e. Teenages should earn their allowance.

   (1) _____

   (2) _____

   (3) _____

f. Teenagers should be given their allowance.

   (1) _____

   (2) _____

   (3) _____

g. Winter is my favorite season.

   (1) _____

   (2) _____

   (3) _____

h. Winter is my least favorite season.

   (1) _____

   (2) _____

   (3) _____

i. Watching television can be a waste of time.

   (1) _____

   (2) _____

   (3) _____

j. Watching television can be a valuable experience.

   (1) _____

   (2) _____

   (3) _____

Practice

Pay special attention to main ideas as you read "Soccer: Before the Game." Then complete the exercises that follow the selection.

Soccer: Before the Game
John Devaney

(1) Giorgio Chinaglia, the high-scoring New York Cosmos star, walks slowly into the empty dressing room, the first to arrive for the game. But that's no surprise because Giorgio is *always* the first player to arrive for a Cosmos home game.

(2) He sits on a stool in front of his locker and fishes out the rubber-cleated shoes he wears during a game. He pulls the leather laces off the shoes and carefully threads each shoe with new laces. Giorgio *always* wears new laces for a game.

(3) Then, he pulls on the pair of blue-and-white wrist bands he will wear for the first half of the game. He puts on a new pair for the second half. Giorgio *always* changes wrist bands after the first half of a game. "Yes," he says with a rueful smile, "I am just a little superstitious, yes I am."

(4) Talent and skill are important to soccer superstars, but most players also believe in the power of luck. "The bigger the star," says Chicago Sting equipment manager Willy Steinmiller, "the more likely he is to be superstitious."

(5) The most superstitious is Ferner, the West German goalkeeper. "I think you will find that is true on most teams," says the rangy, mustached Ferner. "You know why? Luck is important for a keeper. If a ball hits the post of the goal and bounds away, the keeper is a hero. If the ball hits the post and trickles into the cage, he's a bum. So to be good he's got to be lucky. And if you believe in good luck and bad luck, then of course you must be superstitious."

(6) Ferner insists on wearing the same shin guards he's worn for the past nine years. "I have to glue them together before a game," says the Sting equipment manager. Just before a game Ferner asks an equipment man to place a towel on his back. He won't let anyone touch his shoes before a game. And he also demands that he be the last one out of the dressing room. "Sometimes," says the Sting's equipment manager, "one of the referees has to come down to the Sting dressing room and demand that Ferner come out so the game can begin."

(7) The Sting's high scorer, Karl-Heinz Granitza, is superstitious about his T-shirt. He wore the same T-shirt for every game during the 1981 season. "I wore it because we

kept on winning," says Granitza. "I wore it right through to the Soccer Bowl." He'll wear it for the 1982 and 1983 seasons, he says, "because we won the Soccer Bowl and the championship of the league so it must be a lucky T-shirt."

(8)   "We had one player," says Willy Steinmiller, "who always wore the same broken-down studs on his shoes, even though the studs can be easily replaced by screwing them off. He kept wearing those nubby studs until finally they broke off and he had to wear new ones. He said that the older his studs, the more goals he scored in a season."

(9)   A star's superstitions can drive his coach up the locker room wall. "I could never talk tactics or strategy to them before a game," says former California Surf coach Hubert Vogelsinger. "They were thinking too much about their superstitions. I had some who would always put on their shoes first, then the rest of their uniform. There were other players who would put on their entire uniform except their pants, and they wouldn't put those on until just before the game. So they'd be running around before the game naked below their waists.

(10)   "When I'd say, 'OK, let's go out there and play,' there would always be a tremendous fight. There were always three or four guys who wanted to be the player who went out onto the field last."

(11)   No North American Soccer League team has more superstars than the Cosmos have and therefore they have more superstitious players than any team in the league. "It's true," says one Cosmos, "that the better the player, the more likely he is to be superstitious. It's like what the goalkeepers say: Luck is important in scoring goals, and the more goals you score, the more you believe in luck."

(12)   When the team is on the road, Chinaglia always makes sure he sits in the same bus seat during the ride from their hotel to the stadium. "Once I forgot and sat in a different seat," Chinaglia says, his nut-brown eyes smoldering as he remembers. "We lost. I never made that mistake again."

(13)   Most Cosmos players drive to Giant Stadium in East Rutherford, New Jersey, for home games. "I live in New Jersey and it is not too far from the stadium," says the Cosmos goalkeeper, Hubert Birkenmeier. "But I always take the same route to the stadium. If I make a mistake and get on a new road, I go back to my house and I start over again. I make sure I get on the road I always take."

(14)   The team's best midfielder is "Bogey" Bogicevic. "He has a size 33 waist," says the Cosmos equipment manager,

Charlie Kessel. "But he always wears double-X sized pants for the game. They are maybe four or five sizes too large. They really swing in the breeze."

(15)   Bogey simply tightens the drawstring on the shorts. "I like the pants to be baggy, you know," he says. "For me the baggier the shorts, the better my luck."

Exercise 1. Reread paragraphs 1-5. For each paragraph, choose the statement that better expresses the main idea. Circle your answer.

a. The main idea of paragraph 1 is:

(1) Giorgio Chinaglia is the first to arrive for the game.

(2) Giorgio Chinaglia is always the first to arrive for a game.

b. The main idea of paragraph 2 is:

(1) Giorgio Chinaglia wears new laces for the game.

(2) Giorgio Chinaglia always wears new laces for a game.

c. The main idea of paragraph 3 is:

(1) Giorgio Chinaglia always changes wristbands for the second half of the game.

(2) Giorgio Chinaglia puts on a new wristband for the second half of the game.

d. The main idea of paragraph 4 is:

(1) Soccer requires talent and skill.

(2) Most soccer players believe in the power of luck.

e. The main idea of paragraph 5 is:

(1) Ferner and other goalkeepers like him are the most superstitious members of the team, because luck plays an important role in determining whether goalkeepers are "heroes" or "bums."

(2) Ferner believes in good luck and bad luck.

Exercise 2. Reread paragraphs 6-10. If the statement below expresses the main idea of the paragraph, write *True* in the blank at the right. If the statement does not, write *False*.

a. Paragraph 6: Ferner glues his shin guards together before the game.   _____

b. Paragraph 7: Karl-Heinz Granitza, who plays for the Stings, believes his T-shirt is lucky.   _____

c. Paragraph 8: One player on Willy Steinmiller's team believed his studs were lucky.   _____

d. Paragraph 9: Some soccer players put their shoes on first.   _____

128

e. Paragraph 10: Steinmiller would tell the players, "OK, let's go out there and play." _____

Exercise 3. Reread paragraphs 11-15. For each paragraph, write a statement expressing the main idea.

a. Paragraph 11: _____

_____

b. Paragraph 12: _____

_____

c. Paragraph 13: _____

_____

d. Paragraph 14: _____

e. Paragraph 15: _____

Exercise 4. Write *M.I.* by the statement that expresses the main idea of this selection. Write *S.D.* by each statement that contains a supporting detail.

a. The Cosmos star, Giorgio Chinaglia, is superstitious. _____

b. Some players believe that the order in which they go out on the field brings them luck. _____

c. Many soccer players are superstitious and follow pregame routines to bring them good luck. _____

d. Some players believe that the order in which they dress brings them luck. _____

e. One player for the Stings believes his T-shirt brought him luck during the 1981 season. _____

Chapter 6
Dictionary

Why use a dictionary? A dictionary tells you the meaning of a word you do not know. But a dictionary tells you other information as well. For example, it tells you how to pronounce the word, how to use it in a sentence, how to spell it, and what its part of speech is.

In this chapter you will learn how to interpret the information in a dictionary. Of course, dictionaries differ slightly. For more information about your particular dictionary, look at the section called "How to Use Your Dictionary" in the front pages of it.

Lesson 1
Using Guide Words

Two guide words appear at the top of every dictionary page. They name the first and last words that appear on that page. For example, imagine the guide words at the top of the page are *mar* and *mash*. All words in alphabetical order that come between *mar* and *mash* also appear on this page. Guide words help you to find a word quickly.

For example, you probably do not know the meaning of the word *pterodactyl*. What is a pterodactyl? Let's look it up in a dictionary.

The guide word on the left shows the *first word* defined on that page.

The guide word on the right shows the *last word* defined on that page.

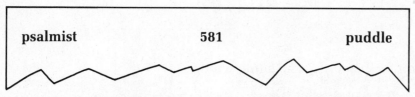

| psalmist | 581 | puddle |

You can see that *pterodactyl* is on page 581. It falls alphabetically between the words *psalmist* and *puddle*.

The dictionary tells you that a *peterodactyl* is an extinct flying reptile. The *p* is silent and the word is pronounced tə'ə-dăk'til.

You don't have to know the meaning or the pronunciation of the guide words in order to use them. Look carefully at the first few letters of each guide word to see if your word fits on that page.

Exercise 1. The guide words at the top of the dictionary page are *fox* and *freckle*. Which of the words below would be found on this page? Write *Yes* next to those words that would be found on this page. Write *No* next to those words that would not be found on this page.

a. free _____

f. fudge _____

b. fraction _____

g. frantic _____

c. Friday _____

h. fog _____

d. frame _____

i. frog _____

e. freak _____

j. foxfire _____

Exercise 2. Look carefully at each word below. If you do not understand the word or do not know how to pronounce it, you may want to look it up later. Your job now is to put an X next to the guide words that show on which page the *italicized* word would be found.

a. *Dinosaur* would appear on the page with the guide words:

_____ daze/devour

_____ dew/dock

_____ doctor/drip

b. *Lizard* would appear on the page with the guide words:

_____ lamp/leak

_____ letter/llama

_____ loaf/lump

c. *Reptile* would appear on the page with the guide words:

_____ rat/rhino

_____ rhyme/ring

_____ road/run

d. *Stegosaurus* would appear on the page with the guide words:

_____ stab/step

_____ stiff/storm

_____ strap/stuff

e. *Swamp* would appear on the page with the guide words:

_____ swab/swan

_____ sweet/swim

_____ switch/sword

Name _____

Lesson 2

Understanding an Entry

An entry word is a word or term defined in the dictionary. The entry is the information about the entry word. A great deal of information is given in each entry, such as definitions, pronunciation, part of speech, and other forms of the word.

Look at the entry below for the entry word *succeed*.

> **suc·ceed** (sək-sēd') *v.* **succeeded, succeeding.** 1. To come after; to follow in time or order. *Our team succeeded the Hawks as champions.* 2. To replace another in office or position. *She succeeded her father to the throne.* 3. To turn out successfully; have the desired result. *Our plan succeeded.* 4. To replace or follow another. *He succeeded to the office of mayor.* [Middle English *succeden,* from Old French *succeder,* from Latin *succedere,* to follow closely, to go after; *sub-* toward, next to + *cedere,* to go.] **suc·ceed'ing·ly**—*adv.*

Each section of the entry is coded by the letters *A, B, C,* etc.

> **suc·ceed** (sək-sēd') *v.* **succeeded, succeeding.** 1. To come after; to follow in time or order. *Our team succeeded the Hawks as champions.* 2. To replace another in office or position. *She succeeded her father to the throne.* 3. To turn out successfully; have the desired result. *Our plan succeeded.* 4. To replace or follow another. *He succeeded to the office of mayor.* [Middle English *succeden,* from Old French *succeder,* from Latin *succedere,* to follow closely, to go after; *sub-* toward, next to + *cedere,* to go.] **suc·ceed'ing·ly**—*adv.*

Part *A* shows you the entry word, *succeed.* It tells you the spelling of this word and how to divide it into syllables. Some dictionaries use a dot to divide words, some a hyphen (-), and others just leave a space between the syllables.

Part *B* shows how to pronounce each syllable of the word and which syllable to stress or accent. For example: (sək-sēd').

Part *C* tells you the part of speech of the first definition. The abbreviation *v.* means verb. Other abbreviations for parts of speech are *n.* (noun), *pron.* (pronoun), *adj.* (adjective), *adv.* (adverb), *prep.* (preposition), *conj.* (conjunction), and *inter.* (interjection). The abbreviation *pl.* means plural.

Part *D* shows you other forms of the entry word. Since *succeed* is a verb, Part *D* shows the principal parts of this verb. When the entry word is a noun, Part *D* shows you the plural form of the word, if the dictionary makers think you might have trouble spelling it. For example, **po·ta·to** (pō-tā'tō) *n., pl.* **potatoes.** When the entry word is an adjective, Part *D* shows you the comparative and superlative forms. For example, **good** (good) *adj.* **better, best.** (Remember: The comparative form is used to compare two things. The superlative form is used to compare three or more things.)

Part *E* contains the definitions. Most words in English have more than one meaning. In the entry each different definition is numbered. Sometimes a sample sentence follows the definition to show you how the word is used. This entry shows four different meanings for *succeed.*

Part *F* shows the origin, or history, of the entry word. This information is enclosed in brackets [   ]. Sometimes the symbol < is used to mean *comes from. Succeed* has a long history. It came from the Middle English word *succeden,* which came from an Old French word, *succeder,* which came from the Latin word *succedere.* The Latin word was made up of two parts: *sub,* which means "toward or next to," and *cedere,* which means "to go."

Part *G* shows a related form of the entry word. *Succeedingly* is the adverb form of the verb *succeed.*

Exercise 1. Read the entry below. Then answer the questions that follow it. Write your answers in the blanks at the right.

> **val•ley** (văl′ē) *n., pl.* **valleys.**   1. A long, low area between a range of mountains.   2. The area of land drained by a river.   3. A hollow or sunken space that looks like a valley. *The boat was trapped in the valley between the two waves.* [Middle English *valey,* from Norman French, from Vulgar Latin *vallata,* from Latin *vallis,* a vale.]

a. The word *valley* has two syllables. Which syllable is stressed?   _____

b. The word *valley* is what part of speech?   _____

c. How do you spell the plural of *valley?*   _____

d. How many meanings does this entry list for *valley?*   _____

e. From which of the following languages does the word *valley* not come: Latin, Spanish, Norman French, Middle English?   _____

Exercise 2. Read the entry below. Then answer the questions that follow it. Write your answers in the blanks at the right.

> **mis•ty** (mĭs′tē) *adj.* **mistier, mistiest.**   1. Made up of or looking like mist.   2. Clouded or veiled as if by mist.   3. Vague, unclear. **mis′ti•ly**—*adv.,* **mis′ti•ness**—*n.*

a. If you break the word *misty* into two syllables, between which two letters can you break it?   _____

b. The word *misty* is what part of speech?   _____

c. The comparative form of *misty* is *mistier.* What is the superlative form?   _____

d. What is the adverb form of *misty?*   _____

e. What is the noun form of *misty?*   _____

Name _____

Finding the Correct Meaning

In English, many words have more than one meaning. This means that a dictionary entry will contain several definitions for the same entry word. For example, look at the entry below.

> **game** (gām) *n.* 1. A pastime; a way of amusing one-self. 2. A sport or contest played by following a set of rules. 3. One instance of such an activity. *The first game lasted 45 minutes.* 4. The equipment used to play certain games. *Marie received several games for her birthday.* 5. A plan or scheme. *His game is to take over the company.* 6. Wild animals, birds, or fish hunted for food or sport. 7. The flesh of these creatures. *adj.* **gamer, gamest.** 1. Of or having to do with such game. 2. Spirited; brave. *v.* **gamed, gaming.** 1. To gamble. [Middle English *game(n),* Old English *gamen,* amusement, fr. Common Germanic *gam-,* to enjoy.]

Now read the sentence below. The sixth meaning of **game** listed under *noun* fits this sentence.

> They hunted for **game** in Africa.

When you read, you must choose the meaning that fits the sentence, or context. You may have to change the definition slightly to match the form of the word used in the sentence.

For example, read the following sentences.

> I played several **games** at school. Among them were football, hockey, and basketball.

Since **games** is plural, you should make the definition plural.

> I played several **sports** at school. Among them were football, hockey, and basketball.

If a verb is used in the past tense, you should rewrite its definition in the past tense.

> The Earl of Sandwich **gamed** while eating.
> The Earl of Sandwich **gambled** while eating.

If an adjective is used to compare two things, you should rewrite its definition to compare two things.

> My new pony is **gamer** than my other horse.
> My new pony is **more spirited** than my other horse.

Exercise. Read the selection below from "The Swimming Nose" by Eve Bunting. Then look up each **boldface** word in a dictionary. Write a definition for each word that fits the sentence it is in.

The shark is sometimes called "the swimming nose" because of its wonderful **sense** of smell. It should be called "the swimming computer." All of its senses work together to make the shark supersensitive to all that is happening in the ocean around it.

The shark's ability to smell is **uncanny.** Two-thirds of its brain is devoted to that sense alone. The smelling is done through the nostrils, which are usually on the underside of the head, and which have nothing whatever to do with the shark's breathing.

An experiment was done to test the shark's sense of smell. Two separate **tanks** were used: one held sharks, and the other held fish. While the fish were swimming quietly, water was piped from their tank to the sharks' tank. The sharks showed little **interest.** Then the fish were **prodded** to make them frightened. When some of this water was piped in to the sharks, things livened up. The sharks began **circling** and snapping at the pipe that carried the fear-scented water! This is scary news for fish.

Scarier for humans were the results of another test. These showed that sharks can smell one drop of human blood in one hundred million drops of water. Any type of blood excites sharks. Skin divers who **spear** fish and tie them to their belts are asking for trouble. Many attacks on skin divers come at waist level. The shark has been **alerted** by the blood of the struggling fish. It follows its nose. And the human is there too when the shark lunges and bites.

Scientists were encouraged when they found that sharks didn't like the smell of human sweat. They tried making an artificial "sweat smell" as a shark **repellent.** Unfortunately, it didn't work all the time.

Questions

a. *Sense means* _____

b. *Uncanny means* _____

c. *Tanks means* (look up *tank*) _____

d. *Interest means* _____

e. *Prodded means* (look up *prod*) _____

f. *Circling means* (look up *circle*) _____

g. *Scarier means* (look up *scare*) _____

h. *Spear means* _____

i. *Alerted means* (look up *alert*) _____

j. *Repellent means* _____

Name _____

Lesson 4

Finding Homophones

Homophones are words that sound alike, but have different meanings and different spellings. For example, the words *vein* and *vain* are homophones. *Vein* means "a vessel that carries blood back to the heart," but *vain* means "feeling too much pride in oneself."

Sleigh and *slay* are also homophones. *Sleigh* means "a vehicle that has runners for traveling on snow and ice." *Slay* means "to kill."

In the comic strip below, Jughead mixes up the homophones *plane* and *plain*. A *plane* is a machine that flies in the air, while a *plain* is a large, flat, and treeless area of land.

ARCHIE

Probably you have seen a sign along the highway saying, "Deer Crossing." This sign warns motorists to watch for these animals. One elementary school wanted to warn motorists to watch for children crossing the street. It put up a sign that said, "Dear Crossing."

Sometimes you need to look up homophones in the dictionary. For example, look at the words *principal* and *principle*. Do you know which means "a general truth or standard" and which means "the head of a school"? If you don't, the following sentence may give you trouble.

The speaker attacked the nation's *principles.*

Look up this homophone in a dictionary. You see that the speaker attacked the nation's standards, not the nation's heads of schools.

Exercise. Read each sentence below. Then use a dictionary to find the meaning of each homophone in parentheses. Choose the one that fits the sentence. Write it in the blank at the right.

a. His watch did not keep good (thyme—time).   _____

b. (Thyme—Time) is a spice that is often used in soups.   _____

c. I began by painting the bottom (stair—stare).   _____

Copyright © 1984 by Harcourt Brace Jovanovich, Inc. All rights reserved

137

d. When you see someone famous, it is difficult not to (stair—stare).

e. After I fell, the (pane—pain) in my ankle was unbearable.

f. The ball went through the right (pane—pain) of glass.

g. John was undecided about painting the (scene—seen) in watercolors or oils.

h. John had never (scene—seen) a more beautiful lake.

i. Maggie walked proudly down the (isle—aisle) to accept the prize.

j. Her prize was a trip to the (Isle—Aisle) of Capri.

k. My great-grandmother lived in England during the (reign—rain—rein) of Queen Victoria.

l. In England, a great deal of (reign—rain—rein) falls in winter.

m. The carpenter used a (plain—plane) to make the table top smooth.

n. The table he was making was (plain—plane) but beautiful.

o. Tim turned (pale—pail) when he thought he saw a ghost.

p. The child played in the sand with his (pale—pail) and shovel.

q. For her part as the queen in the play about sixteenth-century Spain, Marcy wore a white (rough—ruff) around her neck.

r. He sanded the (rough—ruff) edge of the door.

s. Alice wrote all her letters on yellow (stationary—stationery).

t. The train remained (stationary—stationery) for over fifteen minutes.

Lesson 5

Finding Homographs

Homographs are words that are spelled alike but that have different meanings and different word origins. Each homograph has its own dictionary entry. For example, the words *school* and *school* are homographs. Look at the following dictionary entries:

> **school**[1] (sko̅o̅l) *n.* 1. A place where children are educated. 2. A place where people are taught a skill. 3. A college or university. 4. The students who make up this place. *v.* 1. To educate. 2. To train. [Middle English *scole,* fr. Old English *scōl,* fr. Latin *schola,* leisure, school, fr. Greek *skholē,* leisure time devoted to learning.]

school² (skōol) *n.* A large group of fish, whales, porpoises, etc. swimming together. [Middle English *scole,* fr. Middle Dutch *schōle,* troop, group.]

The first entry word has several meanings. All the meanings deal with education or learning. This word comes from a Greek word that means "leisure time devoted to learning."

The second entry word means "a large group of fish, whales, porpoises, etc. swimming together." It comes from a Middle Dutch word that means "troop, group."

For example, read the two sentences below.

Christopher's mother was studying accounting at night *school.*

The diver saw a *school* of fish.

How do you know if a word is a homograph? In the dictionary an entry word is followed by a numeral if there is another entry word spelled by the same letters. For example, **school¹** and **school².**

Suppose you look up a word you do not know. You find that none of the definitions fit the sentence. Check to see if there is another word spelled by the same letters. This word will have its own dictionary entry.

Exercise 1. Read the dictionary entries below. Then read the sentences following the entries. Write *1* in the blank by any sentence that uses the meaning of the first homograph. Write *2* in the blank by any sentence that uses the meaning of the second homograph.

swim¹ (swĭm) *v.* **swam, swum, swimming.** 1. To propel oneself through water by moving part of one's body. 2. To move as though gliding through water. *n.* 1. The period of swimming. 2. The act of swimming. [Middle English *swimmen,* Old English *swimman.*]

swim² (swĭm) *v.* **swam, swum, swimming.** 1. To be dizzy or giddy. 2. To appear to swim. *n.* A state of dizziness; a faint. [Middle English *swime,* dizziness, Old English *swima.*]

a. Her head was swimming from all the ideas they discussed. _____

b. It took her ten minutes to swim to the opposite shore. _____

c. Let's go for a swim! _____

d. The knock on his head caused the room to swim before his eyes. _____

Exercise 2. Read the dictionary entries below. Then read the sentences following the entries. Write *1* in the blank next to any sentence that uses the meaning of the first homograph. Write *2* in the blank next to any sentence that uses the meaning of the second homograph.

lie¹ (lī) *v.* **lay, lain, lying.**   1. To place oneself in a flat or horizontal position. *I lay on the bed.*   2. To be in a flat or horizontal position. *The book lay on the table.*   3. To remain in a certain condition. *Hatred lies in his heart.*   4. To be buried. 5. To extend. *n.*   1. The surface of a plot of land.   2. The way in which something is situated.   3. An animal's hiding place. [Middle English *lien, lay, ley(e)n,* Old English *liegan, laeg, legen.*]

lie² (lī) *n.*   1. A falsehood.   2. Something meant to deceive. *v.* **lied, lying.**   1. To give false information for the purpose of deceiving.   2. To create a false impression. [Middle English *ligen, lien,* Old English *leogan.*]

a. Several islands lie off the coast of Georgia.   _____

b. The farmer decided to let the field lie fallow this year.   _____

c. Trick photography is the art of making photographs lie.   _____

d. The two-month-old baby drank from her bottle while lying in bed.   _____

Lesson 6

Using a Pronunciation Key

You can find out how to pronounce a word by looking it up in the dictionary. In parentheses after the entry word, you will find the word spelled with pronunciation symbols. For example, **live•li•hood** (līv′lē-hood′).

The key to these symbols appears in the front of the dictionary. The key lists each pronunciation symbol used in the dictionary. It illustrates the sound each symbol stands for with a word whose pronunciation most people know. The important parts of this key are usually printed at the bottom of every other page in the dictionary.

Look at the following key. It tells you that the symbol ă stands for the *a* sound you hear in *pat,* and the symbol ā stands for the *a* sound you hear in *pay.* Notice the last symbol, ə, which looks like an upside-down e. It is called a *schwa,* pronounced *shwä.* This sound is never stressed. The pronunciation key shows that ə is pronounced like the *a* in *about,* the *e* in *item,* the *i* in *edible,* the *o* in *gallop,* and the *u* in *circus.*

140

Pronunciation Key

ă	pat	h	hat	ŏ	pot	t	tight
ā	pay	hw	which	ō	toe	th	thin, path
âr	care	ĭ	pit	ô	paw, for	th	this, bathe
ä	father	ī	pie	oi	noise	ŭ	cut
b	bib	îr	pier	o͞o	took	ûr	urge
ch	church	j	judge	o͞o	boot	v	valve
d	deed	k	kick	ou	out	w	with
ě	pet	l	lid, needle	p	pop	y	yes
ē	bee	m	mum	r	roar	z	zebra, dismal, exile
f	fife	n	no, sudden	s	sauce	zh	vision
g	gag	ng	thing	sh	ship, dish	ə	about, item, edible, gallop, circus

Look again at the pronunciation of *livelihood* (līv′lē-ho͞od′). The key tells you that the *l* sounds like the *l* in *lid*, the *ī* like the *ie* in *pie*, the *v* like the *v* in *valve*, the *ē* like the *ee* in *bee*, the *h* like the *h* in *hat*, the o͞o like the *oo* in *took*, and the *d* like the *d* in *deed*. The heavy accent mark tells you to give the first syllable the heavier stress. The light accent mark tells you to give the last syllable the lighter stress.

Many long words have two accent marks. For example, in the word *grand′fa′ther*, the first syllable receives the heavier, or primary, stress, the second syllable receives the lighter, or secondary, stress, and the last syllable is not stressed at all.

Exercise 1. Use the pronunciation symbols to pronounce each word below. Then write the syllable that receives the primary, or heavier, stress in the first blank at the right. In the second blank, write the syllable that receives the secondary, or lighter, stress. If no syllable receives a secondary stress, write *No* in the second blank. An example is done for you.

		Primary	*Secondary*
Example:			
	balderdash (bôl′dər-dăsh′)	bal	dash
a.	bamboozle (băm-bo͞o′zəl)	_____	_____
b.	bankrupt (băngk′rŭpt′)	_____	_____
c.	barbecue (bär′bĭ-kyo͞o′)	_____	_____
d.	barometer (bə-rŏm′ə-tər)	_____	_____
e.	bashful (băsh′fəl)	_____	_____

Exercise 2. Use the pronunciation symbols to pronounce each word below. Then circle the correct answer. (You may want to check your answers against a dictionary.) An example is done for you.

Example:
The first *a* in the word *balderdash* (bôl′dər-dăsh′) has the same sound as the *a* in

(1) fade   (2) back   (3) call

a. The *oo* in *bamboozle* (băm-bōō′zəl) has the same sound as the *oo* in

(1) smooth   (2) book   (3) shook

b. The *u* in *bankrupt* (băngk′rŭpt′) has the same sound as the *u* in

(1) dull   (2) cure   (3) sugar

c. The *a* in *barbecue* (bär′bĭ-kyōō′) has the same sound as the *a* in

(1) sat   (2) late   (3) car

d. The *o* in *barometer* (bə-rŏm′ə-tər) has the same sound as the *o* in

(1) one   (2) old   (3) lock

e. The *u* in *bashful* (băsh′fəl) has the same sound as the *u* in

(1) luck   (2) focus   (3) full

Lesson 7

Using a Dictionary to Pronounce Words You Think You Do Not Know

When you read a word you think you do not know, look it up in a dictionary to find out how to pronounce it. Once you say the word aloud, you may be surprised to find you really do know its meaning after all.

For example, look at the following sentence.

Janice hoped to be an *Olympic* star.

You may not recognize the word *Olympic* when you read it. Now look at how it is pronounced: (ō-lĭm′pĭk). The *o* sounds like the *oe* in *toe*, the *l* like the *l* in *lid*, the *y* like the *i* in *pit*, the *m* like the *m* in *mum*, the *p* like the *p* in *pop*, the *i* like the *i* in *pit*, and the *c* like the *k* in *kick*. The second syllable is accented.

Once you sound out this word, you probably will recognize it. An Olympic star would be a star in the international athletic contests held every four years.

Exercise. In the following selection from "Bruce Jenner" by Louis Sabin, you may not recognize the **boldface** words. Read the selection carefully. Then use the pronunciation key on p. 141 to answer the questions that follow the selection.

His T-shirt read "Feet, Don't Fail Me Now," and on the cool, gray Thursday and Friday in August 1976 his feet performed just as they were supposed to. In fact, every part of Bruce Jenner worked perfectly as he went through the ten demanding events of the **decathlon** at the Montreal Olympics.

For years Jenner had been preparing at home in San Jose, California: running, high jumping, long jumping, pole **vaulting,** putting the shot, throwing the **javelin** and the **discus.** Winning would give him the title of the "Greatest Athlete in the World"—he wanted that more than anything else he could imagine.

Because he wasn't equally strong in all events—no **decathlete** ever is—and was going against the Russian Nikolay Avilov, the Olympic record holder and 1972 gold medalist, Jenner could not afford to let up for a minute. A bad performance in any event could cost **precious** points, and Jenner was gunning for 8,600. Avilov had won in '72 with 8,454 and might equal that, as might Guido Kratschmer of West Germany, another internationally ranked decathlete. So Jenner carefully set out to meet a specific goal for each event.

In the 100-meter dash Jenner aimed for a time of 10.9 seconds and made 10.94. His 23'8¼" long jump was one-quarter inch more than he expected, but his shot put of 47'6" was almost three inches less than he had hoped. As Jenner knew, Avilov and Kratschmer couldn't be counted out yet. They were both too close for comfort.

After Jenner high jumped 6'8", his exact goal, ran the 400 meters in 47.9 and the 110-meter **hurdles** in 14.4, and threw the discus 170' and the javelin 225', he was leading the field and was a bit ahead of his goals. Also he had achieved personal bests in the long jump, high jump, shot put, and the 400-meter. But there were two events to go, and anything could happen.

In the pole vault, one of his stronger events, Jenner wanted to clear 15'9". When the bar was set at 15'5", he missed two attempts and became very nervous. All ready to go for his final try, he was stopped by an official. It was time for a medal-presentation ceremony. Time, also, for a warmed-up decathlete to cool down and be thrown off his form. The delay could kill all his dreams. But when the go-ahead came a few minutes later, Jenner told himself that he'd make it—and he did! He went on to clear 15'9" and get within reach of the gold medal.

The 1,500 meter-run—the last event, in which Jenner's goal was 4 minutes 14 seconds—saw him apparently grow stronger.

Running powerfully and **sprinting** the last 300 meters, he out-distanced almost the entire field. Grinning broadly as he crossed the finish line, with hands raised in fists over his head, he acknowledged the roar of the fans gathered in the Olympic **stadium,** clasped an American flag someone had thrust at him, and jogged a victory lap. And the whole world watched the handsome young American—Bruce Jenner, whose 8,618 points had established a new Olympic record in the ten-event test of **stamina** and courage.

Questions (Write your answers in the blanks below.)
a. Say *decathlon* (dĭ-kăth′lən) aloud. What do you think it means?

_____

What does the dictionary say it means?

_____

_____

b. Say *vaulting* (vôl′tĭng) aloud. What do you think it means?

_____

What does the dictionary say it means?

_____

c. Say *javelin* (jăv′lən) aloud. What do you think it means?

_____

What does the dictionary say it means?

_____

d. Say *discus* (dĭs′kəs) aloud. What do you think it means?

_____

What does the dictionary say it means?

_____

e. Say *decathlete* (dĭ-kăth′lēt′) aloud. What do you think it means?

_____

What does the dictionary say it means?

_____

f. Say *precious* (prĕsh′əs) aloud. What do you think it means?

_____

What does the dictionary say it means?

_____

g. Say *hurdles* (hûrd′ləz) aloud. What do you think it means?

_____

Name _____

What does the dictionary say it means?

_____

h. Say *sprinting* (sprĭnt′ĭng) aloud. What do you think it means?

_____

What does the dictionary say it means?

_____

i. Say *stadium* (stā′dē-əm) aloud. What do you think it means?

_____

What does the dictionary say it means?

_____

j. Say *stamina* (stăm′ə-nə) aloud. What do you think it means?

_____

What does the dictionary say it means?

_____

Lesson 8

Finding the Correct Spelling of a Word

The dictionary shows the correct spelling for each entry word.
However, when you do not know the spelling of a word, you need a
strategy for finding it in the dictionary.

Many dictionaries include a spelling chart in their front pages.
This chart shows you all the letters that spell a certain sound. For
example, look at the following spelling chart.

Sound	As In	Possible Spelling
ă	add	*c*at, pl*ai*d, *c*alf, lau*gh*
ā	ace	m*a*te, b*ai*t, g*ao*l, g*au*ge, p*ay*, st*ea*k, sk*ei*n, w*eigh*, pr*ey*
â(r)	care	d*a*re, f*ai*r, pr*ay*er, wh*e*re, b*ea*r, th*ei*r
ä	palm	d*a*rt, *a*h, s*e*rgeant, h*ea*rt
b	bat	*b*oy, rub*b*er
ch	check	*ch*ip, bat*ch*, righ*t*eous, bas*ti*on, struc*t*ure
d	dog	*d*ay, la*dd*er, calle*d*
ě	end	m*a*ny, *ae*sthete, s*ai*d, s*ay*s, b*e*t, st*ea*dy, h*ei*fer, l*eo*pard, fr*ie*nd, O*e*dipus

Sound	As In	Possible Spelling
ē	even	Caesar, quay, scene, meat, see, seize, people, key, ravine, grief, phoebe, city
f	fit	fake, coffin, cough, half, phase
g	go	gate, beggar, ghoul, guard, vague
h	hope	hot, whom
hw	where	whale
ĭ	it	pretty, been, tin, sieve, women, busy, guilt, lynch
ī	ice	aisle, aye, sleight, eye, dime, pie, sigh, guile, buy, try, lye
j	joy	edge, soldier, modulate, rage, exaggerate, jam
k	cool	can, accost, saccharine, chord, tack, acquit, king, talk, liquor
l	look	let, gall
m	move	drachm, phlegm, palm, make, limb, grammar, condemn
n	nice	gnome, know, mnemonic, note, banner, pneumatic
ng	ring	sink, song, meringue
ŏ	odd	watch, pot
ō	open	beau, yeoman, sew, over, soap, roe, oh, brooch, soul, though, grow
ô	order	ball, balk, fault, dawn, cord, broad, ought
oi	oil	poison, toy
ou	out	ounce, bough, cow
o͞o	pool	rheum, drew, move, canoe, mood, group, through, fluke, sue, fruit
o͝o	took	wolf, foot, could, pull
p	pit	map, happen
r	run	rose, rhubarb, marry, diarrhea, wriggle
s	see	cite, dice, psyche, saw, scene, schism, mass
sh	rush	ocean, chivalry, vicious, pshaw, sure, prescience, schist, nauseous, shall, pension, tissue, fission, potion
t	talk	walked, thought, ptarmigan, tone, Thomas, butter
th	thin	thick
th	mother	this, bathe
ŭ	up	some, does, blood, young, sun
yo͞o	fuse	beauty, eulogy, queue, pew, ewe, adieu, view, fuse, cue, youth, yule
û(r)	burn	yearn, fern, err, girl, worm, journal, burn, Guernsey, myrtle
v	eve	of, Stephen, vise, flivver

146

Name _____

Sound	As In	Possible Spelling
w	win	choir, quilt, *w*ill
y	yet	onion, hallelujah, *y*earn
z	zoo	was, scissors, xylophone, *z*est, mu*zz*le
zh	vision	rouge, pleasure, incision, seizure, glazier
ə		*a*bove, fount*ai*n, dark*e*n, clar*i*ty, parli*a*ment, cann*o*n, porp*oi*se, vici*ou*s, loc*u*st

    Imagine you hear the following sentence: *He gnashed his teeth.*
Because you are not quite certain what *gnash* means, you want to
look it up in the dictionary. Since the word is pronounced ñash, you
look it up under the *n*'s. You can't find it. What should you do?
Check the spelling chart. This chart tells you that the sound /n/ can
be spelled *gn, kn, mn, n, nn,* or *pn.* You can eliminate *n* since you
have already tried it, and *nn* since no words begin with a double *n.*
That leaves you four choices. When you try the first one, you will
find the correct spelling of *gnash.*

_____

Exercise. Study the spelling chart. Then answer the questions that
follow it. Write your answers in the blanks at the right.

a. The sound /ā/ can be spelled *a, ai, ao, au, ay, ea, ei, eig,* and
_____?   _____

b. The letters *te, ti,* and *tu* all spell the sound _____?   _____

c. The letters *a* and *o* both spell the sound you hear in *odd.* What is
this sound?   _____

d. The letters *wh* can spell the sound /h/ you hear in *hope.* What
other sound can *wh* spell?   _____

e. The sound /ng/ is usually spelled *n* or *ng.* What is another way it is
spelled?   _____

f. The letters *gh* can spell the sound /g/ you hear in *ghoul.* What
other sound can they spell?   _____

g. The sound /ou/ that you hear in *out* can be spelled *ou, ough,* and
_____?   _____

h. The sound /t/ can be spelled by the letters *ed, ght, t, th, tt,* and
_____?   _____

i. The schwa sound /ə/ can be spelled in how many different
ways?   _____

j. The letters *gh, lf,* and *ph* all spell the sound _____?   _____

147

Finding Synonyms in a Dictionary

Synonyms are words that have the same or nearly the same meaning. For example, the words *pinch* and *smidgeon* are synonyms. Both mean "a small amount."

BEETLE BAILEY **by Mort Walker**

Is *dollop* a synonym for *pinch*? No. A *dollop* is a large lump.

Name _____

Your dictionary can help you find synonyms. Often, the definition part of the entry contains a synonym for the entry word. For example:

smid•gen (smĭj′ən) *n.* A small amount; a bit; a pinch.

Exercise 1. Match each word in Column A with its synonym in Column B. Use your dictionary to help you.

A	B
_____ **a.** dollop	**(1)** occupy
_____ **b.** entrance	**(2)** satisfied
_____ **c.** inhabit	**(3)** destroy
_____ **d.** upset	**(4)** joy
_____ **e.** content	**(5)** sluggish
_____ **f.** link	**(6)** portal
_____ **g.** ruin	**(7)** calm
_____ **h.** sedate	**(8)** scoop
_____ **i.** lazy	**(9)** join
_____ **j.** delight	**(10)** bothered

Exercise 2. Four words appear below each **boldface** word. Three of these are synonyms for the boldface word. One is not. Circle the one that is not. Use your dictionary to help you.

a. hold	(1) clamp	(2) grasp	(3) loose	(4) clasp
b. mistake	(1) hit	(2) blooper	(3) error	(4) slip
c. question	(1) query	(2) answer	(3) inquire	(4) quiz
d. argue	(1) bicker	(2) search	(3) squabble	(4) wrangle
e. quiet	(1) silence	(2) hush	(3) still	(4) wake
f. toss	(1) retrieve	(2) throw	(3) pitch	(4) sling
g. top	(1) apex	(2) summit	(3) base	(4) peak
h. glum	(1) glad	(2) sullen	(3) dour	(4) gloomy
i. beginning	(1) start	(2) birth	(3) dawn	(4) close
j. grave	(1) serious	(2) funny	(3) heavy	(4) weighty

Finding Antonyms in the Dictionary

Antonyms are words that mean the opposite of each other. For example, the words *brave* and *cowardly* are antonyms. The words *real* and *fake* are antonyms.

ARCHIE

A dictionary can help you find antonyms for some words. Sometimes, the definition part of the entry will tell you what the word is not. For example, look at the entry below.

> **fake** (fāk) *adj.* Having a false appearance; not real or genuine. *n.* A person, act, or thing that is not real or genuine. *v.* **faked, faking.** To pretend.

Since *fake* means "not real or genuine," the words *real* and *genuine* must be antonyms for *fake*. Sometimes the dictionary will include an antonym at the end of an entry. For example:

> **a•ble** (ā′bəl) *adj.* **abler, ablest.** 1. Having enough power or skill to accomplish something. 2. Skilled; talented. *ANT.* inept

---

Exercise 1. Match each word in Column A with its antonym in Column B. Use your dictionary to help you.

	A		B
_____	**a.** artificial	**(1)**	leave
_____	**b.** arrive	**(2)**	incomplete
_____	**c.** melt	**(3)**	calm
_____	**d.** complete	**(4)**	complicated
_____	**e.** excited	**(5)**	common
_____	**f.** minor	**(6)**	genuine
_____	**g.** simple	**(7)**	raise
_____	**h.** silent	**(8)**	freeze
_____	**i.** unusual	**(9)**	noisy
_____	**j.** lower	**(10)**	major

Name _____

Exercise 2. Use your dictionary to help you complete the crossword puzzle that follows. Find the antonym of each of the clue words.

Across

1. curly
2. rude
4. pull
5. hazardous
6. pitiless
8. cheap
12. land
14. praise
15. artificial
18. hot
19. fat
20. bold
21. busy

Down

1. familiar
3. common
5. complex
7. conceal
9. inept
10. graceful
11. full
13. courteous
14. apex
16. depart
17. deny
19. false

151

Lesson 11

Practice

While you read the following selection, pay special attention to the words printed in **boldface.** Then complete the exercise that follows.

Python Mother
Stephen M. Hoffman

Something long and thick parted the tall grass in a field in northern India. It was Batala, an Indian **python,** returning from the river. She had just **quenched** her thirst and was now hurrying back to her nest of eggs.

Each of Batala's eggs was about four inches (10 cm) long and had a leathery shell. There were more than 20 of them heaped in a pile in a circle of flattened grass. Luckily, nothing had disturbed them while she was away.

Batala **coiled** her 12-foot (4-m) body around her eggs, careful not to crush any. She covered them like a shiny brown **igloo,** with her broad head resting on top. Unlike other kinds of snakes, a female Indian python can raise its body temperature to help keep its eggs warm.

Wild dogs, **civets, jackals,** and other animals would steal from Batala's nest if she did not guard it. Once, a **mongoose** slipped out of the grass and **chittered** fiercely at her. Batala **flicked** her tongue at the tiny weasel-like mammal, trying to pick up its scent. She showed no fear. She seemed to know the mongoose would not attack such a huge snake. After a moment the mongoose could see that Batala was not about to leave her nest. With a snarl the mongoose disappeared back into the grass.

Except for hungry leopards, Batala's only real enemies were people, who often killed pythons for their beautiful skins. Some people thought these snakes were poisonous and should be killed for that reason. But Batala had no poison. Great crushing strength and many sharp teeth were her only weapons.

In early May Batala had laid her eggs. For 11 weeks she stayed coiled around them. And now, on this day in August, there was movement beneath her body. Her eggs were **hatching!** Slowly she crawled from the nest.

Tiny heads with tiny waggling tongues poked out through slits in some of the eggs. Each little snake had a bony "tooth" on its nose, which it had used to cut open the tough eggshell. Batala watched as one baby crawled all the way out. It was only two feet (60 cm) long, but it looked just like her.

Batala stayed near her nest for several hours. By evening all the baby snakes had hatched and crawled away. There was nothing more that Batala could do for them. So as night fell, she too moved off into the darkening field.

152

Name _____

Exercise. Look up each of the words below in your dictionary. Then copy the complete dictionary entry for each word.

a. py•thon (_____ **)** ____

_____

_____

_____

_____

b. quench (_____ **)** ____

_____

_____

_____

c. coil (_____ **)** _____

_____

_____

_____

_____

d. ig•loo (_____ **)** _____

_____

_____

_____

_____

e. ci•vet (_____ **)** _____

_____

_____

_____

_____

f. jac•kal (_____ **)** ____

_____

_____

_____

_____

g. mon•goose (_____ **)**

_____

_____

_____

h. chit•ter (_____ **)** __

_____

_____

_____

_____

i. flick (_____ **)** _____

_____

_____

_____

_____

j. hatch (_____ **)** _____

_____

_____

_____

_____

Chapter 7
Context

The context of a word is the group of words or sentences surrounding the word. In this chapter you will learn several strategies for using context clues to find the meaning of words you do not know. In addition, you will learn to choose the meaning of a word that fits the context.

Lesson 1
Understanding Context

The context of a word is the group of words or sentences surrounding the word. Often the context contains clues that help you figure out the meaning of an unfamiliar word. For example, look at the sentence below.

> Gene's teacher, who was just learning to use computers himself, was amazed at Gene's *competence,* or skillfulness, in using the machine.

You may not know the meaning of the word *competence.* The context, that is, the words surrounding *competence,* should help you figure out that *competence* means "skillfulness."

Now look at the following sentences:

> Aretha came home from school, walked into the living room, and put her books on the table. The title of the first book was *BASIC.* Her mother looked at the book and said, "Basic what?"
>
> "Just BASIC," replied Aretha.
>
> "Is it *Basic Mathematics, Basic English, Basic Reading?*" persisted her mother.
>
> "Oh, Mom," replied Aretha. "You know I'm taking a computer course. BASIC is the language we use to talk to computers."

When you started reading this passage, you may not have known what BASIC meant. The context, the rest of the sentences in the passage, helped you figure out that BASIC is a computer language.

Exercise. Read the following selection from "Dining at the Eyrie" by Florence M. Weekes. Use the context to help you figure out the meaning of each **boldface** word. Write these definitions in the blanks following the selection. Then check your answers against a dictionary.

The first time I saw the baby eagle on the big nest of sticks in the hickory tree, it was so tiny I nearly missed it. The **eaglet** had hatched weak and helpless, weighing only about three ounces. You could have held it cupped in your hand. That was the first of April. By the middle of June—in less than three months—it would grow to be as big as its parents. It would stand three feet high and have a wingspan of seven feet.

Growing so big so fast takes a lot of eating. In fact, I only spotted the eaglet that first time because the mother bird was feeding it. I was adjusting my telescope to see what went on in the nest of a bald eagle. I could see that the mother bird was pulling pieces off a fish. Then I realized that the mother was putting tiny bits of the fish into a little bird's mouth.

After that I often visited the nest to watch the eaglet grow up. During the last weeks of its nest life, I watched it every day, often arriving before sunrise and staying until after dark. I was lucky to find a deserted, tumbledown barn where I could watch the nest by pointing my telescope out between cracks in the walls.

A bald eagle's nest is called an **eyrie.** It is usually built, as this one was, high in a tall tree near a lake or river. Eyries are often seven or more feet across, because eaglets must reach full size before they fly free, and sometimes there are two or even three in a nest at one time.

The eaglet in the hickory tree's nest was about three weeks old when I first saw it walking. It stood for only a few seconds and was very shaky. It still had some of its first downy feathers, which are silky and light, but it was well into its second feather covering (called **plumage**). This second plumage was gray, soft, and woolly looking.

At first the mother bird stayed at the nest, while the father bird hunted or stood watch. I often saw him winging his way home with a fish clutched in his talons. The female would look up and greet him with a soft, chittering sound. He would chitter back before alighting on the nest beside her and dropping the fish. Sometimes he would taste a bit or feed some to the baby, but usually he flew to a high perch to watch over them. The mother bird would stand on the fish and tear it up with her sharp, powerful beak.

She gulped down big pieces for herself, but for her baby she broke off tiny bits. She held the **morsels** at the very tip of her beak and gently placed them in the waiting little mouth. As the baby grew, so did its helpings. The mother seemed to know just what the baby could handle.

Eagles eat all parts of a fish, even the bones. One day, when the eaglet was about one month old, the mother fed it the long, slippery **entrails** from a big fish. I wondered how it would manage. I had read about another eyrie where the parents had not had any luck feeding this kind of food to their nestlings.

But this mother eagle handled the situation just fine. She passed one end of the intestine to her youngster, beak to beak. Then, while the eaglet gulped and swallowed, she held the string of food out straight, carefully controlling how fast it reached the eaglet's eagerly snapping beak. Then the young bird, full and satisfied, closed it eyes and slept for the rest of the afternoon.

Definitions

a. *Eaglet* means _____

b. *Eyrie* means _____

c. *Plumage* means _____

d. *Morsels* means _____

e. *Entrails* means _____

Lesson 2

Finding the Meaning That Fits the Context

The English language contains many words that have more than one meaning. When you read, you must choose the meaning that fits the context. For example, you probably know many meanings for the word *cast*. Some of its meanings are: (1) a rigid, or stiff, surgical dressing; (2) the act of throwing out a fishing line; (3) the people who act in a play or movie. Now look at the following sentence:

The doctor put Christopher's broken arm in a *cast*.

Only the first meaning of *cast* fits this sentence.

Now look at the comic strip below. Gonzo expected a party for people wearing surgical dressings. It turned out to be a party for people who act in the show.

MUPPETS by Guy and Brad Gilchrist

157

Exercise 1. Read the selection below, "The Magnetized Knife" by Edward Stoddard. Pay special attention to the words printed in **boldface.** Then, for each boldface word, choose the meaning that fits the context. Put an X in the blank by your answer.

Do this trick at the dinner **table** with a clean knife at your place. Fold your hands, then straighten them out with the fingers still interlaced. Lay them down over the table knife and raise them, backs toward the people watching. You may find it easier to have the **blade** of the knife sticking over the edge of the table to get started. The knife clings to your fingers. You look proud.

But everyone laughs because your thumbs are hidden. So you raise your left thumb. People still laugh. Raise your right thumb—after you have put your left thumb back.

Everyone is sure you are just using your thumbs. So you fool them all by raising both thumbs. The knife still clings to your fingers!

The secret is simple. When you fold your hands, put the second **finger** of the right hand inside instead of through the other fingers. There are only seven fingers and two thumbs showing on the other side, but nobody ever notices this. Besides, your little act with the thumbs takes their **attention** away from your fingers.

You hold the knife between this extra finger and the **base** of your left fingers. That's all there is to it.

Definitions

a. In this selection, *table* means

_____ a piece of furniture

_____ a list of related numbers

b. In this selection, *blade* means

_____ the cutting part of a tool

_____ a leaf of grass

c. In this selection, *finger* means

_____ the part of a glove that covers a finger

_____ any of the five separate parts forming the end of the hand

d. In this selection, *attention* means

_____ the concentration of mental powers upon an object

_____ the way a soldier stands

e. In this selection, *base* means

_____ any of the four objects that mark the four corners of a baseball diamond

_____ the bottom

Name _____

Exercise 2. Read the selection below, "See-Through Saucers" by Bill Severn. Pay special attention to the words printed in **boldface**. Then, for each boldface word, choose the meaning that fits the context.

There are two stacked-together saucers and a **pack** of cards on your table. You ask a friend to take the pack, **shuffle** the cards until he is sure they are well-mixed, and then to deal them face down, one at a time, into the top saucer. "I won't touch the cards at all," you explain. "You can stop dealing whenever you want to, and put the rest of the pack back on the table."

After he has dealt a dozen cards or so, you **cover** them by turning one saucer upside down on top of the other, so the cards are hidden from sight between the two saucers. Then you hold the two saucers together, **shake** them and turn them over to mix the cards some more, and rest the saucers on the table.

"I'd need x-ray eyes to be able to see through those saucers and tell you which card is now on top," you say. "But I'll make a magic guess. . . . It's the Three of Hearts." Your friend lifts off the top saucer and the card facing him is the Three of Hearts!

What you need: A pack of cards and two saucers or small paper plates.

The secret: You set it up ahead of time by taking one card from the pack, say the Three of Hearts, and putting it *face down* in one of the saucers. Put the other saucer on top of it, so the known card is hidden between the stacked-together saucers, and put the pack of cards on the top saucer. Have them that way on your table.

What you do: Sit or stand behind the table, with your friend facing you. Ask him to take the cards and shuffle them. Explain that you won't touch the cards at all. Have him start dealing them face down, one at a time, into the top saucer. After he has dealt some, tell him he can stop dealing whenever he wishes.

When he stops and puts the pack aside, take the top saucer at its right-hand side with your right hand. Remove that top saucer by tipping it toward the left so the cards slide from it into the bottom saucer that is still on the table. That puts them right on top of the hidden Three of Hearts. Then turn the saucer that is in your hand upside down and put it, face-to-face, on top of the saucer on the table.

With a hand on either side, hold the two saucers tightly together and lift them from the table. Say that you are going to mix the cards some more. Shake the held-together saucers back and forth, which really doesn't mix the cards since there isn't room inside for them to change position, although it looks as if they are being mixed. Then turn the saucers upside down together and put them back on the table. The cards inside are now face up, with the Three of Hearts on top.

You talk about needing "x-ray eyes" to see through the saucers, and then call out the name of the card that will be on top. Finally, have your friend lift off the covering saucer to find that your "magic guess" was **right.**

Definitions

a. In this selection, *pack* means

_____ set

_____ container

b. In this selection, *shuffle* means

_____ perform a dance step

_____ mix

c. In this selection, *cover* means

_____ protect

_____ conceal

d. In this selection, *shake* means

_____ upset

_____ move up and down, side to side, etc.

e. In this selection, *right* means

_____ correct

_____ virtuous

Lesson 3

Understanding Words Used As Nouns and Verbs

A noun is a word that names a person, a place, a thing, or an idea. For example, the words *girl, city, apartment,* and *happiness* are nouns. **A verb is a word that expresses action or a state of being.** For example, the words *run* and *is* are verbs. Some words can be used as either nouns or verbs. Look at the following sentences:

He played one night in a *park* in Charlotte, North Carolina.
Many people tried to *park* their cars in the lot.

In the first sentence *park* is a noun that means "a playing field." In the second sentence *park* is a verb that means "to put in a certain place." The meaning of a word in a sentence depends on whether it is used as a noun or as a verb.

Name _____

Exercise. Read the following selection, "The Dog That Made a Box Score" by Furman Bisher. Pay special attention to each **boldface** word. Then follow the directions at the end of the selection.

A large Cuban baseball player named Roberto Gonzalo Ortiz appeared in Charlotte, North Carolina, in 1941, to play baseball for the Charlotte Hornets in the Piedmont League. Ortiz loved to play baseball and the Washington Senators, who owned his contract, thought he played very well. He came as a pitcher who had burning **speed,** but little control. When he started to play for the Hornets, he was switched to the outfield, where his strong arm would **command** respect of base runners.

Because Ortiz could barely speak English, he found himself alone in Charlotte except for one Cuban friend and a small dog, who was the color of cooked **squash.** The Cuban boy was shy but animals loved him, especially his homeless mongrel dog. When the team worked out, the yellow dog romped along with Ortiz. When the team went into the clubhouse, he seemed to wait especially for Ortiz to come out. When the team played, the yellow dog seemed to know that his place was out of the way.

Another thing the dog seemed to know was baseball. The excitement in the stands created when the Charlotte team would work up a **rally** excited him, too. Often the grounds-keeper would be forced to **chase** him out of the park.

One Sunday afternoon, though, while the yellow dog was enjoying the freedom of the park, he completely forgot himself. Out of it he emerged as one of the most famous dogs in baseball lore.

The Charlotte team went to bat in the last of the ninth inning trailing by one **run,** apparently the victim of a tough pitcher. But the pitcher lost his control momentarily, and walked a Hornet batter. The next batter was Roberto Ortiz.

The big Cuban got a **pitch** that he liked and lashed into it. As he hit the ball, the crowd leaped to its feet with a roar. This aroused the yellow dog, who was sleeping in the dirt under the first-base bleachers. The ball had gotten by the center fielder and a run was scoring, tying the game. Ortiz would be trying for every base he could get.

As the Cuban neared first, he was joined by a sudden **blur.** The yellow dog, catching **sight** of his friend, had burst through the open clubhouse gate and was off to join him. Down to second base they went, the big Cuban and the little dog, running like a team. Then around second base, past the shortstop, whom the dog barely missed while making his wide turn.

The throw was coming in from the outfield now and Ortiz was in danger as he neared third. The coach signaled for him to **slide** and as Ortiz slid, the yellow dog slid, too. The umpire's hands signaled safe. Both Ortiz and his dog had made it.

How the game ended is really not important. What is important took place the next day. In the box score of the game, the Charlotte *News* made a special place for the little yellow dog. He appeared underneath Ortiz's name: "y—Yellow Dog." Below, in the space usually reserved for pinch hitters and pinch runners, appeared this explanatory line: "y—Yellow Dog ran with Ortiz in the 9th."

Directions. Read each sentence below. In the blank, write *v.* if the **boldface** word is used as a verb. Write *n.* if it is used as a noun. Look up the boldface word in your dictionary. Write the meaning that fits the sentence.

a. "He came as a pitcher who had burning **speed,** but little control."

_____

b. "When he started to play for the Hornets, he was switched to the outfield, where his strong arm would **command** respect of base runners."

_____

c. "Because Ortiz could barely speak English, he found himself alone in Charlotte except for one Cuban friend and a small dog, who was the color of cooked **squash**."

_____

d. "The excitement in the stands created when the Charlotte team would work up a **rally** excited him, too."

_____

e. "Often the groundskeeper would be forced to **chase** him out of the park."

_____

f. "The Charlotte team went to bat in the last of the ninth inning trailing by one **run,** apparently the victim of a tough pitcher."

_____

_____

g. "The big Cuban got a **pitch** that he liked and lashed into it."

_____

h. "As the Cuban neared first, he was joined by a sudden **blur**."

_____

i. "The yellow dog, catching **sight** of his friend, had burst through the open clubhouse gate and was off to join him."

_____

j. "The coach signaled for him to **slide** and as Ortiz slid, the yellow dog slid, too."

_____

Name _____

Finding the Meaning of a Familiar Word with an Unfamiliar Meaning

Many words have more than one meaning. Some words that you know well with one meaning may have another, less familiar, meaning.

For example, you certainly know a meaning for the word *play*. Now look at the following sentences:

> When Ellen put her feet into her friend's sneakers, her feet had so much *play* that she couldn't even walk. The sneakers kept falling off.

You may not know a meaning of play that fits these sentences. Look again at the context. The context should help you see that *play* means "space for movement."

Now look at the next sentence.

> He made a *nice* distinction between the talent of the two writers.

You may not know a meaning of *nice* that fits this sentence. The context does not give you enough clues to figure out its meaning. Check a dictionary. You will find that one meaning of *nice* is "showing the ability to see slight differences." This meaning fits the context.

Sometimes when you are reading, you see a word you are sure you know, but the sentence or the paragraph does not make sense when you use the meaning you know. Keep an open mind, look back, and let the context help you discover the word's meaning. If the context does not provide enough clues, find all the meanings of the word in the dictionary and then choose the meaning that fits the context.

Exercise 1. In the sentences below, each **boldface** word is used with a meaning that may be unfamiliar to you. For each sentence, put a check in the blank next to the definition that fits the context.

a. There were 100 people in the experiment. Ninety people received the new medicine, but ten people were in the **control** group and received sugar pills.

_____ command

_____ people used as a standard of comparison

b. The miner made a **narrow** escape from the collapsing tunnel.

_____ barely successful

_____ small in width, tight

c. The gymnast learned to keep a **fast** grip on the ropes.

_____ firm

_____ swift

d. The gold that the prospector found amounted to a **pretty** fortune.

_____ excellent

_____ large in size

e. The President promised to take a **hard** line on defense.

_____ making few concessions or allowances; giving up little

_____ difficult to understand

f. We left the lecture early because the room was hot and the speech was **dry.**

_____ dull, matter-of-fact

_____ free from water

g. He made **vain** promises that he knew he wouldn't keep.

_____ conceited

_____ lacking substance; worthless

h. The old woman remembered an **air** she had heard when she was a child.

_____ tune

_____ colorless gas

i. The rancher had **title** to the land and everything on it.

_____ name of a book, play, or movie

_____ legal right

j. The carpenter took **just** measurements before she cut the wood.

_____ exact

_____ fair

Exercise 2. Look back at Exercise 1. Which meaning did you choose for each boldface word? For each word, write a sentence using this meaning.

a. control _____

b. narrow _____

c. fast _____

164

d. pretty _____

e. hard _____

f. dry _____

g. vain _____

h. air _____

i. title _____

j. just _____

Exercise 3. You certainly know the meaning of the words *sweet*, *soft*, *hard*, and *sparkling*. Look up each of these words in a dictionary and write what they mean when they describe water.

a. sweet water _____

b. soft water _____

c. hard water _____

d. sparkling water _____

Lesson 5

Using Definition Clues to Find the Meaning of an Unfamiliar Word

Writers sometimes give definitions of words they think their readers may not know. These definitions may be signaled by words or by punctuation marks. Words that sometimes signal definitions include: *means, are, is, were, was.* For example, read the sentences below.

> In a musical score, the word *piano* means "softly."
> A *kannel* is a stringed musical instrument that comes from Estonia.

Punctuation marks that signal definitions include: commas, dashes, and parentheses. For example, read the sentences below.

> One of the most popular instruments of the sixteenth and seventeenth centuries was the *lute*, a stringed instrument with a pear-shaped body.
> In a brass instrument sound is produced when the air in the column begins to vibrate—move back and forth rapidly.
> *Percussion instruments* (musical instruments in which sound is produced by striking or shaking) are important in orchestras and bands.

Exercise 1. While you read the recipe below, look for definition clues that help you define each **boldface** word. Then write your definitions on the lines below the recipe.

Lee's Vegetable Soup
(Serves four to six people)

4 tbsp butter	salt and pepper to taste
1 tbsp vegetable oil	3 cups beef, chicken or vegetable broth
1 large onion	
2 medium carrots	½ cup cooked peas
¼ cup parsley	1 large cooked potato
2 **stalks** (long stems that end in leaves) celery	1 tomato

First, prepare your vegetables. **Mince** (cut into very small pieces) the onion, parsley, and celery. Slice the carrots into rounds, and **dice**—cut into the shape of small cubes—the tomato and the potato.

In a **kettle,** a large metal pot with a lid, melt the butter and add the oil. When the oil is very hot, add the onion and **sauté** a few more minutes. *Sauté* means to fry in just a little oil or fat. Stir in the tomato, salt, and pepper. Add the **broth,** which is the liquid in which the meat, fish, or vegetables have been cooked. **Simmer** (cook over a low flame) for thirty to forty minutes. Add the peas and potatoes, and cook for five more minutes. Serve **piping hot** (extremely hot).

If you want your vegetables to be in a clear broth, **skim** (remove the small bits of floating matter) the soup during the last five minutes. If you want the broth to be thick, **purée**—mash and strain—one cup of the soft-boiled vegetables. This can be done during the last ten minutes of the time the soup is simmering.

Definitions
a. *Stalks* means _____

b. *Mince* means _____

c. *Dice* means _____

d. *Kettle* means _____

e. *Sauté* means _____

f. *Broth* means _____

g. *Simmer* means _____

h. *Piping hot* means _____

i. *Skim* means _____

j. *Purée* means _____

Name _____

Exercise 2. On the blanks provided, write a sentence for each of the
words below. Be sure to use the meaning you wrote for Exercise 1.

a. stalks _____
_____

b. mince _____
_____

c. dice _____
_____

d. kettle _____
_____

e. sauté _____
_____

f. broth _____
_____

g. simmer _____
_____

h. piping hot _____
_____

i. skim _____
_____

j. purée _____
_____

Lesson 6

Using Comparison Clues to Find the Meaning of an Unfamiliar Word

When you read, you often find words whose meanings you do
not know. A writer may give you clues to the meaning of an unfamiliar word by making a comparison. A comparison shows how
two people, things, or ideas are alike. When you know one, you
know the other.

For example, in the sentence below, you may not know the meaning of the word *ominous*. The sentence, though, gives you a comparison that helps you figure out the meaning of this word.

> Like the threatening clouds of yesterday afternoon, today's clouds are also *ominous*.

The words *like* and *also* tell you that the clouds of yesterday and today are alike. How are they alike? They are both *threatening*. So that is what *ominous* means.

Look at another example:

> Jose's dog growls and jumps up when the mail carrier approaches.
> Eva's dog is even more *ferocious*. It shows its teeth and snaps at the mail carrier.

You may not know the meaning of the word *ferocious*. Look at the context. The sentences tell you that both dogs are ferocious, but Eva's dog is even more so. Jose's dog growls and jumps up. Eva's dog bares its teeth and snaps. *Ferocious* must mean "very fierce."

Exercise. Each sentence below contains a comparison that helps you figure out the meaning of the **boldface** word. Read each sentence. Then put an X in the blank next to the meaning of each boldface word.

a. In the same way that earlier people have wanted to know their families' history, Americans today also search for their **roots.**

_____ secrets

_____ birthdates

_____ family history

b. The **ancestors** on your mother's side, like the people from whom your father descended, are part of your family tree.

_____ ancients

_____ people from whom you are descended

_____ mother's friends

c. Elena's **maternal** ancestors came from Haiti, as did the mother's side of Katherine's family.

_____ related through one's mother

_____ friendly and charming

_____ long-ago

d. Karl's **paternal** ancestors came from Sweden, as did the father's side of Kristen's family.

_____ Swedish

_____ fatherly

_____ related through one's father

e. Like the **pedigree** of the Queen of England, your list of ancestors may include dukes and duchesses.

_____ list of ancestors

_____ list of dukes and duchesses

_____ list of dogs

f. Like the **lineage** of most Americans, your ancestry probably includes the common men and women who made this country great.

_____ ancestry

_____ common men and women

_____ American relatives

g. Just as the first names Jennifer, Kate, and Diana are popular today, years ago the **forenames** Patience, Priscilla, and Charity were popular.

_____ tops of heads

_____ first names

_____ names of triplets

h. Like the people who chose **surnames** such as Carpenter and Miller, Michael's great-great-grandfather chose Shoemaker, the name of his occupation, as his last name.

_____ last names

_____ the names of their jobs

_____ the names of the places where they lived

i. In Greece some last names were formed by adding "pulos" to the end of the first name of an ancestor on the father's side of the family. Similarly, in Poland some last names were formed by adding "wiecz" to the end of the first name of a **forebear** on the paternal side of the family.

_____ uncle

_____ father

_____ ancestor

j. In Norway, Sweden, and Denmark, many last names such as Jacobssen, Johnson, and Anderson are **patronymics.** In Ireland, England, and Scotland, many last names such as O'Brien (son of Brien), Fitzgerald (son of Gerald), and MacGregor (son of Gregor) were also formed from the first name of an ancestor on the father's side of the family.

_____ a first name

_____ a name based on the name of a paternal ancestor

_____ a Norwegian, Swedish, or Danish name

Lesson 7

Using Contrast Clues to Find the Meaning of an Unfamiliar Word

A writer may give you clues to the meaning of an unfamiliar word by showing a contrast. This means that the writer shows you how two things, people, or ideas are different. Often, knowing what something is not helps you to understand what it is. For example, look at the sentence below.

> Unlike his relaxed cousin Suzy, John is very _tense._

You may not know the meaning of the word _tense._ Now look at the context. The sentence tells you that John is unlike his cousin Suzy. How are they different? John is tense and Suzy is relaxed. Therefore, _tense_ must be "not relaxed."

Now look at the next sentences.

> Felicia is usually quite talkative in class. On the other hand, Rhonda is usually _taciturn._

Probably you do not know the meaning of the word _taciturn._ Now look at the context. The sentences contrast Felicia and Rhonda. How are they different from one another? Felicia is usually quite talkative and Rhonda is usually taciturn. Therefore, _taciturn_ must mean "not talkative."

Exercise. Use contrast clues to help you choose the best meaning for the **boldface** word in each item below. Put an X in the blank by the correct answer.

a. During the magic show, Chris was all smiles, but John wore a **scowl** on his face.

_____ scarf

_____ smile

_____ angry frown

b. Throughout the first act, John complained and wanted to leave, while Chris was **content** just to be in the theater.

_____ satisfied, happy

_____ puzzled

_____ unhappy, wanting to be somewhere else

c. Unlike the **tedious** first act, the second act was quite exciting.

_____ too short

_____ boring

_____ confusing

d. During the first act, nothing had amazed John, whereas during the second act, he was **astonished** by the tricks.

_____ misled

_____ bored

_____ amazed, surprised

e. The set for the first act had been quite **crude**, while the set for the second act was well made.

_____ odd

_____ funny

_____ not well made

f. In costume, the magician had appeared to be very large, but when she took off her outer robes, the audience could see that she was **petite**.

_____ pretty

_____ huge

_____ tiny, small

g. Although the magician was **dexterous** in performing card tricks, the audience feared she would not be as skillful with her hands during the knife-throwing act.

_____ clumsy

_____ skillful with her hands

_____ careful

h. Chris was very still and quiet when the magician threw the first knife, but he was **animated** and cheering wildly by the end of the act.

_____ fearful

_____ silent

_____ lively

i. Before the show the magician had been too nervous to eat, but by the end of the show she was **ravenous.**

_____ not hungry

_____ very hungry

_____ satisfied

j. For her last trick she made a turkey dinner **materialize** out of thin air. Then she reversed the trick and made the dinner disappear before the audience's eyes.

_____ appear as if from nowhere

_____ disappear

_____ cook

Lesson 8

Using Examples to Find the Meaning of an Unfamiliar Word

Writers sometimes give examples that help you define an unfamiliar word. For instance, read the sentences below.

> Jason is a skilled *acrobat*. For example, he can stand on his head and walk on his hands. He can do cartwheels, walkovers, and backflips. He can even perform roundoffs and butterflies.

You may not know the meaning of the word *acrobat*. The context, though, gives you six examples of what an *acrobat* does. These examples should help you figure out that an *acrobat* is "a person trained to perform gymnastic feats and exercises."

Now look at the next sentences.

> Acrobats must be *limber*. Not only must they be able to touch their toes, but they must be able to bend over backwards, too.

You may not know the meaning of the word *limber*. The context provides two examples that should help you figure out its meaning.

Acrobats must be able to touch their toes and bend over backwards. *Limber* means "flexible; agile."

When you read, look for examples that help you figure out the meaning of an unfamiliar word. Be sure, though, to check your meaning in a dictionary.

Exercise 1. Read the following items. Use the example clues to help you choose the meaning of each **boldface** word. Put an X in the blank next to your answer.

a. North American Indians held many **tournaments,** such as wrestling matches, spear-throwing contests, and lacrosse meets.

_____ parties

_____ contests

_____ classes

b. In some American Indian tribes, many games and sports were played for **pedagogical** reasons. For example, spear-throwing and arrow-shooting contests allowed hunters to practice marksmanship, and races helped warriors to improve their speed in running.

_____ educational

_____ rest and leisure

_____ hunting

c. Some games and sports had a **recreational** purpose. For example, darts, juggling, and kickball gave tribespeople the opportunity to relax and have fun.

_____ refreshing one's mind or body

_____ teaching new skills

_____ improving one's health

d. There were several different ways of matching wrestling **adversaries.** For instance, the tribe's two smallest boys began the contest. The winner wrestled the next largest boy, and the winner of that contest wrestled the next largest until the two strongest boys faced each other.

_____ games

_____ parties

_____ opponents

e. North American Indians had many **hibernal** sports and games. For example, they played shinny, which was a type of ice hockey. They also held sled races and snowshoe races.

_____ winter

_____ summer

_____ spring

Exercise 2. Look up each of the words below in your dictionary. Then for each word list four examples that would help readers find its meaning.

a. athletics

_____
_____
_____
_____

b. gear

_____
_____
_____
_____

c. bait (for fishing)

_____
_____
_____
_____

d. garment

_____
_____
_____
_____

e. puppet

_____
_____
_____
_____

Lesson 9

Using Indirect Context Clues

The context often contains indirect clues that help you make an intelligent guess about the meaning of an unfamiliar word. These clues do not tell you exactly what the unfamiliar word means. But by studying these clues carefully and using your common sense, you should be able to figure out the meaning of this word. For example, look at the paragraph below from "Skateboarding: Homemade Safety" by Ken Fulton.

> Serious skateboarders want to act and look **professional,** and that means wearing protection. All stars in sports from hockey to skiing to bicycle motocross **shield** their bodies from injury because they don't want to sit on the sidelines.

In the first sentence of this paragraph, you may not know the meaning of the word *professional.* Now look at the clues. *Professional* is the way that *serious* skateboarders want to act and look. Stars in sports are professional. On the basis of these clues, you probably figured out that *professional* means "like someone who earns his or her living at a certain activity."

In the second sentence of this paragraph, you may not have been familiar with the word *shield.* The meaning of the word has something to do with not getting injuries. It is something stars in sports do "because they don't want to sit on the sidelines." *Shield* must mean "protect."

When you read, look for indirect context clues that help you figure out the meaning of an unfamiliar word. Be sure, though, to check your guesses against a dictionary.

Exercise 1. Continue reading this selection from "Skateboarding: Homemade Safety" by Ken Fulton. Pay special attention to indirect context clues that help you figure out the meaning of each **boldface** word. After you finish reading the selection, write the meaning of each boldface word in the blank provided. Check your definitions with a dictionary.

> Being safe doesn't have to be expensive. In fact, it can cost nothing. Consider borrowing a friend's safety gear, using gear from other sports, or even making your own equipment.
>
> For example, the elbow and knee pads used by basketball players are perfect for protecting a skater's **joints.** The helmet you use for bicycling is also good for skating. If your family has a garden, you may have hard, rubber, gardener's knee pads you can use.

Your local drug store probably sells elastic bandages. Pad and wrap them loosely—you don't want to cut off your **circulation**—around your elbows and knees for quick and easy protection.

Just a little imagination can **transform** ordinary items into skateboard armor. Like an old pair of socks.

Measure from the top of the sock toward the foot and make a mark when you have measured enough to completely cover your elbow or knee. Then measure the same amount again down the sock. Add two extra inches, then cut off the rest of the sock.

Next, double the sock and you have a tube with a pocket between the two layers. Stuff a portion of that pocket with several layers of newspaper, cloth, or a piece of foam rubber. Put stuffing only where your elbow or knee will be.

Sew the sock layers together on either side of the padding to prevent **shifting.** Then sew the two layers together to seal the pocket of the tube. This elbow/knee pad can be taped in place, or you can sew elastic into the edges of the tube to hold the pad to your arm or leg.

Homemade elbow pads can also be made from the **miniature** plastic footballs. Cut the football in half lengthwise and insert a large piece of foam into each half. Then sew a wide elastic band across the open middle of the football, and you have protection with a tough outer skin and a soft inner cushion.

Pro skaters don't have to spend a lot of money to be safe. But no skater is a pro unless he wears the safety gear of his sport.

Definitions

a. joints _____

b. circulation _____

c. transform _____

d. shifting _____

e. miniature _____

Exercise 2. Read the following selection, "Be a Weather-Wise Hiker" by Greg Stone. Pay special attention to indirect context clues. Write the meaning of each **boldface** word in the blank provided. Check your definitions with a dictionary.

"Boy, look at that **halo** around the moon," said Tom, twisting in his sleeping bag for a better view. "I guess we're in for rainy weather."

I soon learned Tom was right. The next morning, the sky was covered with high, thin clouds, as if some cosmic spider had spun a silvery-white web. By afternoon, they were a solid blanket and had moved lower. The first showers hit that evening and continued off and on for two days.

176

That beautiful glow around the moon was a warning. The halo was caused by moonlight shining through ice crystals that make up those high, wispy clouds. Such clouds, called *cirrus* by weathermen, are frequently the **forerunners** of an approaching warm front, which usually means a long period of wet weather.

Here are a few simple rules to help tell what weather is likely in the next six hours.

There are two keys: *wind* and *clouds*.

Wind. What direction is it blowing *from*? Be sensitive to any change in *direction*. Observing tree leaves, clouds, and ripples on a lake is a good way to tell wind direction.

If the wind moves from south, to west, or north, that's a sign of fair weather. (Sailors call this a *veering* wind.) However, if the wind *backs* around the other way, changing from north, to west, to south, watch out. That usually means bad weather.

Violent storms have their own wind directions. Watch the wind to tell how quickly a storm is moving past. Beginning with winds from the northeast, they'll switch to east, southeast, south, southwest, west, and finally northwest. The worst rain or snow is usually over by the time the wind gets into the south. Once it switches to west and northwest, it will be dry and cooler.

Clouds. Don't let chubby, little white *cumulus* clouds, which appear on a sunny day, bother you. When the sun sets and the land cools, they'll go away.

On a hot, humid day, powder puffs may cover the sky and turn blue-black or a dirty yellow. It may be a *line* **squall** developing. A mass of cold air is moving in and tossing these clouds up ahead of it like snow off a plow. You may be in for a series of short, violent storms.

If you see lightning, note the direction. If it's to the west or northwest, the storm carrying it is moving *toward* you. If it's to the south or southeast, don't worry. That storm has already passed.

Also watch for clouds that start high and thin and keep getting lower and thicker. The lower the clouds, the nearer the rain.

Here are a few other weather signs to watch for:

Rainbows in the morning, take warning. Bad weather is to the west, and in the northern hemisphere, weather generally moves from west to east. A rainbow in the afternoon will be to the east and means bad weather has already gone by.

Morning dew is a sign of good weather. If you awake to dry ground, look for showers by afternoon.

Smoke from a chimney rises straight up in fair weather. As bad weather approaches, the smoke tends to drift out **parallel** to the ground in a lazy, ragged line.

Watch birds. They "know enough to come in out of the rain," and they'll start roosting before a storm.

Tree leaves "show their backs" when a foul-weather wind blows. That's because they've grown in a pattern according to the **prevailing,** fair-weather winds. Wind from an unusual direction tends to flip them over.

With rain coming, don't pitch your tent directly under trees, or with trees just to the west. After the rain, the wind will be out of the west and will continue to shake drops out of trees onto your campsite.

Definitions

a. halo _____

b. forerunners _____

c. squall _____

d. parallel _____

e. prevailing _____

Lesson 10

Practice

Pay special attention to context clues as you read the following selection. Then complete the exercise that follows.

Pointers for Better Pictures
Linda Benedict-Jones

Photography has become very popular these days. There are, of course, many different kinds of people who take pictures.

Professional photographers make their living by taking pictures. Some take pictures for advertisements, some take pictures for magazines and newspapers, and still others take pictures of weddings, anniversaries, graduations, and other ceremonies.

There are also **artistic** or creative photographers who use a camera in the same way that a writer uses a pen or a painter uses a brush. In other words, artistic photographers use their cameras to say something that *they* want to say, instead of working on assignments for other people.

A third kind of photographer is the **amateur.** "Amateur" is French. It means someone who loves to do something. Perhaps one day you will be a professional or an artistic photographer but, if you simply love taking pictures, we can consider you an amateur photographer right now.

Just as there are different kinds of photographers, there are also different ways of taking pictures. To begin with, there are dozens of different kinds of cameras. Some cameras are bigger than your teacher's desk, others are as small as a matchbox!

These cameras are used for special purposes, of course, and are not useful for amateurs.

If you are thinking about getting your own camera, it should be a size that fits in your hands comfortably. If it's too big and heavy, you won't enjoy using it and you'll end up leaving it in your room all the time.

Once you have a camera, the next thing to decide is what film to use. You can decide to take your pictures either in color or black and white. The more interested in photography you become the more you will want to develop your own film and make your own prints in a darkroom. If you are using color film, this is quite difficult. But if you are using black-and-white film, you can learn to do it all by yourself.

When you have chosen your film, loaded it in your camera, you are almost ready. There are a couple of things you should check before you begin shooting. First check the **lens.** You must clean it *very carefully* with a special lens tissue. Try never to put your finger on your lens or allow it to get dirty. If your lens is dirty, your pictures will look dirty.

If your camera has any special **settings,** you must make sure they are correctly set for the film you are using. For example, all films have speed (or ASA) numbers. If you have an ASA dial on your camera, it must be set for the number on your packet of film.

Perhaps your camera has settings for the weather. If you are going out on a cloudy day, be sure your camera is set for cloudy; if it is a bright, sunny day, be sure it is set for that.

If you forget to set your camera properly, you will take all your pictures at the wrong **exposure,** and they will either be too dark or too light.

Finally you are ready to shoot. Of course, you want to take good pictures, but what makes a picture good? Well, that is the most difficult question to answer. It's difficult because what *you* think is a good picture might be very different from what someone else thinks is a good picture.

Still, there are things that will help you take better pictures. Some of them are:

Hold your camera very steady with your arms against your body for support. Breathe out slowly as you click the **shutter.**

Press the shutter gently with a slow squeeze.

Remember to keep your camera level while you are taking the picture. If you **tilt** your camera, you will wind up with a slanted horizon line.

If you want to take a picture of a person's face, get close enough so the face is the most important thing in your **viewfinder.** Try to keep the background simple for this kind of portrait.

If you want to take a picture of a group of people, remember not to cut off the tops of their heads when you look through your viewfinder.

If you are taking a picture of a small child or a dog or cat, kneel or stoop down to its level. Otherwise, you will get a picture of the top of its head.

If you are taking pictures on a bright, sunny day, don't let the sun come directly into your lens while you are shooting. If you do, it will cause a **flare** on your film and ruin your picture. It is best to keep the sun at your side or at your back.

Noon is the worst time for taking pictures of people. At noon the sun is directly above our heads and creates ugly shadows under people's eyes and noses. There is usually a nicer light for people, and for other shots, before ten o'clock in the morning and after two o'clock in the afternoon. If you have to take pictures of people during the middle of the day, have them stand in the open shade of a tree.

One of the most important things to remember about photography, however, is that you should enjoy taking pictures and that you should do it as often as possible. You don't have to wait until Christmas Eve or your sister's birthday party to be able to use your camera. Take pictures when you are playing with your friends, or on vacation with your family, or just on a walk by yourself. And if you try to keep in mind some of these pointers, you'll probably take lots of good pictures.

Exercise. In the blanks provided, write the meaning of each **boldface** word as it is used in the selection. Check your answers in a dictionary.

a. **professional** _____

b. **artistic** _____

c. **amateur** _____

d. **lens** _____

_____

e. **setting** _____

f. **exposure** _____

g. **shutter** _____

h. **tilt** _____

i. **viewfinder** _____

j. **flare** _____

Name _____

Chapter 9
Word Origins

Words, like people, have interesting histories. In this chapter you will learn some of these histories. You will look at words based on the names of real people and real places. You will see how words have changed in meaning as they have grown older. In addition, you will learn about words that came into English from other languages.

Lesson 1

Understanding Words Based on Place Names

The origin of a word is the source from which the word came into our language. Many English words are based on the names of cities, regions, or even countries.

For example, the names of many foods we buy come from place names. The *sardine* is named after Sardinia, an island where this small fish was found. The *tangerine* was named for the city in Africa from which these oranges were first imported—Tangier, Morocco. The *turkey* was named by mistake. Early European settlers in America saw fowls they thought were the turkey cock of Africa that was imported by way of Turkey. Later, they found that the fowl was not at all the same, but the name *turkey* stuck. The dinnerware we call *china* was named after the country where it was made.

BEETLE BAILEY by Mort Walker

Usually, the origin of a word can be found in the dictionary at the end of the entry. Look for the explanation in brackets [. . . .]. Here is the dictionary entry for *tangerine*.

> **tan•ger•ine** (tăn′jə-rēn′) *n.* A citrus fruit with easily peeled deep-orange skin and sweet, juicy pulp. [Short for *tangerine orange*, "orange of Tangier."]

Exercise 1. Each of the foods below is named after a specific place. Use your dictionary to find out the name of each place. Write this name in the blank provided. The country where this place is located is filled in for you.

Food	Place	Country
a. tangerine	_____	Morocco
b. cantaloupe	_____	Italy
c. frankfurter	_____	Germany
d. hamburger	_____	Germany
e. mocha	_____	Yemen

Exercise 2. Below is a list of English words. Each comes from the name of a specific place—a country, region, city, or other geographical place. Look up each word in a dictionary and write down its modern meaning. An example is done.

Word	Origin	Modern Meaning
Example:		
marathon	At the battle of Marathon 2,500 years ago, 10,000 Athenians defeated 100,000 Persians. A great runner ran the 26 miles to Athens to tell the good news.	*A 26-mile race; any endurance test*
a. cashmere	From Kashmir, Tibet, home of the Kashmir goat.	_____
b. meander	Acting like the River Maiandros, which wound through the plains of Meander.	_____
c. babel	In the Bible, the Tower of Babel (Babylon), where people talked so many languages they couldn't understand each other.	_____
d. laconic	From the Spartans who lived in Laconia and were famous for saying as little as possible.	_____

210

Exercise 3. For each word in Exercise 2, write a sentence.

a. cashmere: _____

b. meander: _____

c. babel: _____

d. laconic: _____

Lesson 2

Understanding Words Based on People

The origin of a word is the source from which the word came into our language. A great many English words are based on the names of people. For example, in the menu below, all the **boldface** words are based on people's names.

A Menu of People's Names

Cereal—choice of corn or wheat flakes
Peanut butter **sandwich**

Baldwin apples

Graham crackers

To find the origins of words in dictionaries, look for the explanation within brackets [. . . .]. Here is the dictionary entry for *pasteurization*.

pas•teur•i•za•tion (păs′chər-ə-zā′shən, păs′tər-ə-zā′shən) n. To heat (milk, wine, etc.) from 140° to about 155°F. in order to destroy bacteria causing fermentation. [Invented by Louis Pasteur.]

Exercise 1. Each of the following foods is named for a person. Look up the food in your dictionary, and write down the name of that person. Write your answers in the blanks at the right. An example is done.

Food	Origin and Definition	Person
Example: Baldwin apple	Named for the engineer and army officer who first grew these apples (1740–1870).	*Loami Baldwin*
a. sandwich	Two or more slices of bread, which hold a filling. Named for a man who hated to leave the gambling table and wanted something to eat with one hand.	
b. cereal	Any grain used for food, such as wheat, oats, or corn. Named for the Roman goddess of grain.	
c. filbert	A hazelnut that grows in France and England. It ripens on the day named for a French saint. Who is this French saint?	
d. graham	Made from whole-wheat flour. Named for the American vegetarian who used it in many products, such as crackers.	

Exercise 2. People have given their names to many kinds of human invention, discovery, and activity. The following list of words are based on the names of real people. Look up each one and write down the name of the person. Write your answers in the blanks at the right. An example is done.

Word	Origin and Definition	Person
Example: to boycott	A certain captain collected rents for an Irish earl. About 1800, the captain raised the rents. The tenants refused to pay. Local shops refused to deal with him. His mail was not delivered. He fled to England. DEFINITION: To join together and refuse to buy from or deal with.	*Captain Charles* *Cunningham* *Boycott*
a. martinet	This French general built up the first regular army in Europe during the reign of Louis XV. He was known for strict training. DEFINITION: A very strict taskmaster. A stickler for details.	
b. sideburns	A Civil War general had them. By flipping the two parts of the word around, you will have his name. DEFINITION: Whiskers on the side of the face.	

212

Name _____

c. macadam   A Scottish engineer who lived in the 1770s   _____
invented a way of building roads using broken
stone.
                          DEFINITION: A type of roadbed made with
layers of small stone and tar or asphalt.

d. pasteurization   A French chemist discovered a way to kill dis-   _____
ease-producing bacteria.
                          DEFINITION: The process of destroying
most disease-producing bacteria with high
heat.

Lesson 3

Understanding Words That Have Changed in Meaning

Over the years, the meaning of a word may change. For example,
think about the word *apple*. *Apple* once referred to almost any fruit.
Now it refers to only the fruit of the apple tree. This change in meaning helps explain the word *pineapple*. The fruit of the pine tree used
to be called a *pineapple*. Then the tropical fruit was discovered.
People said it looked like the fruit of the pine tree. So they named the
tropical fruit a *pineapple*, and the old *pineapple* became a *pine cone*.

Exercise 1. Read each of the following stories about words. Then
look up each of the **boldface** words in a dictionary, and answer the
questions that follow the stories. Write your answers in the blanks
provided.

A **buffet** (bə-fā) used to mean a low stool. It was pronounced
differently than it is now. One version of the old nursery rhyme
went, "Little Miss Muffet sat on a buffet." Later, **buffet** was
used to refer to a much larger piece of furniture.

a. What is the piece of furniture called a **buffet** used for today?

_____

b. **Buffet** also came to refer to the meal served on this piece of furniture. What kind of meal is a **buffet?**

_____

Silly once meant "blessed" or "good." It went through many
changes. A **silly** person was innocent, plain, and simple. Later,
a **silly** person was weak.

c. Today, **silly** has a new meaning. What is a synonym for **silly?**

_____

The word **tell** first meant "to count." It still means this when used in certain contexts. For example, *untold* wealth is not secret money. There is simply so much money that no one has counted it. Look at the following sentence: *All told*, there are 58 basketball players competing. The expression *all told* means "counting everyone."

d. What does a bank *teller* do?

_____

Exercise 2. Read the following selection, "Pretzels: A Long and Twisted History" by Bebe Faas Rice. Then answer the questions that follow.

What do you think of when you hear the word *pretzel*? Picnics and parties and late-night snacks?

Actually, pretzels began as a Lenten food. Many early Christians of the Roman Empire did not eat milk, eggs, or fat during Lent as a way of showing religious devotion. Since bread was an important staple in their diet, they had to make it using only flour, salt, and water. They rolled the dough into slender ropes, shaping them in the form of two arms crossed in prayer. These were called *bracellae,* a Latin word meaning "little arms."

In later centuries, the Germans changed the word for crossed arms of dough to *brezels*. That's how we got the modern-day word *pretzels*.

For hundreds of years pretzels were eaten only during Lent. With the arrival of Easter, they would disappear for another year.

It wasn't until the 1800s that people began to eat the tasty little breads year-round.

In the United States, the Pennsylvania Dutch make soft pretzels. They are served warm and are yeasty and delicious. They are easy to make, and it's fun to twist the dough into the traditional "little arms" shape.

You might want to invite a group of friends over for a pretzel-making party at your house during this Lenten season.

a. The original word for *pretzel* was *bracellae*. What does this Latin word mean?

_____

b. Why did the early Christians call this food *bracellae*?

_____

_____

c. What word did the Germans use for *pretzels*?

_____

214

Name _____

d. When did people start eating this Lenten food all year round?

_____

e. How are pretzels today different from the pretzels the early Christians ate?

_____

Lesson 4

Understanding Words from the American Indians

Many words we use today came into English from the languages of the American Indians. For example, we eat some of the same foods Sitting Bull and Pocahontas did, and we call them by almost the same names they did. All the foods underlined below are from American Indian languages, mostly Algonquin.

When early settlers came to America, they found new plants, foods, animals, and places. They used American Indian words to name these things, but they changed the pronunciation a little to make the new words easier to say. For example, the word *succotash* comes from the Algonquin *misickquatash*, which means "ear or kernel of corn."

To find the origins of words in dictionaries, look for the explanation within brackets [. . . .]. Here is the dictionary entry for *succotash*.

> **suc·co·tash** (sŭk′ə-tăsh′) *n.* Corn kernels and lima beans cooked together. [Algonquin *misickquatash*, ear or kernel of corn.]

Exercise 1. Each word in Column A comes from the Algonquin language. Match each word in Column A with the original Algonquin word in Column B. Write your answers in the blanks at the left. Use your dictionary to help you. (The spelling of the Algonquin words will differ slightly depending on the dictionary you use.)

<table>
<tr><td align="center">A</td><td align="center">B</td></tr>
<tr><td>_____ a. skunk</td><td>(1) misickquatash</td></tr>
<tr><td>_____ b. succotash</td><td>(2) askutasquash</td></tr>
<tr><td>_____ c. squash</td><td>(3) mkussin</td></tr>
<tr><td>_____ d. moccasin</td><td>(4) skekakwa or squnck</td></tr>
<tr><td>_____ e. raccoon</td><td>(5) arakunen</td></tr>
</table>

Exercise 2. The names for almost half of our states are based on words from American Indian languages. Match each word in Column A with the information about its original meaning and language in Column B. Write your answers in the blanks at the left. Use your dictionary to help you.

<table>
<tr><td align="center">A</td><td align="center">B</td></tr>
<tr><td>_____ a. Massachusetts</td><td>(1) Clear water—Dakota Sioux</td></tr>
<tr><td>_____ b. Oklahoma</td><td>(2) At the big hill—Algonquin</td></tr>
<tr><td>_____ c. Mississippi</td><td>(3) Big lake—Ojibwa</td></tr>
<tr><td>_____ d. Michigan</td><td>(4) Red people—Choctaw</td></tr>
<tr><td>_____ e. Minnesota</td><td>(5) Big river—Ojibwa</td></tr>
</table>

Lesson 5

Understanding Words from Foreign Languages

English words have come from nearly every language on earth. For example, the word *boss* comes from Dutch. *Mustache* comes from French. *Kindergarten* comes from German.

In the comic strip below, Nancy's friend Sluggo names four very long words, but only one of them—*upholsterer*—comes from the language spoken long ago in England, Old English.

NANCY by Ernie Bushmiller

An *upholsterer* is a person who upholsters, or rebuilds furniture. The other three words come from German: A *delicatessen* is a shop that sells cooked food. *Pumpernickel* is a dark sourish bread made from rye flour. *Liverwurst* is a sausage made from liver.

The origin of words can be found in dictionaries. Look for the explanation within brackets [. . . .]. Here is the dictionary entry for *delicatessen*. The first language this word came from is Latin.

> **del•i•ca•tes•sen** (dĕl′ĭ-kə-tĕs′ən) n. A shop that sells freshly prepared foods ready for serving. [Fr. German, *delikatessen*, delicacy; fr. French, *délicatesse*, fr. Italian *delicatezza*, fr. Latin *delicatus*.]

Some dictionaries use abbreviations to indicate foreign languages. Some of these abbreviations are:

ME	(Middle English)	Gk	(Greek)
OE	(Old English)	F	(French)
G	(German)	Sp	(Spanish)
L	(Latin)		

Exercise 1. Look up each word below in your dictionary. In the blank, write the name of the first language from which the word came.

a. ketchup _____

b. goulash _____

c. coffee _____

d. waffle _____

e. tea _____

f. tomato _____

g. spaghetti _____

h. tortilla _____

i. cider _____

j. macaroon _____

Exercise 2. Read the following selection, "Terror at 10,000 Feet" by George Shea. Pay special attention to the words printed in **boldface**. After you finish reading the selection, look up each boldface word in your dictionary. Write the first language from which the word came in the blank next to the word.

Al Howard was the only **pilot** in his part of Alaska. He was a good pilot, and a careful one. But today he had a bad feeling about flying. He woke up feeling dizzy. *I should not fly today,* Al thought to himself.

Then the telephone rang.

It was Helen Winters. Helen ran the airfield. "Al," she said, "can you get out here right away?"

"I'm not flying today," Al told her. "I'm not feeling very . . ."

Helen broke in. "Al, it's an **emergency.** It's Dan Stewart. He's very sick. He could die. The doctor wants him in a hospital right away."

"All right," Al said. "I'll be right there."

When Al reached the airfield, Dan Stewart was already there. He was covered with a **blanket.** His 12-year-old daughter, Janie, was with him. Together, Al and Janie helped get Dan into the small airplane. Janie sat in front. She had been up with Al before.

The weather was good. The trip would only take an hour. Soon, they were 10,000 feet in the air, heading over the mountains. Then it happened.

Al called out, "Janie!" He **slumped** over. Al had blacked out.

Janie started to shake him. "Al! Al!" she cried. "Wake up!"

A moment later, the airplane turned nose-down. It went into a dive.

Janie pushed Al to the side. Then she reached for the control stick. She pulled back on it the way she had seen Al do. The airplane came out of the dive. It started climbing. Then it shook. It began to lose speed.

Janie had pulled too hard!

Janie pushed the stick forward, little by little. The airplane stopped shaking. It picked up speed.

Good, Janie thought. She looked out the window. Suddenly, she was filled with **terror.** In front of her was a mountain. The airplane was headed right for it!

Again, Janie pulled back the stick. This time she pulled slowly. The airplane shook. But it went up. "Come on," Janie said. "Come on! Go over! Come on!" She could not take her eyes off the mountain. Any second the airplane would plow right into it. Janie froze. *I'm going to die,* she thought.

The mountain seemed inches away. Then, unbelievably, Janie saw blue sky. The airplane had cleared the mountain! Janie pushed the control stick forward. Then Al moved. He opened his eyes. "Good girl," he whispered. "Hold on another minute. Then I think I can take over."

Half an hour later, Al landed the airplane. In minutes, they were on their way to the hospital. "I'm sure your dad will make it," Al said. "We will all make it, thanks to you."

They rode along. Janie looked out the window. She wished for only two things. She wanted her dad to be OK. And she wanted her knees to stop shaking.

a. pilot _____

b. emergency (look up *emerge*) _____

c. blanket _____

d. slump _____

e. terror _____

Lesson 6
Practice

Read the following selection. Then complete the exercises that follow.

A Is for Antediluvian
Charles W. Ferguson

Of course you could just say "before the Flood," because that is what antediluvian means. But antediluvian, besides being a beautiful word with little bells ringing in it, is also a comical word. And if you learn the life story of the word and see how people have used it for its humor as well as for its loveliness, you will understand a great deal more than the word itself.

Antediluvian tells us, among other things, how our English-American language is made up of older languages. Rome was located in a country called Latium and Romans spoke a language called Latin. Roman legions carried Latin with them and left it wherever they went. They conquered what is now England and left their language there, so that when the English made up words, even centuries after the Romans had left, they often turned to Latin.

When they wanted a word to mean "before the Flood," when they wanted to say it all in one word, they took two Latin words and put them together. They took ante, which means before. Ante is a prefix—a fixed beginning of a word that you will find in many other words. You will hear it in anteroom, a small room you go into before you enter a big one. You will hear it in antebellum, which means before the war, bellum being the Latin word for war. And you'll find it in the letters you see written every day. A.M. stands for ante meridiem and it tells you of the morning, of the time before the sun reaches the meridian and is directly overhead.

The Latin word for flood is diluvium. You have heard a flood referred to as a deluge. The Flood in the word antediluvian is the one in which Noah took two of every beast, according to the Bible story, and kept them secure in his Ark. It was a turning point and starting-over point in the history of the Jews. It happened way, way back there, and anything that happened before the Flood was thought of as very, very old. It belonged to another time.

It is not surprising that by 1726 (or long before our American Revolution) people had started using the word antediluvian to mean a thing was out-of-date—so much out-of-date that it was comical. It was something unbelievably old. People would say that a tottering old man was antediluvian. Charles Lamb, the English essayist, spoke of "an antediluvian makeshift of a building."

The word still hangs on in our speech and you will hear it occasionally. This means that it serves a purpose, that there is a place for it. It's a nice word with a funny meaning and that's one way you will hear it. Today you hear people say to a fellow who does not have the latest car but insists on driving one that is behind the times, "Where did you get that antediluvian model?"

The word can be used in a more serious way. Benjamin Franklin, writing of the good things he saw ahead of his day and thinking how health might be improved, foresaw a time "when our lives might be lengthened beyond the antediluvian standard." It is also a word that can help draw pictures. S. J. Perelman, describing a night scene from a hut on stilts in the jungle, writes: "An amber spotlight simulating the full moon had been turned on, and it made the beasts seem even more antediluvian than normally." Here, as in *The Hunting of the Snark*, the word gives a creepy feeling:

There was silence supreme! Not a shriek, not a scream,
Scarcely even a howl or groan,

As the man they called "Ho" told his story of woe
In an antediluvian tone.

Exercise 1. Write a definition for each of the words below.

a. antediluvian: _____

b. anteroom: _____

c. antebellum: _____

d. ante meridiem: _____

e. deluge: _____

Exercise 2. Write sentences using each word below.

a. antediluvian: _____

_____

b. anteroom: _____

_____

c. antebellum: _____

_____

d. ante meridien: _____

_____

e. deluge: _____
_____

Exercise 3. Write a definition for each of the words below.

a. antecede: _____

b. antecedent: _____

c. antechamber: _____

d. antedate: _____

Exercise 4. Write sentences using each of the words below.

a. antecede: _____
_____

b. antecedent: _____
_____

c. antechamber: _____
_____

d. antedate: _____
_____

Chapter 10

Figurative Language

What is figurative language? **Figurative language is a vivid and colorful way of expressing your thoughts.** Figurative language creates a picture in your reader's mind. This picture gets your thought across in a strong and sometimes startling way.

Figurative language is not meant to be taken literally, or exactly. The words in figurative language take on a new meaning all their own. That's why the comic strip below is funny. When you say, "I'm going to sit down and tickle the ivories," you are using figurative language. This is a colorful, and somewhat humorous, way of saying that you are going to play the piano.

MUPPETS **by Guy and Brad Gilchrist**

Lesson 1

Identifying Figurative and Literal Language

In literal language, words mean exactly what they say. For example, read the following sentence.

From the helicopter, Carla could see the blazing forest fire.

In the sentence above, each word is used with its usual dictionary meaning. The fire really is *blazing*, or burning brightly.

In figurative language, words do not mean exactly what they say. Figurative language suggests a new meaning for the words in a vivid way. For example, look at the following sentences.

> Carla saw the outlaw steal the horse. Her eyes blazed as she rode after him.

Here, *blazed* is used figuratively. Carla's eyes were not actually burning brightly. The word *blazed*, however, creates a vivid, or colorful, picture of how Carla's eyes shone brightly with anger.

Now read the next two items.

> The hang glider jumped from the cliff. What a thrilling experience! He was floating on air.
>
> What a soft mattress! I'm floating on air.

In the first item, all the words are used literally. Once the hang glider jumps from the cliff, he really is floating on air. In the second item, the words are used figuratively. The person is on a mattress. He is not really floating on air; he just feels as if he is.

Exercise. Read the selection below from "The Sound of Summer Running" by Ray Bradbury. Then follow the directions at the end of the selection.

> Late that night, going home from the show with his mother and father and his brother Tom, Douglas saw the tennis shoes in the bright store window. He glanced quickly away, but his ankles were seized, his feet suspended, then rushed. The earth spun; the shop awnings slammed their canvas wings overhead with the thrust of his body running. His mother and father and brother walked quietly on both sides of him. Douglas walked backward, watching the tennis shoes in the midnight window left behind.
>
> "It was a nice movie," said Mother.
>
> Douglas murmured, "It was. . . ."
>
> It was June and long past time, for buying the special shoes that were quiet as a summer rain falling on the walks. June and the earth full of raw power and everything everywhere in motion. The grass was still pouring in from the country, surrounding the sidewalks, stranding the houses. Any moment the town would capsize, go down and leave not a stir in the clover and weeds. And here Douglas stood, trapped on the dead cement and the red-brick streets, hardly able to move.
>
> "Dad!" He blurted it out. "Back there in that window, those Cream-Sponge Para Litefoot Shoes . . ."
>
> His father didn't even turn. "Suppose you tell me why you need a new pair of sneakers. Can you do that?"
>
> "Well . . ."
>
> It was because they felt the way it feels every summer when you take off your shoes for the first time and run in the grass. They felt like it feels sticking your feet out of the hot covers in wintertime to let the cold wind from the open window blow on

224

them suddenly and you let them stay out a long time until you pull them back in under the covers again to feel them, like packed snow. The tennis shoes felt like it always feels the first time every year wading in the slow waters of the creek and seeing your feet below, half an inch further downstream, with refraction, than the real part of you above water.

"Dad," said Douglas, "it's hard to explain."

Somehow the people who made tennis shoes knew what boys needed and wanted. They put marshmallows and coiled springs in the soles and they wove the rest out of grasses bleached and fired in the wilderness. Somewhere deep in the soft loam of the shoes the thin hard sinews of the buck deer were hidden. The people that made the shoes must have watched a lot of winds blow the trees and a lot of rivers going down to the lakes. Whatever it was, it was in the shoes, and it was summer.

Douglas tried to get all this in words.

"Yes," said Father, "but what's wrong with last year's sneakers? Why can't you dig *them* out of the closet?"

Well, he felt sorry for boys who lived in California where they wore tennis shoes all year and never knew what it was to get winter off your feet, peel off the iron leather shoes all full of snow and rain and run barefoot for a day and then lace on the first new tennis shoes of the season, which was better than barefoot. The magic was always in the new pair of shoes. The magic might die by the first of September, but now in late June there was still plenty of magic, and shoes like these could jump you over trees and rivers and houses. And if you wanted, they could jump you over fences and sidewalks and dogs.

"Don't you see?" said Douglas. "I just *can't* use last year's pair."

For last year's pair were dead inside. They had been fine when he started them out, last year. But by the end of summer, every year, you always found out, you always knew, you couldn't really jump over rivers and trees and houses in them, and they were dead. But this was a new year, and he felt that this time, with this new pair of shoes, he could do anything, anything at all.

They walked up on the steps to their house. "Save your money," said Dad. "In five or six weeks—"

"Summer'll be over!"

Lights out, with Tom asleep, Douglas lay watching his feet, far away down there at the end of the bed in the moonlight, free of the heavy iron shoes, the big chunks of winter fallen away from them.

"Reasons. I've got to think of reasons for the shoes."

Well, as anyone knew, the hills around town were wild with friends putting cows to riot, playing barometer to the atmospheric changes, taking sun, peeling like calendars each day to take more sun. To catch those friends, you must run much faster than foxes or squirrels. As for the town, it steamed with enemies grown irritable with heat, so remembering every winter argument and insult. *Find friends, ditch enemies!* That was the Cream-Sponge Para Litefoot motto. *Does the world run too fast? Want to be alert, stay alert? Litefoot, then! Litefoot!*

He held his coin bank up and heard the faint small tinkling, the airy weight of money there.

Whatever you want, he thought, you got to make your own way. During the night now, let's find that path through the forest. . . .

Downtown, the store lights went out, one by one. A wind blew in the window. It was like a river going downstream and his feet wanting to go with it.

In his dreams he heard a rabbit running running running in the deep warm grass.

Directions. Write *L* next to each item in which all the words are used with a literal meaning. Write *F* next to each item in which the words are used with a figurative meaning.

a. "Late that night, going home from the show with his mother and father and his brother Tom, Douglas saw the tennis shoes in the bright store window." _____

b. "He glanced quickly away, but his ankles were seized, his feet suspended, then rushed." _____

c. "The earth spun; the shop awnings slammed their canvas wings overhead with the thrust of his body running." _____

d. "His mother and father and brother walked quietly on both sides of him." _____

e. "It was June and long past time for buying the special shoes that were quiet as a summer rain falling on the walks." _____

f. "Somehow the people who made tennis shoes knew what boys needed and wanted." _____

g. "They put marshmallows and coiled springs in the soles and they wove the rest out of grasses bleached and fired in the wilderness." _____

h. "Well, he felt sorry for the boys who lived in California where they wore tennis shoes all year and never knew what it was to get winter off your feet, peel off the iron leather shoes all full of snow and rain and run barefoot for a day and then lace on the first new tennis shoes of the season, which was better than barefoot." _____

i. "The magic might die by the first of September, but now in late June there was still plenty of magic, and shoes like these could jump you over trees and rivers and houses." _____

j. "In his dreams he heard a rabbit running running running in the deep warm grass." _____

Lesson 2

Understanding Figurative Expressions

Figurative expressions contain words and phrases used without their usual, or dictionary, meanings. The words in figurative expressions work together to form a new meaning all their own. For example, read the sentence below.

> After Maria struck out for the third time, she said, *"I feel lower than a snake's belly."*

Maria doesn't mean that she is down on the ground. She has simply chosen a colorful way of saying that she feels very bad.

Now read the comic strip below.

HAGAR THE HORRIBLE by Dik Browne

When Hagar says that he has the eyes of an eagle, he means that he has extremely good eyesight. When he says that he has the brain of a fox, he means that he is smart and cunning. When he says that he has the heart of a lion, he means that he is brave. What do you think Hagar's wife, Helga, means by her comment?

Exercise. Finish reading "The Sound of Summer Running" by Ray Bradbury. Then read each of the figurative expressions that follow the selection.

Old Mr. Sanderson moved through his shoe store as the proprietor of a pet shop must move through his shop where are kenneled animals from everywhere in the world, touching each one briefly along the way. Mr. Sanderson brushed his hands over the shoes in the window, and some of them were like cats to him and some were like dogs; he touched each pair with concern, adjusting laces, fixing tongues. Then he stood in the exact center of the carpet and looked around, nodding.

There was a sound of growing thunder.

One moment, the door to Sanderson's Shoe Emporium was empty. The next, Douglas Spaulding stood clumsily there, staring down at his leather shoes as if these heavy things could not be pulled up out of the cement. The thunder had stopped when his shoes stopped. Now, with painful slowness, daring to look only at the money in his cupped hand, Douglas moved out of the bright sunlight of Saturday noon. He made careful stacks of nickels, dimes, and quarters on the counter, like someone playing chess and worried if the next move carried him out into sun or deep into shadow.

"Don't say a word!" said Mr. Sanderson.

Douglas froze.

"First, I know just what you want to buy," said Mr. Sanderson. "Second, I see you every afternoon at my window; you think I don't see? You're wrong. Third, to give it its full name, you want the Royal Crown Cream-Sponge Para Litefoot Tennis Shoes: 'LIKE MENTHOL ON YOUR FEET!' Fourth, you want credit."

"No!" cried Douglas, breathing hard, as if he'd run all night in his dreams. "I got something better than credit to offer!" he gasped. "Before I tell, Mr. Sanderson, you got to do me one small favor. Can you remember when was the last time you yourself wore a pair of Litefoot sneakers, sir?"

Mr. Sanderson's face darkened. "Oh, ten, twenty, say, thirty years ago. Why . . . ?"

"Mr. Sanderson, don't you think you owe it to your customers, sir, to at least try the tennis shoes you sell, for just one minute, so you know how they feel? People forget if they don't keep testing things. United Cigar Store man smokes cigars, don't he? Candy-store man samples his own stuff, I should think. So . . ."

"You may have noticed," said the old man, "I'm wearing shoes."

"But not sneakers, sir! How you going to sell sneakers unless you can rave about them and how you going to rave about them unless you know them?"

Mr. Sanderson backed off a little distance from the boy's fever, one hand to his chin. "Well . . ."

"Mr. Sanderson," said Douglas, "you sell me something and I'll sell you something just as valuable."

"Is it absolutely necessary to the sale that I put on a pair of the sneakers, boy?" said the old man.

"I sure wish you could, sir!"

The old man sighed. A minute later, seated panting quietly, he laced the tennis shoes to his long narrow feet. They looked detached and alien down there next to the dark cuffs of his business suit. Mr. Sanderson stood up.

"How do they *feel?*" asked the boy.

"How do they feel, he asks; they feel fine." He started to sit down.

"Please!" Douglas held out his hand. "Mr. Sanderson, now could you kind of rock back and forth a little, sponge around, bounce kind of, while I tell you the rest? It's this: I give you my money, you give me the shoes, I owe you a dollar. But, Mr. Sanderson, *but*—soon as I get those shoes on, you know what *happens?*"

"What?"

"Bang! I deliver your packages, pick up packages, bring you coffee, burn your trash, run to the post office, telegraph office, library! You'll see twelve of me in and out, in and out, every minute. Feel those shoes, Mr. Sanderson, *feel* how fast they'd take me? All those springs inside? Feel all the running inside? Feel how they kind of grab hold and can't let you alone and don't like you just *standing* there? Feel how quick I'd be doing the things you'd rather not bother with? You stay in the nice cool store while I'm jumping all around town! But it's not me really, it's the shoes. They're going like mad down alleys, cutting corners, and back! There they go!"

Mr. Sanderson stood amazed with the rush of words. When the words got going the flow carried him; he began to sink deep in the shoes, to flex his toes, limber his arches, test his ankles. He rocked softly, secretly, back and forth in a small breeze from the open door. The tennis shoes silently hushed themselves deep in the carpet, sank as in a jungle grass, in loam and resilient clay. He gave one solemn bounce of his heels in the yeasty dough, in the yielding and welcoming earth. Emotions hurried over his face as if many colored lights had been switched on and off. His mouth hung slightly open. Slowly he gentled and rocked himself to a halt, and the boy's voice faded and they stood there looking at each other in a tremendous and natural silence.

A few people drifted by on the sidewalk outside, in the hot sun.

Still the man and boy stood there, the boy glowing, the man with revelation in his face.

"Boy," said the old man at last, "in five years, how would you like a job selling shoes in this emporium?"

"Gosh, thanks, Mr. Sanderson, but I don't know what I'm going to be yet."

"Anything you want to be, son," said the old man, "you'll be. No one will ever stop you."

The old man walked lightly across the store to the wall of ten thousand boxes, came back with some shoes for the boy, and wrote up a list on some paper while the boy was lacing the shoes on his feet and then standing there, waiting.

The old man held out his list. "A dozen things you got to do for me this afternoon. Finish them, we're even Stephen, and you're fired."

"Thanks, Mr. Sanderson!" Douglas bounded away.

"Stop!" cried the old man.

Douglas pulled up and turned.

Mr. Sanderson leaned forward. "How do they *feel?*"

The boy looked down at his feet deep in the rivers, in the fields of wheat, in the wind that already was rushing him out of the town. He looked up at the old man, his eyes burning, his mouth moving, but no sound came out.

"Antelopes?" said the old man, looking from the boy's face to his shoes. "Gazelles?"

The boy thought about it, hesitated, and nodded a quick nod. Almost immediately he vanished. He just spun about with a whisper and went off. The door stood empty. The sound of the tennis shoes faded in the jungle heat.

Mr. Sanderson stood in the sun-blazed door, listening. From a long time ago, when he dreamed as a boy, he remembered the sound. Beautiful creatures leaping under the sky, gone through brush, under trees, away, and only the soft echo their running left behind.

"Antelopes," said Mr. Sanderson. "Gazelles."

He bent to pick up the boy's abandoned winter shoes, heavy with forgotten rains and long-melted snows. Moving out of the blazing sun, walking softly, lightly, slowly, he headed back toward civilization. . . .

Directions. Write the meaning of each figurative expression on the blank below it.

Example

"Old Mr. Sanderson moved through his shoe store as the proprietor of a pet shop must move through his shop where are kenneled animals from everywhere in the world, touching each one briefly along the way."

Literal Meaning: *Old Mr. Sanderson treasured the goods in his store and treated them lovingly.*

a. "Mr. Sanderson brushed his hands over the shoes in the window, and some of them were like cats to him and some were like dogs; he touched each pair with concern, adjusting laces, fixing tongues."

Literal Meaning: _____

_____

b. "The thunder had stopped when his shoes stopped."

Literal Meaning: _____

c. "Mr. Sanderson backed off a little distance from the boy's fever, one hand to his chin."

Literal Meaning: _____

_____

230

d. "The tennis shoes silently hushed themselves deep in the carpet, sank as in a jungle grass, in loam and resilient clay."

Literal Meaning: _____

_____

_____

Lesson 3

Understanding Idioms

An idiom is a group of words that has a special meaning all its own. For example, look at the following sentence.

Whenever he was criticized, Jan got *hot under the collar*.

The idiom *hot under the collar* means "angry." Its meaning has little to do with the dictionary meaning of the individual words.

An idiom is a type of figurative expression. It differs from other figurative expressions in one important way. Usually, an idiom has been used so often in everyday speech that it has lost its figurative power.

In the cartoon below, a telephone is called a "hot line." Yet telephone wires never get warm to the touch. A *hot line* means "a fast, direct connection to someone for use during times of crisis."

ARCHIE

Exercise 1. In the sentences below, the idioms are printed in **bold-face.** Read each sentence. Then choose the correct meaning for each idiom. Put an X next to your answer.

Example

Carl started to walk on stage. Suddenly he **got cold feet.**

____X____ lost his courage

_____ felt a draft on his feet

a. His blood ran cold.

_____ he was terrified

_____ he lost his fever

b. The director, **a cold fish,** scowled at Carl from the wings.

_____ a person who loves cold fish

_____ an unfriendly person

c. Brenda, the play's star, had given him **a cold shoulder** earlier in the day.

_____ a joint disease

_____ unfriendly treatment

d. The producer muttered, "Why did I pay this kid **in cold cash** before the show?"

_____ in real money

_____ in money stored in a refrigerator

e. No one was helping Carl. They were all **throwing cold water on** his dreams.

_____ moistening

_____ discouraging

Exercise 2. Read each statement below. Each idiom is printed in **boldface.** Write the meaning of each idiom on the line provided. You may use your dictionary to help you. (Since the key word in each idiom is *hot,* look up *hot* in your dictionary.)

a. Carl knew he was **in hot water.**

_____

b. The producer was getting **hot under the collar.**

_____

c. Why had he wanted to become an actor? All Carl wanted to do now was to get off this **hot seat.**

_____

d. His parents had not wanted him to go on the stage. All year long the subject had been a **hot potato** at home.

_____

e. Carl smiled when he remembered how his parents finally gave their consent. His confidence returned. He knew his dream of a career on the stage was not just **hot air,** and now he would make the audience know it too.

_____

Exercise 3. Read each statement below. Each idiom is printed in **boldface.** Write the meaning of each idiom on the line provided. You may use your dictionary to help you. (Look up the key word in each idiom.)

a. Actors often get **cold feet.**

_____

b. Good speakers think **on their feet.**

_____

c. When you are famous, **the world is often at your feet.**

_____

d. Midland High was beaten **hands down** by St. Theresa's.

_____

e. The man told the judge that **his hands were clean.**

_____

Lesson 4

Understanding Similes

A simile is a direct comparison between two essentially, or basically, unlike things. A simile contains the word *like* or *as*. For example, each of the sentences below contains a simile.

> The clouds looked *like* white kittens.
> The clouds were as fluffy *as* the fur of white kittens.

How are clouds and white kittens alike? They are both soft and fluffy.

The comic strip below contains several similes. To Tiger, the big cloud looks like a white dog. To Hugo, it looks like a whipped-cream dessert. To Punkinhead, it looks like a horse. Julian, however, sees only what is actually there. He can name the cloud—cumulonimbus. He can explain how it is formed. He is good at describing clouds literally, not figuratively.

TIGER by Bud Blake

Exercise 1. Each of the sentences below contains a simile. For each sentence, the two things being compared are underlined. Read each sentence. Then choose the description that tells how the two things being compared are alike. Put an X in the blank next to your choice.

Example

When Peggy blushed, her <u>cheeks</u> turned as red as a <u>cardinal</u>.

_____ Both were soft.

_____ Both smelled good.

___**X**___ Both were bright red.

a. Kirsten's <u>hair</u> is like <u>corn silk</u>.

_____ Both are long.

_____ Both are fine and pale yellow.

_____ Both grow quickly.

b. Margie swam like a <u>dolphin</u>.

_____ Both are smart.

_____ Both are short.

_____ Both are graceful in the water.

c. His <u>voice</u> had the same effect on me as <u>a nail scraping against a chalkboard</u>.

_____ Both make horrible sounds.

_____ Both make pleasant sounds.

_____ Both are soft.

d. After four hours of sunbathing on the beach, her <u>throat</u> was as dry as <u>dust</u>.

_____ Both are dry.

_____ Both have baked for four hours.

_____ Both are light.

e. <u>I have as much of a chance of winning the race</u> as <u>a chimpanzee has of writing a novel</u>.

_____ Both have a good chance.

_____ Both are talented.

_____ Both have almost no chance at all.

Exercise 2. Each of the following sentences contains a simile. Read each sentence. Draw a line under the two things being compared. Then choose the description that tells how the two things being compared are alike. Put an X in the blank next to your choice.

a. The old house was as dark as a country road at midnight.

_____ Both are dusty.

_____ Both are dark.

_____ Both are empty.

b. The puppy's skin was like velvet.

_____ Both are soft and smooth.

_____ Both smell good.

_____ Both have a rich color.

c. The old woman's memories were as vivid as a Vermont forest in autumn.

_____ Both are colorful and lively.

_____ Both are old.

_____ Both are tired.

d. The child's hair smelled like a spring morning.

_____ Both are pretty.

_____ Both are warm.

_____ Both smell clean and fresh.

e. At six o'clock this morning the woodpecker outside my window sounded like a drummer in a rock band.

_____ Both are loud and persistent, or refusing to stop.

_____ Both are good musicians.

_____ Both are early risers.

Exercise 3. Complete each of the following similes. Write your answers on the blanks provided.

a. Jack's jokes are as old as _____

_____.

b. From inside our warm house, the snowstorm looked like _____

_____.

c. The snow fell as silently as _____

_____.

d. The old love letters were as fragile as _____

_____.

e. When Chris hit the homer, the crowd went as wild as _____

_____.

Lesson 5

Understanding Metaphors

   A metaphor is an implied, or suggested, comparison between two essentially unlike things. It does not contain the word *like* or *as.* For example, in the following poem, "What the Rattlesnake Said" by Vachel Lindsay, the speaker, who is the rattlesnake, uses two metaphors. The rattlesnake compares the moon to a prairie-dog and the sun to a broncho.

>   The moon's a little prairie-dog.
>   He shivers through the night.
>   He sits upon his hill and cries
>   For fear that *I* will bite.
>
> 5   The sun's a broncho. He's afraid
>   Like every other thing,
>   And trembles, morning, noon and night,
>   Lest *I* should spring, and sting.

In the next poem, "Fog" by Carl Sandburg, the poet compares the fog to a cat.

>   The fog comes
>   on little cat feet.
>
>   It sits looking
>   over harbor and city
> 5   on silent haunches
>   and then moves on.

The comic strip below contains two metaphors. First the mother compares the child to a little ray of sunshine. Then the child starts to cry. At this point the mother compares the child to thunder and lightning.

SNUFFY SMITH by Fred Lasswell

_____

Exercise 1. Each sentence below contains a metaphor. For each sentence, the two things being compared are <u>underlined</u>. Read each sentence. Then choose the description that tells how the two things are alike. Put an X in the blank next to your choice.

a. The <u>eighth-grade classroom</u> was a <u>beehive of activity</u>.

_____ Both contain students.

_____ Both were very busy places.

_____ Both were painted yellow.

b. The new <u>secretary</u> was a <u>pair of scissors</u> that cut through the red tape of the office.

_____ Both were sharp and efficient, or able to get the job done.

_____ Both were new.

_____ Both liked red tape.

c. Her <u>hands</u> were <u>hummingbirds</u> darting from one task to another.

_____ Both move quickly.

_____ Both are colorful.

_____ Both move slowly.

d. His <u>wit</u> was a <u>hammer</u> with which he beat down all in his way.

_____ Both are humorous.

_____ Both can be used to beat down or pound.

_____ Both were sharp.

e. The <u>snow</u> was a <u>prison</u> around the buried skier.

_____ Both are rooms.

_____ Both are underground.

_____ Both prevent escape.

Exercise 2. Read the two poems below. Then answer the questions that follow.

Ways of Composing
Eve Merriam

typewriter:
a mouthful of teeth chattering
afraid to be quiet

a pencil can lie down and dream
dark and silver silences

From the Japanese
Eve Merriam

The summer night
is a dark blue hammock
slung between the white pillars of day.

I lie there
5 cooling myself
with the straw-colored
flat round fan
of the full moon.

a. In "Ways of Composing," to what does the poet compare a typewriter?

_____

b. How are these two things alike?

_____

c. The poet says, "a pencil can lie down and dream/dark and silver
silences." Why are the silences *silver*?

_____

d. Which method of composing do you think the poet prefers—a
typewriter or a pencil? Why?

_____

e. In "From the Japanese," to what does the poet compare a summer
night?

_____

f. How are these two things alike?

_____

g. To what does the poet compare the days?

_____

h. How are these two things alike?

_____

i. To what does the poet compare the full moon?

_____

j. How are these two objects alike?

_____

Understanding Jargon

Jargon is the language—words and phrases—used by people in a special group or a particular profession. For example, tap dancers use words like *flap, shuffle,* and *ball change* to name certain steps.

Many expressions in jargon are types of idioms. The individual words do not mean exactly what they say but work together to form a new meaning. For example, look at the caption at the bottom of this photograph.

The expression *4-for-4* means "four hits during four times at bat."

Royals' George Brett saluting his 4-for-4 day Sunday against Blue Jays.

Every sport has its own jargon. In the comic strip below, Valerie shows she knows baseball jargon.

DRABBLE by Fagan

Here are the meanings of the expressions she uses:

To *pull a pitch* is to hit the ball to the field on the same side of the plate as the batter stands. A right-handed batter stands on the left side of home plate.

A *low and away pitch* is below the strike zone and to the side of the plate away from the batter.

A *little bleeder* is a slow, badly batted ground ball that just gets through the infield.

Exercise. In the following sports broadcast, all the terms come from baseball. The jargon is underlined. Mark an X in front of the words that give the best meaning for the underlined words. An example is done.

Example

Hi, folks! This is your faithful sportscaster, U. R., here, broadcasting a double decker live from Yankee Stadium.

_____ two decks of cards

_____ a two-level boat

___X___ two games

a. His honor, the ump, has just hollered, "Play ball!"

_____ the judge

_____ the umpire

_____ the Supreme Court judge

b. The <u>opener</u> today will be a battle between pitching giants.

_____ the first game of a double header

_____ the moment the ball park opens

_____ the first event, usually a comedy

c. Pitching for the Yankees today is Marv L. Uss, who <u>blanked</u> fourteen players last Tuesday.

_____ walked

_____ struck out

_____ stared down

d. Pitching for the Royals is Super Arm, whose <u>bullets and benders</u> have been working well all season.

_____ rifles and pistols

_____ slow balls and spitballs

_____ fast balls and curves

e. The <u>night cap</u> may seem a little dull after this game.

_____ hot cocoa

_____ second game of a double header

_____ last game of the week

f. Leading off for the Pirates is O.U. Slammer, who has been on <u>a clouting spree</u> for five weeks.

_____ getting many hits

_____ hitting people over the head

_____ buying many things

g. There is the first pitch, <u>smoking over the plate</u>! Strike One!

_____ catching fire

_____ forming a gray line

_____ moving quickly; a fast ball

h. There is the second pitch! Slammer <u>fans the breeze</u>. Strike Two!

_____ swings and misses

_____ cools off the catcher

_____ leans into the wind

i. Pitch number three coming. CRACK! What <u>a slugger</u> he is!

_____ a prizefighter

_____ a long-ball hitter

_____ a steady hitter

j. It is a <u>four-bagger</u>, folks!

_____ home run

_____ three-base hit

_____ base on balls

Lesson 7

Practice

As you read the following selection, pay special attention to figurative language. Then complete the exercise that follows this selection.

The Blue Rose
Maurice Baring

(1)   There lived once upon a time in China a wise Emperor who had one daughter. His daughter was remarkable for her perfect beauty. Her feet were the smallest in the world; her eyes were long and slanting and bright as brown onyxes, and when you heard her laugh it was like listening to a tinkling stream or to the chimes of a silver bell. Moreover, the Emperor's daughter was as wise as she was beautiful, and she chanted the verse of the great poets better than anyone in the land. The Emperor was old in years; his son was married and had begotten a son; he was, therefore, quite happy with regard to the succession to the throne, but he wished before he died to see his daughter wedded to someone who should be worthy of her.

(2)   Many suitors presented themselves to the palace as soon as it became known that the Emperor desired a son-in-law, but when they reached the palace they were met by the Lord Chamberlain, who told them that the Emperor had decided that only the man who found and brought back the blue rose should marry his daughter. The suitors were much puzzled by this order. What was the blue rose and where was it to be found? In all, a hundred and fifty suitors had presented themselves, and out of these, fifty at once put away from them all thought of winning the hand of the Emperor's daughter, since they considered the condition imposed to be absurd.

(3)   The other hundred set about trying to find the blue rose. One of them—his name was Ti-Fun-Ti—he was a merchant and was immensely rich—at once went to the largest shop in the town and said to the shopkeeper, "I want a blue rose, the best you have."

(4)   The shopkeeper, with many apologies, explained that he did not stock blue roses. He had red roses in profusion, white, pink, and yellow roses, but no blue roses. There had hitherto been no demand for the article.

(5)   "Well," said Ti-Fun-Ti, "you must get one for me. I do not mind how much money it costs, but I must have a blue rose."

(6)   The shopkeeper said he would do his best, but he feared it would be an expensive article and difficult to procure. Another of the suitors, whose name I have forgotten, was a warrior, and extremely brave; he mounted his horse, and taking with him a hundred archers and a thousand horsemen, he marched into the territory of the King of the Five Rivers, whom he knew to be the richest king in the world and the possessor of the rarest treasures, and demanded of him the blue rose, threatening him with a terrible doom should he be reluctant to give it up.

(7)   The King of the Five Rivers, who disliked soldiers and had a horror of noise, physical violence, and every kind of fuss (his bodyguard was armed solely with fans and sunshades), rose from the cushions on which he was lying when the demand was made, and tinkling a small bell, said to the servant who straightway appeared, "Fetch me the blue rose."

(8)   The servant retired and returned presently bearing on a silken cushion a large sapphire which was carved so as to imitate a full-blown rose with all its petals.

(9)   "This," said the King of the Five Rivers, "is the blue rose. You are welcome to it."

(10)   The warrior took it, and after making brief, soldier-like thanks, he went straight back to the Emperor's palace, saying that he had lost no time in finding the blue rose. He was ushered into the presence of the Emperor, who as soon as he heard the warrior's story and saw the blue rose which had been brought sent for his daughter and said to her: "This intrepid warrior has brought you what he claims to be the blue rose. Has he accomplished the quest?"

(11)   The Princess took the precious object in her hands and after examining it for a moment said: "This is not a rose at all. It is a sapphire; I have no need of precious stones." And she returned the stone to the warrior with many elegantly expressed thanks. And the warrior went away in discomfiture.

(12)   The merchant, hearing of the warrior's failure, was all the more anxious to win the prize. He sought the shopkeeper and said to him: "Have you got me the blue rose? I trust you have; because, if not, I shall most assuredly be the means of your death. My brother-in-law is chief magistrate, and I am allied by marriage to all the chief officials in the kingdom."

(13)   The shopkeeper turned pale and said: "Sir, give me three days and I will procure you the rose without fail." The merchant granted him the three days and went away. Now the shopkeeper was at his wit's end as to what to do, for he knew well there was no such thing as a blue rose. For two days he did nothing but moan and wring his hands, and on the third day he went to his wife and said, "Wife, we are ruined."

(14)   But his wife, who was a sensible woman, said: "Nonsense. If there is no such thing as a blue rose we must make one. Go to the chemist and ask him for a strong dye which will change a white rose into a blue one."

(15)   So the shopkeeper went to the chemist and asked for a dye, and the chemist gave him a bottle of red liquid, telling him to pick a white rose and to dip its stalk into the liquid and the rose would turn blue. The shopkeeper did as he was told; the rose turned into a beautiful blue and the shopkeeper took it to the merchant, who at once went with it to the palace saying that he had found the blue rose.

(16)   He was ushered into the presence of the Emperor, who as soon as he saw the blue rose sent for his daughter and said to her: "This wealthy merchant has brought you what he claims to be the blue rose. Has he accomplished the quest?"

(17)   The Princess took the flower in her hands and after examining it for a moment said: "This is a white rose; its stalk has been dipped in a poisonous dye and it has turned blue. Were a butterfly to settle upon it, it would die of the potent fume. Take it back. I have no need of a dyed rose." And she returned it to the merchant with many elegantly expressed thanks.

(18)   The other ninety-eight suitors all sought in various ways for the blue rose. Some of them traveled all over the world seeking it; some of them sought the aid of wizards and astrologers, and one did not hesitate to invoke the help of the dwarfs that live underground; but all of them, whether they traveled in far countries or took counsel with wizards and demons or sat pondering in lonely places, failed to find the blue rose.

(19)   At last they all abandoned the quest except the Lord Chief Justice, who was the most skillful lawyer and statesman in the country. After thinking over the matter for several months he sent for the most famous artist in the country and said to him: "Make me a china cup. Let it be milkwhite in colour and perfect in shape, and paint on it a rose, a blue rose."

(20)   The artist made obeisance and withdrew, and worked for two months at the Lord Chief Justice's cup. In two months' time it was finished, and the world has never seen such a beautiful cup, so perfect in symmetry, so delicate in texture, and the rose on it, the blue rose, was a living flower, picked in fairyland and floating on the rare milky surface of the porcelain. When the Lord Chief Justice saw it he gasped with surprise and pleasure, for he was a great lover of porcelain, and never in his life had he seen such a piece. He said to himself, "Without doubt the blue rose is here on this cup and nowhere else."

(21)   So, after handsomely rewarding the artist, he went to the Emperor's palace and said that he had brought the blue rose. He was ushered into the Emperor's presence, who as he saw the cup sent for his daughter and said to her: "This eminent lawyer has brought you what he claims to be the blue rose. Has he accomplished the quest?"

(22)   The Princess took the bowl in her hands and after examining it for a moment said: "This bowl is the most beautiful piece of china I have ever seen. If you are kind enough to let me keep it I will put it aside until I receive the blue rose, for so beautiful is it that no other flower is worthy to be put in it except the blue rose."

(23)   The Lord Chief Justice thanked the Princess for accepting the bowl with many elegantly turned phrases, and he went away in discomfiture.

(24)   After this there was no one in the whole country who ventured on the quest of the blue rose. It happened that not long after the Lord Chief Justice's attempt a strolling minstrel visited the kingdom of the Emperor. One evening he was playing his one-stringed instrument outside a dark wall. It was a summer's evening, and the sun had sunk in a glory of dusty gold, and in the violet twilight one or two stars were twinkling like spearheads. There was an incessant noise made by the croaking of frogs and the chatter of grasshoppers. The minstrel was singing a short song over and over again to a monotonous tune. The sense of it was something like this:

"I watched beside the willow trees
    The river, as the evening fell,
The twilight came and brought no breeze,
    Nor dew, nor water for the well.

"When from the tangled banks of grass
    A bird across the water flew,
And in the river's hard grey glass
    I saw a flash of azure blue."

246

(25)   As he sang he heard a rustle on the wall, and looking up, he saw a slight figure white against the twilight, beckoning to him. He walked along under the wall until he came to a gate, and there someone was waiting for him, and he was gently led into the shadow of a dark cedar tree. In the dim twilight he saw two bright eyes looking at him, and he understood their message. In the twilight a thousand meaningless nothings were whispered in the light of the stars, and the hours fled swiftly. When the east began to grow light, the Princess (for it was she) said it was time to go.

(26)   "But," said the minstrel, "to-morrow I shall come to the palace and ask for your hand."

(27)   "Alas!" said the Princess, "I would that were possible, but my father has made a foolish condition that only he may wed me who finds the blue rose."

(28)   "That is simple," said the minstrel. "I will find it." And they said good night to each other.

(29)   The next morning the minstrel went to the palace, and on his way he picked a common white rose from a wayside garden. He was ushered into the Emperor's presence, who sent for his daughter and said to her: "This penniless minstrel has brought you what he claims to be the blue rose. Has he accomplished the quest?"

(30)   The Princess took the rose in her hands and said: "Yes, this is without doubt the blue rose."

(31)   But the Lord Chief Justice and all who were present respectfully pointed out that the rose was a common white rose and not a blue one, and the objection was with many forms and phrases conveyed to the Princess.

(32)   "I think the rose is blue," said the Princess. "Perhaps you are all colour blind."

(33)   The Emperor, with whom the decision rested, decided that if the Princess thought the rose was blue it was blue, for it was well known that her perception was more acute than that of anyone else in the kingdom.

(34)   So the minstrel married the Princess, and they settled on the sea coast in a little-seen house with a garden full of white roses, and they lived happily for ever afterwards. And the Emperor, knowing that his daughter had made a good match, died in peace.

Exercise. Refer to the story to answer each of the questions below.

a. Look at paragraph 1. To what does the author compare the Princess's eyes?

_____

b. To what does he compare the sound of her laughter?

_____

c. Look at paragraph 2. What does the expression "to win someone's hand" mean?

_____

d. In paragraph 8, the soldier receives a sapphire. How is a sapphire like a blue rose?

_____

e. Look at paragraph 12. What do we mean by the expression "It will be the means of your death"?

_____

f. Look at paragraph 13. What is the meaning of the expression "at wit's end"?

_____

g. In paragraph 20, the author compares the surface of the porcelain with milk. How are they alike?

_____

h. Look at paragraph 24. Rewrite these words in literal language: ". . . the sun had sunk in a glory of dusty gold, and in the violet twilight one or two stars were twinkling like spearheads."

_____

i. In his song, the minstrel compares what to "hard grey glass"?

_____

j. What do you think "the blue rose" is?

_____

Chapter 11
Imagery

Imagery is language that helps you form a picture of what something is like. In the comic strip below, Sally has trouble picturing rivers, mountains, and borders because she has never seen them.

PEANUTS by Charles Schulz

Writers try to help you imagine the things they are writing about by using language that appeals to your five senses and that creates vivid pictures in your mind.

Lesson 1
Recognizing Sensory Language

Sensory language contains words and phrases that appeal to one or more of the five senses. The five senses, of course, are sight, hearing, taste, smell, and touch. These words and phrases create vivid images, or word pictures in your mind.

For example, read the passage below from *Zia* by Scott O'Dell.

> After one of the big storms that come in from the islands, our shore is covered with small clams. The clams are no larger than the end of your finger and the wind spread them out on the beach so thick it's hard to walk. The clams are blue and when you look either way, up or down the beach, all you can see for leagues are these tiny blue clams. That's why we call it the Blue Beach.
>
> The great storms always come in the winter but this one came in June and the beach was covered with clams up to your ankles. Usually we raked them up, my brother and I, into baskets and took them back to the Mission. There we washed them and cooked them in a little fresh water. They made wonderful

soup, these little blue clams, and we would make a whole meal out of a bowl of soup and a handful of tortillas.

On this morning, after the storm had raged all night, we went to the beach early to gather clams. But the storm had washed up so much that we forgot the clams for a while and went running along the beach searching for other things.

The author of this passage, Scott O'Dell, uses sensory words to make you experience the beach for yourself. He appeals to your sense of sight. For example, imagine a beach covered with small blue clams "no larger than the end of your finger." O'Dell appeals to your sense of taste. Imagine a soup from these clams and eating a bowl of soup and tortillas. Since clams and tortillas have strong aromas, these details also appeal to your sense of smell. O'Dell appeals to your sense of touch. Imagine the feeling of walking on all those clam shells. Finally, O'Dell appeals to your sense of hearing. Imagine the sound of someone walking on a beach covered with clam shells.

Details that appeal to your senses create vivid impressions. In the comic strip below, Charlie Brown and Pigpen remember certain houses because of their cooking odors: garlic, spaghetti, cabbage. Charlie Brown's house, however, has hardly any memorable odors at all. It smells like an odorless TV dinner.

PEANUTS by Charles Schulz

Exercise 1. The five senses are sight, hearing, smell, taste, and touch. Read each group of items below. Then write the name of the sense to which each group appeals.

Example
spotted, streaked, glittering, shiny   *sight*

a. salty, sour, sweet, bitter   _____

b. snoring, whispering, hissing, shouting   _____

c. red, purple, blue, yellow   _____

d. smooth, rough, hot, wet   _____

e. skunk, perfume, garlic, incense   _____

Exercise 2. Column *A* contains words that appeal to your sense of touch. Column *B* contains words that describe how each item in Column *A* feels. Match each word in Column *A* with the best description of how it feels in Column *B*.

	A		B
_____	**a.** rose stems	(1)	soft, feathery
_____	**b.** rose petals	(2)	prickly
_____	**c.** winter wind	(3)	velvety
_____	**d.** pillow	(4)	stinging, biting
_____	**e.** pancake syrup	(5)	sticky

Exercise 3. Read the paragraph below from *The Thanksgiving Treasure* by Gail Rock. Then answer the questions that follow it.

We loved speeding along the back roads on our bikes, and being out in the countryside gave us a great sense of freedom. There were few houses outside of town, just acres and acres of cornfields and wheatfields and grazing cattle. There were hardly any trees, except those that farmers had planted around their houses and for windbreaks along the sides of fields, so you could see for miles. Sound seemed to carry farther out in the country too. You could hear a dog barking a mile away, or a distant train whistle, or the hum of big truck tires on another highway far to the North, and if you were lucky enough to ride past a meadowlark in the summer wheat, he would fling sweet notes right in your ear. The larks had gone South by this time of the year though, and the cold wind struck our faces as we pedaled past the brown stubble of harvested corn.

a. This paragraph appeals mainly to two of the five senses—sight and hearing. The first detail that appeals to sight is *country back roads*. How many houses are there along these back roads?

_____

b. The paragraph says that the countryside is filled with acres and acres of three things. What are these three things?

_____

c. The paragraph says that there are hardly any trees, with two exceptions. What is the first exception?

_____

d. What is the second exception?

_____

e. How does this lack of trees affect how far a person can see?

_____

f. The paragraph says, "Sound seemed to carry farther out in the country too." What can you hear from a mile away?

_____

g. The paragraph says you can hear two other distant sounds. What is the first of these?

_____

h. What is the second of these distant sounds?

_____

i. What is the last detail the paragraph mentions that appeals to your sense of hearing?

_____

j. How does the paragraph describe the sound produced by this creature?

_____

Lesson 2

Visualizing a Setting

The setting of a story is where and when it takes place. Writers help you visualize, or picture in your mind, the setting by including details that appeal to your senses.

For example, read the paragraph below from _A Swiftly Tilting Planet_ by Madeleine L'Engle.

> The big kitchen of the Murrys' house was bright and warm, curtains drawn against the dark outside, against the rain driving past the house from the northeast. Meg Murry O'Keefe had made an arrangement of chrysanthemums for the dining table, and the yellow, bronze, and pale-gold blossoms seemed to add light to the room. A delectable smell of roasting turkey came from the oven, and her mother stood by the stove, stirring the giblet gravy.

The writer of this paragraph, Madeleine L'Engle, includes details that help you feel as though you are in that kitchen. She appeals to your sense of sight. The kitchen is big and bright. Its curtains are drawn against the dark. There is an arrangement of chrysanthemums with "yellow, bronze, and pale-gold blossoms." L'Engle appeals to your sense of smell. The room is filled with the smell of the flowers and of the roasting turkey and giblet gravy. The roasting turkey and giblet gravy also appeal to your sense of taste. L'Engle appeals to

252

Name _____

your sense of hearing. There is rain driving past the house. Lastly, she appeals to your sense of touch. The room is warm.

Not all paragraphs that include sensory details appeal to all five senses. Some appeal to only one sense, or to two or three, or to four.

Exercise 1. The painting below is called *Breezing Up*. It is by the great American artist Winslow Homer. Read the list of vivid phrases below the picture. Write *Yes* in the blank by each phrase that describes the setting shown in this picture. Write *No* by each phrase that does not.

Winslow Homer: *Breezing Up*. National Gallery of Art, Washington, D.C.

a. storm clouds in the sky _____

b. alone on the vast ocean _____

c. lightning streaking the sky _____

d. strong wind in the sail _____

e. bright sun turning the ocean to gold _____

f. boy wrapped in blanket on the front of the boat _____

g. ocean smooth as glass _____

h. tasting salt spray _____

i. wooden boat with one sail _____

j. storm brewing _____

Exercise 2. Write a paragraph describing *Breezing Up*. Be sure to use vivid details that appeal to the senses. You may use phrases from Exercise 1.

_____

_____

_____

_____

_____

Exercise 3. The following paragraph from *Time Cat* by Lloyd Alexander creates a vivid impression of the sleeping quarters in a wing of the Imperial palace in ancient Japan. The details in it appeal to three of the five senses: sight, hearing, and smell. Read the paragraph carefully. Then, for each sense, list at least one detail that appeals to it.

> Later, after everyone had been properly fed, a procession of servants led Jason, Gareth, and the kittens to their sleeping quarters in another wing of the palace. There the walls were made of sliding paper screens, opened to the gentle night air. The scent of flowers filled the room; in the moonlight, across the Imperial grounds, Jason saw garden after garden and rows of blossoming cherry trees, and heard the rustle of a miniature waterfall. Throughout the gardens the breeze stirred hanging bamboo rods which gave a melodious, woodeny kind of ring. Crickets chirped in tiny wicker cages.

a. sight: _____

_____

b. hearing: _____

c. smell: _____

Lesson 3

Understanding Vivid Verbs

Verbs are the action words in sentences. For example, the words *help*, *dance*, and *run* are verbs. Some verbs are particularly vivid and sharp. They give you a clear picture of the action. For example, read the following two sentences:

The candle *shone* in the dark.
The candle *flickered* in the dark.

Both sentences contain verbs, but the verb in the second sentence creates a more vivid picture. *To flicker* means "to shine with an unsteady or wavering light."

Name _____

Exercise. The poem below, "I Speak, I Say, I Talk" by Arnold L. Shapiro, contains many vivid verbs. Read the poem. Then write the meaning of each vivid verb on the blank provided. The first one is done for you.

                    Cats purr.
                    Lions roar.
                    Owls hoot.
                    Bears snore.
                5   Crickets creak.
                    Mice squeak.
                    Sheep baa.
                    But I SPEAK!

                    Monkeys chatter.
                10 Cows moo.
                    Ducks quack.
                    Doves coo.
                    Pigs squeal.
                    Horses neigh.
                15 Chickens cluck.
                    But I SAY!

                    Flies hum.
                    Dogs growl.
                    Bats screech.
                20 Coyotes howl.
                    Frogs croak.
                    Parrots squawk.
                    Bees buzz.
                    But I TALK!

Example

purr means: ___*"To make a soft, vibrating sound"*_____

a. *roar* means: _____

b. *hoot* means: _____

c. *snore* means: _____

d. *creak* means: _____

e. *squeak* means: _____

f. *baa* means: _____

g. *chatter* means: _____

h. *moo* means: _____

i. *quack* means: _____

j. *coo* means: _____

k. *squeal* means: _____

l. *neigh* means: _____

m. *cluck* means: _____

n. *hum* means: _____

o. *growl* means: _____

p. *screech* means: _____

q. *howl* means: _____

r. *croak* means: _____

s. *squawk* means: _____

t. *buzz* means: _____

Lesson 4

Understanding Vivid Adverbs

An adverb is a word that modifies a verb, an adjective, or another adverb. An adverb answers one of the following questions: Where? When? How? How much? Vivid adverbs give you an exact picture of the way an action was done. They pack a lot of meaning. For example, read the following sentence:

> The House of Dies Drear stood *mysteriously* on the hill.

The adverb *mysteriously* tells you exactly how the house stood there. It stood there in a manner full of mystery; that is, it had an air about it of the secret or unknown.

Now read the next sentence.

> The cries of the escaped slaves echoed *plaintively* through the night.

The adverb *plaintively* tells you exactly how the cries echoed. They echoed in a manner full of sorrow and woe. They expressed all the troubles the escaped slaves had lived through.

Many adverbs end in the suffix -*ly*. Sometimes you can find the adverb as the entry word in the dictionary. Many times, though, you have to look up the adjective form, the form without the -*ly* ending. Then add the meaning "in a manner" to the adjective meaning. For example, imagine you want to look up the word *furiously* in the dictionary. First drop the -*ly* ending. Then look up the word *furious*. Add the words "in a manner" to the dictionary definition of *furious*. *Furiously* means "in a manner full of violent anger."

Name _____

Exercise 1. The House of Dies Drear had been a stop on the Underground Railroad. When Thomas Small and his family move into the house, they are caught up in a mystery that happened over 100 years ago. In the selection below, from *The House of Dies Drear* by Virginia Hamilton, Thomas falls into one of the tunnels the runaway slaves had used. Read the selection. Pay special attention to the adverbs printed in **boldface.** Then look up each of these adverbs in your dictionary and write its meaning on the blanks provided.

Thomas got to his feet and made his way down the rock stairway into darkness. At the foot of the stairs was a path with walls of dirt and rock on either side of it. The walls were so close, Thomas could touch them by extending his arms a few inches. Above his head was a low ceiling carved out of rock. Such cramped space made him uneasy. The foundation of the house had to be somewhere above the natural rock. The idea of the whole three-story house of Dies Drear pressing down on him caused him to stop a moment on the path. Since he had fallen, he hadn't had time to be afraid. He wasn't now, but he did begin to worry a little about where the path led. He thought of ghosts, and yet he did not **seriously** believe in them. "No," he told himself, "not with the flashlight. Not when I can turn back . . . when I can run."

And besides, he thought, I'm strong. I can take care of myself.

Thomas continued along the path, flickering his tiny beam of light this way and that. Pools of water stood in some places. He felt a coldness, like the stream of air that came from around the button on the oak doorframe. His shoes were soon soaked. His socks grew cold and wet, and he thought about taking them off. He could hear water running a long way off. He stopped again to listen, but he couldn't tell from what direction the sound came.

"It's just one of the springs," he said. His voice bounced off the walls **strangely.**

Better not speak. There could be tunnels leading off this one. You can't tell what might hear you in a place like this.

Thomas was scaring himself. He decided not to think again about other tunnels or ghosts. He did think for the first time of how he would get out of this tunnel. He had fallen five feet, and he wasn't sure he would be able to climb back up the crumbling brick walls. Still, the path he walked had to lead somewhere. There had to be another way out.

Thomas felt his feet begin to climb; the path was slanting up. He walked slowly on the slippery rock; then **suddenly** the path was very wide. The walls were four feet away on either side, and there were long stone slabs against each wall. Thomas sat down on one of the slabs. It was wet, but he didn't even notice.

"Why these slabs?" he asked himself. "For the slaves, hiding and running?"

He opened and closed a moist hand around the flashlight. The light beam could not keep back the dark. Thomas had a lonely feeling, the kind of feeling running slaves must have had.

And they dared not use light, he thought. How long would they have to hide down here? How could they stand it?

Thomas got up and went on. He placed one foot **carefully** in front of the other on the path, which had narrowed again. He heard the faint sound of movement somewhere. Maybe it was a voice he heard, he couldn't be sure. He swirled the light around over the damp walls, and fumbled it. The flashlight slid out of his hand. For a long moment, he caught and held it between his knees before **finally** dropping it. He bent **quickly** to pick it up and stepped down on it. Then he **accidentally** kicked it with his heel, and it went rattling somewhere over the path. It hit the wall, but it had gone out before then. Now all was very dark.

"It's not far," Thomas said. "All I have to do is feel around."

He felt around with his hands over smooth, moist rock; his hands grew cold. He felt water, and it was icy, slimy. His hands trembled, they ached, feeling in the dark, but he could not find the flashlight.

"I couldn't have kicked it far because I wasn't moving." His voice bounced in a whisper off the walls. He tried crawling backward, hoping to hit the flashlight with his heels.

"It's got to be here . . . Papa?" Thomas stood, turning toward the way he had come, the way he had been crawling backward. He didn't at all like walking in the pitch blackness of the tunnel.

"I'll go on back," he said. "I'll just walk back as quick as I can. There'll be light coming from the veranda steps. I'll climb up that wall and then I'll be out of this. I'll get Papa and we'll do it together."

He went **quickly** now, with his hands extended to keep himself from hitting the close walls. But then something happened that caused him to stop in his tracks. He stood still, with his whole body tense and alert, the way he could be when he sensed a storm before there was any sign of it in the air or sky.

Thomas had the queerest notion that he was not alone. In front of him, between him and the steps of the veranda, something waited.

"Papa?" he said. He heard something.

The sound went, "Ahhh, ahhh, ahhh." It was not moaning, nor crying. It wasn't laughter, but something forlorn and lost and old.

Thomas backed away. "No," he said. "Oh please!"

"Ahhh, ahhh," something said. It was closer to him now. Thomas could hear no footsteps on the path. He could see nothing in the darkness.

258

He opened his mouth to yell, but his voice wouldn't come. Fear rose in him; he was cold, freezing, as though he had rolled in snow.

"Papa!" he managed to say. His voice was a whisper. "Papa, come get me . . . Papa!"

"Ahhhh." Whatever it was, was quite close now. Thomas still backed away from it, then he turned around, away from the direction of the veranda. He started running up the path, with his arms outstretched in front of him. He ran and ran, his eyes wide in the darkness. At any moment, the thing would grab him and smother his face. At any time, the thing would paralyze him with cold. It would take him away. It would tie him in one of the tunnels, and no one would ever find him.

"Don't let it touch me! Don't let it catch me!"

Thomas ran smack into a wall. His arms and hands hit first; then, his head and chest. The impact jarred him from head to foot. He thought his wrists were broken, but ever so slowly, painful feeling flowed back into his hands. The ache moved **dully** up to the sockets of his shoulders. He opened and closed his hands. They hurt so much, his eyes began to tear, but he didn't seem to have broken anything.

Thomas felt **frantically** along the wall. The wall was wood. He knew the feel of it right away. It was heavy wood, perhaps oak, and it was man made, man hewn. Thomas pounded on it, hurting himself more, causing his head to spin. He kept on, because he knew he was about to be taken from behind by something ghostly and cold.

"Help me! It's going to get me!" he called. "Help me!"

Thomas heard a high, clear scream on the other side of the wall. Next came the sound of feet scurrying, and then the wall slid **silently** up.

"Thomas Small!" his mother said. "What in heaven's name do you think you are doing inside that wall!"

Directions. On the blanks provided, write the meaning of each adverb below. Use your dictionary to help you.

a. seriously: _____

b. strangely: _____

c. suddenly: _____

d. carefully: _____

e. finally: _____

f. quickly: _____

g. accidentally: _____

h. dully: _____

i. frantically: _____

j. silently: _____

Exercise 2. In *The House of Dies Drear,* Thomas became frightened when he started to imagine ghosts of slaves following him through the tunnel. Below are ten adverbs you might see in a ghost story. Look up each adverb in a dictionary. For each adverb, write a sentence using it.

a. eerily: _____

_____

b. fearfully: _____

_____

c. diabolically: _____

_____

d. soundlessly: _____

_____

e. anxiously: _____

_____

f. dreadfully: _____

_____

g. forlornly: _____

_____

h. sorrowfully: _____

_____

i. dauntlessly: _____

_____

j. apprehensively: _____

_____

Lesson 5

Understanding Modifiers

A modifier is a word or group of words that limits, or makes more definite, the meaning of another word. Modifiers add details to objects, characters, or actions in a story. Modifiers tell how, how much, which one, when, or where. They help the reader form clearer pictures of details in the story.

For example, read the paragraph below from "The Legend of Mount St. Helens" by Eric A. Kimmel.

> Three mountains overlook the majestic Columbia River as it flows to the Pacific Ocean. On the Oregon side is the massive, hump-backed silhouette of Mount Hood. Directly to the north in Washington are the craggy slopes of Mount Adams. To the west is the dazzling white cone of Mount Saint Helens. Before the coming of Lewis and Clark, the Indians of the Columbia region worshipped these mountains. According to their legends, Mount Hood and Mount Adams were brothers. The Indians called Mount Hood "Wy'east," and Mount Adams "Klickatat." Saint Helens was "Loo-Wit," and this is the story they told about her.

Look at the first sentence in the paragraph above. The word *three* is a modifier. It tells you how many mountains. The word *majestic* is a modifier. It tells you what kind of river. Look at the second sentence. The words *massive* and *hump-backed* are modifiers. They tell you what kind of silhouette. Look at the third sentence. The word *craggy* is a modifier. It tells you what kind of slopes. Look at the fourth sentence. The word *white* is a modifier. It tells you what kind of cone. The word *dazzling* is a modifier. It tells you how white.

Exercise. Continue reading this selection from "The Legend of Mount St. Helens" by Eric A. Kimmel. Pay special attention to modifiers. Then answer the questions that follow the selection.

> In the time before time, when gods walked and talked with people, the two great mountain chiefs Wy'east and Klickatat fell in love with a beautiful maiden. Each was determined to win her for his wife, so they dressed in their finest clothes to court her. Their shirts and leggings were white doeskin trimmed with ermine fur and embroidered with porcupine quills. Eagle-feather bonnets covered their heads, and snow-white moccasins were on their feet.
>
> The maiden lived in a village on the shores of Trout Lake. Klickatat came down from the north to court her; Wy'east came

up from the south. They met by the Bridge of the Gods, the great stone rainbow bridge that spanned the Columbia in ancient times. Each brother knew quite well where the other was going, and their tempers flared.

"Where did you find those rags?" Wy'east taunted Klickatat.

"From what garbage heap did you pick that shirt?" Klickatat shouted back. One insult led to another, and soon the two brothers were roaring and stamping so hard the ground shook. They threw off their beautiful white robes and painted their faces black and red—the colors of war. Their anger grew so hot they spit liquid fire. Columns of smoke poured from their mouths, blackening the sun and turning day to night. Animals and men fled from their fury. The earth trembled.

Wy'east picked up a huge stone and hurled it across the river at his brother. Klickatat picked up another and hurled it back. Soon enormous boulders were flying through the air. Some fell on land, knocking down tall trees and ripping up the soil. Others fell in the river, causing huge waves. Still others struck the Bridge of the Gods, which shuddered like a leaf in a high wind.

"Stop! This quarrel must cease! The Bridge shall be destroyed!" It was Loo-Wit who spoke. She was an old, bent woman who watched over the Bridge. She pleaded with the two brothers to come to their senses, but Wy'east and Klickatat were beyond reason. As she begged them to listen, a fiery boulder crashed into the center of the Bridge. The Bridge of the Gods collapsed, and Loo-Wit, broken and burned, fell into the river with it.

The Bridge of the Gods had been made by the Great Spirit himself at the beginning of all things. Its destruction frightened the brothers. They put off their quarrel, and each withdrew to his own place. All that remained to mark where the beautiful Bridge had stood were the rushing rapids of Celilo Falls. Clinging to a rock in the middle of the rapids was Loo-Wit, crying for help. The Great Spirit took pity on her. He pulled her from the rapids and healed her wounds with magic herbs.

"Your devotion shall be rewarded," he said to her. "Make any wish, and I shall grant it."

"O Great Spirit, there is no joy in being old. I wish to be young again," said Loo-Wit. "Give me the form of a young woman once more. That is my greatest wish."

The Great Spirit smiled on her request. He made her the youngest, most beautiful of maidens. But since Loo-Wit had only asked for the form and not the spirit of a young woman, she remained old at heart. She took no pleasure in the company of young people. Their games and dances were not for her, and she cared nothing for the handsome youths who came to court her. Though young, she found no happiness. And so she moved far away to the west, away from the other mountains. There she is to this day: the youngest and most beautiful, and yet the oldest and saddest mountain of all.

Name _____

On 27 March 1980, Mount St. Helens erupted for the first time in 122 years. Less than two months later, the top third of the mountain was blown away in a spectacular explosion of ash and steam. Her once pure white slopes are now black and scarred. Loo-Wit has become a broken old woman again.

Is this the end of the legend? Loo-Wit has spoken. Will Klickatat and Wy'east answer?

Directions. Read each sentence below. Then answer the questions. Write your answers in the blanks provided.

a. "In the time before time, when gods walked and talked with people, the two great mountain chiefs Wy'east and Klickatat fell in love with a beautiful maiden."

(1) Which word tells you what kind of mountain chiefs? _____

(2) Which word tells you what kind of maiden? _____

b. "Their shirts and leggings were white doeskin trimmed with ermine fur and embroidered with porcupine quills."

(1) Which word tells you what kind of doeskin? _____

(2) Which word tells you what kind of fur? _____

(3) Which word tells you what kind of quills? _____

c. "Eagle-feather bonnets covered their heads, and snow-white moccasins were on their feet."

(1) Which word tells you what kind of bonnets? _____

(2) Which word tells you what kind of moccasins? _____

d. "They threw off their beautiful white robes and painted their faces black and red—the colors of war."

(1) Which two words tell you what kind of robes? _____

(2) Which two words joined by the word *and* tell you how they painted their faces? _____

e. "She took no pleasure in the company of young people."

Which word tells you how much pleasure? _____

Lesson 6
Understanding Sounds That Create Vivid Impressions

Sounds can create vivid impressions. For example, the letter *s* spells two sounds. The first is /s/, which you hear in the word *see*. The second is /z/, which you hear in the word *please*. These two sounds often create an impression of suspense and mystery.

Read aloud the stanza below from "The Wreck of the *Hesperus*" by Henry Wadsworth Longfellow. Notice how many times the sounds spelled by the letter *s* are repeated.

It was the schooner *Hesperus*,
    That sailed the wintry sea;
And the skipper had taken his little daughter
    To bear him company.

Exercise. Finish reading "The Wreck of the *Hesperus*" aloud. Pay special attention to the sounds spelled by the letter *s*. Then follow the directions at the end of the poem.

It was the schooner *Hesperus*,
    That sailed the wintry sea;
And the skipper had taken his little daughter
    To bear him company.

5 Blue were her eyes as the fairy flax,
    Her cheeks like the dawn of day,
And her bosom white as the hawthorn buds
    That ope in the month of May.

The skipper he stood beside the helm,
10   His pipe was in his mouth,
And he watched how the veering flaw did blow
    The smoke now west, now south.

Then up and spake an old sailor,
    Had sailed to the Spanish Main,
15 "I pray thee, put into yonder port,
    For I fear a hurricane.

"Last night, the moon had a golden ring,
    And tonight no moon we see!"
The skipper, he blew a whiff from his pipe,
20   And a scornful laugh laughed he.

Colder and louder blew the wind,
    A gale from the northeast,
The snow fell hissing in the brine,
    And the billows frothed like yeast.

264

25 Down came the storm, and smote amain
        The vessel in its strength;
    She shuddered and paused, like a frightened steed,
        Then leaped her cable's length.

    "Come hither! come hither! my little daughter,
30   And do not tremble so;
    For I can weather the roughest gale
        That ever wind did blow."

    He wrapped her warm in his seaman's coat
        Against the stinging blast;
35 He cut a rope from a broken spar,
        And bound her to the mast.

    "O father! I hear the church bells ring;
        Oh, say, what may it be?"
    "'Tis a fog bell on a rock-bound coast!"
40   And he steered for the open sea.

    "O father! I hear the sound of guns;
        Oh, say, what may it be?"
    "Some ship in distress, that cannot live
        In such an angry sea!"

45 "O father! I see a gleaming light;
        Oh, say, what may it be?"
    But the father answered never a word,
        A frozen corpse was he.

    Lashed to the helm, and stiff and stark,
50   With his face turned to the skies,
    The lantern gleamed through the gleaming snow
        On his fixed and glassy eyes.

    Then the maiden clasped her hands and prayed
        That saved she might be;
55 And she thought of Christ, who stilled the wave
        On the Lake of Galilee.

    And fast through the midnight dark and drear,
        Through the whistling sleet and snow,
    Like a sheeted ghost, the vessel swept
60   Toward the reef of Norman's Woe.

    And ever the fitful gusts between,
        A sound came from the land;
    It was the sound of the trampling surf
        On the rocks and the hard sea sand.

65 The breakers were right beneath her bows,
        She drifted a dreary wreck,
   And a whooping billow swept the crew
        Like icicles from her deck.

   She struck where the white and fleecy waves
70   Looked soft as carded wool,
   But the cruel rocks, they gored her side
        Like the horns of an angry bull.

   Her rattling shrouds, all sheathed in ice,
        With the masts went by the board;
75 Like a vessel of glass, she stove and sank;
        Ho! Ho! the breakers roared!

   At daybreak, on the black sea beach,
        A fisherman stood aghast,
   To see the form of a maiden fair,
80   Lashed close to a drifting mast.

   The salt sea was frozen on her breast,
        The salt tears in her eyes;
   And he saw her hair, like the brown seaweed,
        On the billows fall and rise.

85 Such was the wreck of the *Hesperus*,
        In the midnight and the snow!
   Christ save us all from a death like this,
        On the reef of Norman's Woe!

Directions. Read aloud each of the words below. Decide whether the letter s spells the sound /s/ or the sound /z/. Use your dictionary to help you. Write your answers in the blanks below.

Sound		**Sound**	
a. his	_____	**f.** whistling	_____
b. sailor	_____	**g.** breakers	_____
c. hissing	_____	**h.** glass	_____
d. vessel	_____	**i.** aghast	_____
e. corpse	_____	**j.** mast	_____

Name _____

Lesson 7

Finding Imagery in Poetry

Poets use imagery to create vivid impressions. For example, read the haiku below by Sonia Sanchez.

> (for Gwen Brooks)
> woman. whose color
> of life is like the sun, whose
> laughter is prayer.

The poet creates a vivid impression of her fellow poet Gwendolyn Brooks through comparisons. She compares Gwendolyn Brooks' "color of life," or spirit, with the sun, and her laughter with prayer.

Now read the two stanzas below from "The Pit Ponies" by Leslie Norris.

> They come like the ghosts of horses, shyly,
> To this summer field, this fresh green,
> Which scares them.
>
> They have been too long in the blind mine,
> 5 Their hooves have trodden only stones
> And the soft, thick dust of fine coal,

Look carefully at the first stanza. Notice the careful choice of language in l. 1. The poet says that the pit ponies "come like the *ghosts* of horses, shyly." Why does the poet use the word *ghosts*? The ponies have lived so long in the blind mine that they are like ghosts of real ponies. They do not know how to behave in the real world. They come "shyly" and the grass "scares them."

In the second stanza, the poet creates a vivid impression of the ponies' life in the mine. Since the mine is "blind," or closed at one end, it is dark. It is filled with stones and "the soft, thick dust of fine coal." Notice the vivid verb the poet uses. He doesn't say that the ponies' hooves have *walked* on only stones. He tells you precisely how they walked: "Their hooves have *trodden* only stones."

Exercise. Finish reading "The Pit Ponies" by Leslie Norris. Then answer the questions that appear after the poem.

> They come like the ghosts of horses, shyly,
> To this summer field, this fresh green,
> Which scares them.
>
> They have been too long in the blind mine,
> 5 Their hooves have trodden only stones
> And the soft, thick dust of fine coal,

And they do not understand the grass.
For over two years their sun
Has shone from an electric bulb

10   That has never set, and their walking
Has been along the one, monotonous
Track of the piled coal trucks.

They have bunched their muscles against
The harness, and pulled and hauled.
15   But now they have come out of the underworld

And are set down in the sun and real air,
Which are strange to them. They are humble
And modest, their heads are downcast, they

Do not attempt to see very far. But one
20   Is attempting a clumsy gallop. It is
Something he could do when he was very young,

When he was a little foal a long time ago
And could run fleetly on his long foal's legs,
And almost he can remember this. And look,

25   One rolls on her back with joy in the clean grass!
And they all, awkwardly and hesitantly, like
Clumsy old men, begin to run, and the field

Is full of happy thunder. They toss their heads,
Their manes fly, they are galloping in freedom.
30   The ponies have come above ground, they are galloping!

Questions

a. While underground, why did the ponies' "sun" never set?

_____

b. Do you think the fact that their "sun" never set made the ponies' lives monotonous, or repetitious and dull? Why or why not?

_____

c. Read ll. 10-12. What else about their lives was monotonous?

_____

d. In ll. 17-18 the poet uses the modifiers *humble* and *modest* to describe the ponies when they first come above ground. What do these two modifiers mean?

_____

_____

e. Look again at ll. 19-21. One of the ponies attempts a gallop. What word describes this gallop?

_____

f. Look again at ll. 22-24. The pony almost remembers what it was like to run when he was a foal. Which adverb tells you how he ran?

_____

g. In l. 25 the poet says, "One rolls on her back with joy in the clean grass!" How does this image, or picture, make you feel?

_____

h. In ll. 26-27 the poet tells you that the ponies begin to run. How are they like "clumsy old men"?

_____

i. Look at the metaphor in ll. 27-28. Why is the field "full of happy thunder"?

_____

j. What overall feeling does this poem create?

_____

Lesson 8

Practice

Read the following selection. It is written by a woman who lost her sight and hearing when she was a child. Then complete the exercises that follow it.

from The Story of My Life
Helen Keller

I recall many incidents of the summer of 1887 that followed my soul's sudden awakening. I did nothing but explore with my hands and learn the name of every object that I touched; and the more I handled things and learned their names and uses, the more joyous and confident grew my sense of kinship with the rest of the world.

When the time of daisies and buttercups came Miss Sullivan took me by the hand across the fields, where men were preparing the earth for the seed, to the banks of the Tennessee River, and there, sitting on the warm grass, I had my first lessons in the beneficence [kindness] of nature. I learned how the sun and the rain make to grow out of the ground every tree that is pleasant to the sight and good for food, how birds build their nests and live and thrive from land to land, how the squirrel, the deer, the lion and every other creature finds food and shelter. As my knowledge of things grew I felt more and more the delight of the world I was in. Long before I learned to do a sum in arithmetic or describe the shape of the earth, Miss Sullivan had taught me to find beauty in the fragrant woods, in every blade of grass, and in the curves and dimples of my baby sister's hand. She linked my earliest thoughts with nature, and made me feel that "birds and flowers and I were happy peers."

But about this time I had an experience which taught me that nature is not always kind. One day my teacher and I were returning from a long ramble. The morning had been fine, but it was growing warm and sultry when at last we turned our faces homeward. Two or three times we stopped to rest under a tree by the wayside. Our last halt was under a wild cherry tree a short distance from the house. The shade was grateful, and the tree was so easy to climb that with my teacher's assistance I was able to scramble to a seat in the branches. It was so cool up in the tree that Miss Sullivan proposed that we have our luncheon there. I promised to keep still while she went to the house to fetch it.

Suddenly a change passed over the tree. All the sun's warmth left the air. I knew the sky was black, because all the heat, which meant light to me, had died out of the atmosphere. A strange odor came up from the earth. I knew it, it was the odor that always precedes a thunderstorm, and a nameless fear clutched at my heart. I felt absolutely alone, cut off from my friends and the firm earth. The immense, the unknown, enfolded me. I remained still and expectant; a chilling terror crept over me. I longed for my teacher's return; but above all things I wanted to get down from that tree.

There was a moment of sinister silence, then a multitudinous stirring of the leaves. A shiver ran through the tree, and the wind sent forth a blast that would have knocked me off had I not clung to the branch with might and main. The tree swayed and strained. The small twigs snapped and fell about me in showers. A wild impulse to jump seized me, but terror held me fast. I crouched down in the fork of the tree. The branches lashed about me. I felt the intermittent jarring that came now and then, as if something heavy had fallen and the shock had traveled up till it reached the limb I sat on. It worked my suspense up to the highest point, and just as I was thinking the tree and I should fall together, my teacher seized my hand and helped me down. I clung to her, trembling with joy to feel the earth under my feet once more. I had learned a new lesson— that nature "wages open war against her children, and under softest touch hides treacherous claws."

After this experience it was a long time before I climbed another tree. The mere thought filled me with terror. It was the sweet allurement of the mimosa tree in full bloom that finally overcame my fears. One beautiful spring morning when I was alone in the summerhouse, reading, I became aware of a wonderful subtle fragrance in the air. I started up and instinctively stretched out my hands. It seemed as if the spirit of spring had

270

passed through the summerhouse. "What is it?" I asked, and the next minute I recognized the odor of mimosa blossoms. I felt my way to the end of the garden, knowing that the mimosa tree was near the fence, at the turn of the path. Yes, there it was, all quivering in the warm sunshine, its blossom-laden branches almost touching the long grass. Was there ever anything so exquisitely beautiful in the world before! Its delicate blossoms shrank from the slightest earthly touch; it seemed as if a tree of paradise had been transplanted to earth. I made my way through a shower of petals to the great trunk and for one minute stood irresolute; then, putting my foot in the broad space between the forked branches, I pulled myself up into the tree. I had some difficulty in holding on, for the branches were very large and the bark hurt my hands. But I had a delicious sense that I was doing something unusual and wonderful, so I kept on climbing higher and higher, until I reached a little seat which somebody had built there so long ago that it had grown part of the tree itself. I sat there for a long, long time, feeling like a fairy on a rosy cloud. After that I spent many happy hours in my tree of paradise, thinking fair thoughts and dreaming bright dreams.

Exercise 1. Look up each of the following vivid words in your dictionary. Write their meanings on the lines provided.

a. sultry

_____

b. clutch

_____

c. enfold

_____

d. sinister

_____

e. multitudinous

_____

f. strained

_____

g. crouches

_____

h. treacherous

_____

i. exquisitely

_____

j. irresolute

_____

Exercise 2. The following details from the selection appeal to the senses of touch, hearing, smell, and sight. (Taste is not included.) In the blank to the right of each detail, write the sense to which it appeals.

a. "sitting on the warm grass" _____

b. "fragrant woods" _____

c. "curves and dimples of my baby sister's hand" _____

d. "all the sun's warmth left the air" _____

e. "it was the odor that always precedes a thunderstorm" _____

f. "the small twigs snapped" _____

g. "mimosa tree in full bloom" _____

h. "odor of mimosa blossoms" _____

i. "blossom-laden branches almost touching the long grass" _____

j. "the bark hurt my hands" _____

Name _____

Chapter 12
Flexibility and Study Skills

In this chapter you will learn several skills that will help you to read more efficiently. You will learn how to set a purpose for reading and how to adjust your speed to your purpose. In addition, you will practice several skills that will help you to be more successful with your school work.

Lesson 1
Setting a Purpose for Reading

Setting a purpose for reading helps you to read more efficiently. How do you set a purpose for reading? First, get a general idea of what the selection is about. (The title usually gives you a good idea.) Second, write down several questions to which you want to find answers in this selection. To write these questions, you might use the formula newspaper reporters use to get a story. They ask: Who? What? Where? When? Why? and How?

Exercise. Read "Clara Driscoll's Rescue Mission" to answer each of the questions below. Write your answers in the blanks provided.

a. Who was Clara Driscoll? _____

_____

b. What was her rescue mission? _____

c. Where did her rescue mission take place? _____

d. When did it take place? _____

e. Why did it take place? (What was the reason for her rescue mission?) _____

_____

_____

f. How did she go about accomplishing her rescue mission? _____

_____

g. Did she receive support from others? If so, from whom? _____

h. Did she accomplish her mission? _____

_____

i. How did the public react to Clara Driscoll after the mission was over? _____

_____

j. Why is Clara Driscoll called "the heroine of the Alamo"? _____

Clara Driscoll's Rescue Mission
V. Kathryn Oler

In January, 1901, nineteen-year-old Clara Driscoll sent an angry letter to a San Antonio, Texas newspaper. Clara was upset because the Alamo*—the site of one of the most important events in Texas history—was being used as a grocery and liquor store, and because the former Alamo church was in bad repair. Clara's letter said that Texans should be proud of the Alamo and should preserve it for future generations to see.

Born on April 2, 1881, Clara grew up on her father's large cattle ranch in southern Texas. Here she learned to ride a horse, shoot a gun, and rope cattle. She attended school in New York and Paris and traveled around the world as a young woman. But she always valued her Texas heritage, and she considered the Alamo a part of that heritage.

At the time of Clara's letter, the Alamo church was owned by the state of Texas. The long barrack building where most of the Alamo's 188 defenders were killed, belonged to the Hugo-Schmeltzer Company. This company had built the grocery and liquor store around and above the old barrack building. Other people wanted to dismantle the barrack building to build a hotel or a marketplace for selling Alamo souvenirs.

After she wrote her letter, Clara discovered a group called the Daughters of the Republic of Texas (DRT). These women had formed their group so that they could work to preserve Texas history. Clara joined the DRT and convinced the group to try to raise the $75,000 needed to buy the Alamo land.

Under Clara's leadership, the DRT tried many ways to raise the money. Dances and gift sales were held. Letters were sent to people all over the United States and Mexico asking for a fifty-cent donation plus the names of three other people who might give fifty cents. Clara wrote special letters to schoolchildren. She promised to send a story called "The Fall of the Alamo" and a photograph of the mission to any child who sent in one dollar. Clara also asked the Texas state legislature to provide money. The legislature agreed, but the governor vetoed the plan.

All the efforts of the DRT raised less than $7000. To make matters worse, a company from the East had the money to buy the land and wanted to build a hotel on it. Time was running out.

---

*Alamo. A mission that was the site of a battle between Texans and Mexican troops in 1836.

On February 10, 1904, Clara wrote a check using her own money to pay the amount needed to buy the land. She insisted that the title for the land be put in the name of the DRT and not in her own name. At 22, Clara Driscoll was a heroine. She was called the Custodian, the Savior, and the Queen of the Alamo. In time, the Texas legislature gave funds to pay back Clara, and the DRT restored the chapel and courtyard.

After the Alamo project, Clara Driscoll went on to write novels and Broadway plays and to run the large Driscoll cattle and oil empire. Upon her death in 1945, she left the Driscoll fortune as a fund to build and operate a hospital for children in Corpus Christi, Texas. The heroine of the Alamo was buried in San Antonio in the Alamo Cemetery, close to where the original Alamo heroes were killed.

Lesson 2

Reading for Specific Purposes

When you set a purpose for reading a selection, you improve your reading efficiency. Setting a purpose involves two steps. The first step is to jot down questions before you read the selection. The second step is to look for the answers to these questions while you read the selection. For example, the article on p. 276 is called "Muscles and Weight Training." One question you might ask before you read is "Why would I want to take up weight training?" Then you would read to find the answer to this question.

Exercise. Read "Muscles and Weight Training" to find answers to the following questions. Write your answers in the blanks below.

a. What do muscles do when they contract?

_____

b. What do muscles do when they relax?

_____

c. How does weight training make a person stronger?

_____

d. Will women who take up weight training develop bulging muscles?

_____

e. What is one reason why a person might want to take up weight training?

_____

_____

f. Why is it important to learn weight training from an expert or someone with experience in the field?

_____

_____

g. If you want a noticeable increase in strength, how many times a week should you exercise?

_____

h. About how long does it take before any change in strength occurs?

_____

i. During an exercise, when should you inhale?

_____

j. Why should you exercise without using weights before every weight-lifting workout?

_____

Muscles and Weight Training
Thomas A. Blumenfeld, M.D.

Muscles are responsible for all movements of the body. A muscle does its work by becoming shorter (_contracting_) and then returning to its original length (_relaxing_). Large muscles (like those in the arms or legs) are composed of thousands of long, slender cells called _muscle fibers_.

Each muscle fiber contains a thousand or more long thread-like structures called _myofibrils_. Each myofibril is made up of many small _filaments_. And each filament is made up of proteins.

Muscle fibers at the end of the muscle are attached to strong, tough, non-elastic cords called _tendons_. And the tendons are attached to bone. When the muscle contracts it causes the attached bones to move at the joint between them.

Why Weight-Train?

Why are people who are not weight-lifters interested in weight training? One of the things weight training can do is make your muscles larger. (However, because of differences in body chemistry, girls' and women's muscles just won't grow to the bulging sizes that boys' and men's muscles will.) And, as your muscles grow larger, they also become stronger.

Why do the muscles grow larger? Because weight training does several things: (1) It increases the number of myofibrils in each muscle fiber. (2) It increases the total amount of protein in

276

each muscle fiber. (3) It increases the number of tiny blood vessels in the muscle. This, in turn, means that more blood "feeds" these muscle fibers with oxygen and nutrients. (4) It increases the size and strength of the tendons and ligaments (bands of tissue) associated with the enlarging muscles.

Why does weight training work? Because when muscles are exercised or forced to work against greater-than-normal loads, the muscles become stronger.

You may want to begin a weight training program to increase your strength, endurance, athletic performance or body appearance. You should learn how to perform weight training exercises from a physical education instructor, or a coach, or from a book written by an expert on the subject.

Why?

Because if the exercises are not performed properly, muscle imbalance may develop and you could get hurt.

Some things to keep in mind when you are on a weight training program are:

(1) Exercising three times a week (Mondays, Wednesdays, and Fridays, for example) will cause a noticeable increase in strength in about four weeks.

(2) Start off slowly using small weights (a couple of pounds). With the weights you use, you should be able to properly perform a particular exercise 30 times (even if you don't regularly do each exercise that many times). This amount of weight will be a bit different for different exercises. And it will depend on the strength of the muscles used in each exercise.

(3) Do not rely on remembering how heavy the weights you used were the last time you worked out. Make a chart of the exercises you did, the amount of weight used for each exercise, and how many times you performed each one.

(4) In the first few weeks, you may feel some muscle soreness, but it will gradually disappear.

(5) When weight lifting, you should inhale during the easy part of the exercise and exhale during the strenuous part. You should not hold your breath during lifting. Why? Because it increases blood pressure and you may faint.

(6) Before every weight lifting workout, spend 10 to 15 minutes exercising without using weights—to increase the blood flow to the muscles and joints. These exercises should be calisthenics to exercise the arms, shoulders, back and legs.

Adjusting Rate to Purpose

How quickly or slowly you read a selection depends on why you are reading it. For example, if you were reading a chapter in a textbook to study for a test, you would read slowly and carefully. If you were reading a chapter to get a general idea of what it was about, you would skim it, or read it quickly. If you were reading to find a specific piece of information, you would scan the chapter, or read it quickly until you came to the information you needed. If you were reading for enjoyment, you would read at the speed you find most comfortable.

Exercise 1. Below are some purposes you might have for reading "When the Music Stops—Fix It Yourself." Write *Slowly* by each item where you would read the article slowly. Write *Skim* by each item where you would read it to get a general idea. Write *Scan* by each item where you would read it to find specific information. Write *Own Speed* by each item where you would read it simply for enjoyment.

Speed

a. At the local Y, you are taking a course in repairing stereo systems. Your teacher is giving a test tomorrow on this article.

_____

b. While you are playing your stereo system, it begins to smoke. You want to know what to do.

_____

c. Your parents have just bought a new stereo system. You see this article in a magazine and want to know whether you should cut it out and save it for future use.

_____

d. While waiting for a friend in the library, you thumb through a magazine. You see this article and think you would enjoy reading it.

_____

e. You cannot receive a particular radio station on your receiver. You want to know what to do.

_____

When the Music Stops—
Fix It Yourself
Ken Fulton

Your stereo system will probably function for years without a problem, but eventually it *will* fail. When it does, fight the urge to bundle the whole system off to a repairman. If the trouble is due to dirt, a loose connection, or something overlooked, you can fix the problem yourself.

Keep a few simple items to help in your work: a spare set of speaker cables, a small mirror, cotton-tipped swabs, and isopropyl alcohol.

Before troubleshooting, remember that if any piece of your equipment begins to smoke, crackle, or pop, or if you smell

Name _____

something burning, *unplug it immediately.* Whether you've done *anything* or not, don't just turn it off, *pull the plugs.*

And when switching wires for tests, unplug the system first. Then plug it in again after the switch is made.

A system breakdown will happen either slowly over time, or abruptly. If it is abrupt, ask yourself: What did I do last? What might someone else have done? For example: Did someone change a fuse and forget to turn the current back on? Did someone turn off a wall switch that is "always" on? Has someone pushed a button or flicked a switch from its normal position?

Sometimes a signal is lost because controls and switches have not been moved for long periods of time. Avoid this by occasionally rotating all switches and controls through all positions, whether you normally use them or not. This includes levers and pushbuttons.

If most of your system is working, zero in on the trouble by determining if the problem appears on all the amplifier (or receiver) functions—tuner, turntable, tape deck. If the problem is not in all the amplifier functions, then it is likely in an individual component.

When the problem seems to be in only one channel of a component, switch that component's left and right shielded cables *at the amplifier.* (In a receiver, there are no tuner-to-amp cables.) If the trouble changes channels, replace the cable. If the problem remains on the same channel, then that component will probably need service.

For poor sound from the phonograph, check first for dirt on the stylus. Next check the connections of the cartridge in the tone arm, using a small mirror to peek up underneath.

You should not try to fix the motor or changer mechanism of a turntable that doesn't run, or operates erratically.

If you've narrowed the trouble to the tape deck, demagnetize the tape heads and clean them with a special cleaning solvent or ordinary isopropyl alcohol. Do not use rubbing alcohol. Also clean the rubber roller that presses the tape against the tape heads.

If you have trouble receiving a particular radio station on your tuner (receiver), check other stations. If nearly all the others are O.K., then the trouble may be with the antenna. Check the antenna connections and adjust the antenna's reception direction.

When only one station is bad, the fault may be with the broadcaster. But if your trouble extends over most of the dial, you need professional help.

Problems occurring in all the component functions mean the fault is probably in the amplifier (or receiver), or the speakers.

If you have noise, distortion, or silence in one speaker, switch the cables from left to right speaker *at the speakers* (if possible). If the problem doesn't move to the other loudspeaker, then that speaker is the cause. If the trouble moves, then you have an amplifier or speaker-cable problem. So, interchange the speaker connections *at the amplifier*, thus returning the speaker hookup to the original left-right setup. If the trouble stays in the same speaker this time, then replace your cable. If the trouble moves again, the problem is in the amplifier, and you'll have to have it serviced.

Exercise 2. Now read "When the Music Stops—Fix It Yourself" by Ken Fulton for enjoyment. Did you or did you not enjoy it? Why? Write two or three sentences explaining your answer.

_____

_____

_____

_____

_____

_____

Lesson 4

Scanning

Scanning is reading to find specific facts or details. When you scan, you sweep your eyes over the page until you find the specific piece of information you want. You do not read any of the other information. For example, the article on p. 281 is called "Douglas Ewart Carves His Own Special Style." Suppose you want to find out what instrument Douglas Ewart plays. You would sweep your eyes quickly over the page until you found this information. You would ignore all the other information.

Here are some tips for scanning.

1. Before you start scanning, decide which facts or details you want to find.
2. Start looking for the information you think would be at the beginning of the selection. (Experience will help you become expert at this.)
3. Run your finger quickly across and down the page. Search for key words for the information you want; for example, people's names or place names (which begin with capital letters) and numerals.
4. When you find the information you are looking for, stop and write it down. If you happen to see some information you will need later, write this down, too.

Name _____

Exercise. Scan "Douglas Ewart Carves His Own Special Style" by Mary Lewis to find the following information. Write your answers in the blanks below.

a. What are four categories of music?

_____

b. How old was Douglas Ewart when this article was written?

_____

c. What instruments does Douglas Ewart play?

_____

d. Where was Douglas Ewart born?

_____

e. On Jamaica what instrument did Ewart learn to love?

_____

f. What two American musicians influenced him when he was young?

_____

g. When Douglas Ewart moved to the United States, in what city did he take music lessons?

_____

h. When was the Association for the Advancement of Creative Musicians formed?

_____

i. Who are two other members of the AACM?

_____

j. What material does Douglas Ewart most often use to make flutes?

_____

Douglas Ewart Carves His Own Special Style
Mary Lewis

The world of music contains a rainbow of styles. Jazz, rock, blues, and classical music are just a few of the **categories** familiar today. Each **category** is known for a certain musical form, yet each is supported by the places a musician plays, the radio stations playing the music, and even by the way a musician dresses when he or she performs.

This rainbow of musical **categories** can sometimes cause problems for a musician. For example, it's nice to be known as the "King of the Blues," but what if the blues "King" wants to play punk rock? For one thing, he will run the risk of losing his fans, because most people enjoy only one or two styles of music and refuse to listen to any other kind. Record companies often won't allow a change, either; the people in charge of these companies are worried about record sales, not necessarily whether a musician should experiment with a variety of musical forms. It's not often that a musician or singer manages to successfully mix different types of music with a positive response from fans.

Some musicians refuse to be placed within a musical **category.** While listening to their music, it would be hard to attach labels such as "jazz" or "classical" alongside their tunes. Even words like "different" or "unusual" don't really describe anything musically. What is unusual about these musicians, is the fact that some of them are able to receive high praise from critics and still gain a faithful audience. They may not be millionaires or get spots on a list of top selling records, yet they are success stories.

One such story belongs to musician Douglas Ewart. At age 34, Douglas has recorded several albums, played flute and other woodwind instruments while touring Europe, received praise from music experts, and has gained fans worldwide. Yet his success hasn't come in the usual ways. You aren't likely to hear his music played on your favorite radio station, nor do you see his albums displayed at the front of popular record stores. This is partly because of Douglas' music; his songs have been sometimes described as "jazz," but Douglas says that his music has no **category.**

Douglas' musical direction today stems, of course, from his past. Born in Jamaica, Douglas was strongly affected by the neighboring Rastafarians. He learned about great Blacks such as Marcus Garvey and Jomo Kenyatta from Rastafarians, and he also learned to love the steel drum sounds many Rastafarians played. But his real musical enjoyment came through a relative who was always getting American jazz records and playing the songs of Dizzy Gillespie and Charles Mingus. When Douglas was 17, his family moved to the United States; Douglas came with a growing interest in becoming a musician.

Four years later, Douglas began taking music classes in his new hometown, Chicago. Douglas didn't attend the usual kind of music school—he wanted to grow and experiment with different types of musical sounds and he'd heard just the kind of music he liked from a group called the Association for the Advancement of Creative Musicians (AACM). AACM was formed in 1965, and although the group was just two years old, the AACM members had started a school as a way of helping other young musicians gain important skills. Douglas learned to play the flute and saxophone as well as he learned to compose music, a skill that gives Douglas double strength as a musician. Once he completed all the classes at the AACM school, Douglas not only became an admired flute player

282

among AACM members, he also had the added skill of being able to write music.

Because AACM suited Douglas' interest in constant growth and experimentation in music, he became an active member. Fellow members, Anthony Braxton and George Lewis, began hiring Douglas to join their recordings and concerts, and sometimes Douglas wrote music for them. By age 25, Douglas was happily headed down a musical road to success.

Perhaps because of his interest in tinkering with music, Douglas began making his flutes while still attending the AACM school. As a child growing up in Jamaica, Douglas had carved many a kite or spinning top from the wild bamboo growing nearby. While a music student, Douglas took a piece of bamboo from his parents' rug and carved his first flute. Today, Douglas makes most of the flutes he plays, and he usually makes his flutes from bamboo since this material is naturally hollow and can be easily carved to give a melodious sound. Always interested in experimenting, Douglas sometimes makes flutes from other materials such as wood, plastic, or metal. He then carefully studies the different sounds each kind of flute gives to come up with a unique sound all his own.

Douglas is now head of AACM and as chairperson, he spends a lot of his time taking care of the group's business: organizing concerts, gathering members for meetings, keeping the school running smoothly, and giving advice to younger members. In addition to his own writing and performing, Douglas the craftsman finds time to enjoy yet another hobby: making leather goods, a craft Douglas began in 1974 when he decided to make a leather harness to hold his sax while he plays. Douglas has since displayed his leather bags, wallets, and address books at many art fairs in Chicago.

Labels don't stick easily to Douglas Ewart. He is, of course, a musician, and his specialty is the four flutes he loves to play: the nay (say: Naah), originally from North Africa; the shakuhachi (say: SHAY cu hatch CHEE), originally from Japan; the panpipes, originally from Greece; and the more commonly used transverse flute. He is a craftsman who spends and enjoys many hours making flutes and leather goods. While it might be difficult to place Douglas' music in a **category** usually named, two words come easily to mind that best describe this man: change and growth.

Lesson 5

Skimming

Skimming is reading quickly to get a general idea of what a selection is about. Skimming gives you a quick overview of the contents.

A good technique for skimming is to know first of all why you are skimming. For example, do you simply want to find out whether you would like to read this article slowly and carefully later, or do you want to get a general idea about the topic of the article? Once you know your purpose, look at the title of the article. Then read the first and last paragraphs of the article. Next, run your finger down the middle of the page, letting your eyes search the lines of print quickly and letting your mind register key words and impressions. Finally, decide whether you have accomplished your purpose. If you haven't, repeat the process.

Henry Moore: *Reclining Figure*, 1936. Wakefield Art Gallery and Museums

284

Exercise. Skim "Henry Moore: A Great Sculptor" to get a general idea of its contents. Then decide which of the statements below are true and which are false. In the blanks at the right, put *T* by each statement that is true and *F* by each statement that is false.

a. Henry Moore is considered one of England's greatest sculptors. _____

b. The sculpture called *Reclining Figure, 1936*, is very small. _____

c. Henry Moore wants his works to look exactly like the people you see every day. _____

d. Henry Moore mostly makes sculptures of the human figure. _____

e. Henry Moore didn't decide to become a sculptor until he was thirty-five years old. _____

f. Henry Moore enjoyed teaching more than sculpting. _____

g. Although Henry Moore studied ancient art from Greece and Rome, he was more interested in primitive art. _____

h. When Henry Moore began his career as a sculptor, he didn't have to worry about money. _____

i. Carving is a very easy task. _____

j. Henry Moore stopped sculpting when he turned sixty-five. _____

Henry Moore: A Great Sculptor
Joan J. Gazdik

Does the sculpture on page 284 look like a piece of wood eaten away by wind and water? Does it remind you of something to crawl through at the playground? Look again. There are head and shoulders, elbows and arms, and legs and feet. It's a sculpture of a human figure carved by England's greatest sculptor, Henry Moore.

This sculpture is called *Reclining Figure, 1936*. It is carved from a giant piece of elm tree and is nearly seven feet long. The surface is rounded and smooth. If you are close to it, it doesn't look like much. As you slowly walk back from it, you can begin to see a person. From every side it looks a little bit different. You may even get the feeling that there is something inside the wood that wants to burst out.

Henry Moore didn't want his sculptures to look like the people you see every day. This is something from Moore's imagination—something like a dream. Every person who looks at it sees it a little differently. "You don't need to represent the features of a face to suggest the human qualities that are special to a particular person," Moore said. "If you see a friend in the distance, you don't recognize him by the color of his eyes but by the total effect made by his figure."

Most of Moore's work is on the same subject—the human figure. Yet every time he does one, it turns out to be different. Some of the figures are lying down. Some are propped up on an elbow. A few are standing. Many of them are even in two separate pieces. They all seem to have a special quality that tells us they are by Henry Moore.

He doesn't do the same thing over and over because he has run out of ideas. He is trying to explore different ways of looking at something, each time challenging our imaginations to keep up with him. He thinks that every time you look at one of his sculptures, you should see something that you missed before.

Henry decided he wanted to be a sculptor when he was eleven years old and heard a story in Sunday school about Michelangelo. From then on he knew what he would do. Nothing could stop him. His father, who worked in mines all his life, wanted his seven children to have an easier life than he had. He wanted Henry to become a teacher before becoming an artist, just to have something to fall back on.

Moore was never very happy with teaching and was delighted when he received a scholarship to the Royal College of Art. He was a hard-working student. At the college, students studied ancient art from Greece and Rome. Henry preferred another style of art. He spent every Wednesday and Sunday afternoon studying primitive art at the British Museum. He liked the way it looked—blocky and simple. He would go to the bookshops and stay for hours looking through many books on early Mexican art. He didn't have enough money to buy them, but after looking at the same book over and over for a month, he'd know it so well that he didn't have to.

He had ideas for big sculptures, but large pieces of stone and wood were expensive. Because Henry and his wife, Irina, didn't have much money and Henry needed to sell as many sculptures as he could, he tried to make thirty small sculptures a year. Sometimes he'd just begin carving with no special idea in mind. Slowly, the wood or stone would begin to look like something to him and he'd work at getting the piece the way he wanted it.

As Moore grew older, it seemed as if his sculptures got bigger. Many are so large that they have been placed in the countryside, right in the middle of hills or valleys. Some sculptures are in front of buildings in New York and London.

Once someone asked Moore how he got ideas for his work. "I really don't know," he replied. "Sometimes I may scribble some doodles . . . then with those sketches I sit down and something begins."

Often the inspiration comes from things he's found. Shells, pebbles, bones, and animal skulls cover his studio. He likes the shapes of these things. His tiny sculptures made from plaster, called *maquettes*, look very much like these natural things. Moore does a small sculpture, not much bigger than a person's hand, as a practice piece. Then he turns it over and over in his

hands, all the while thinking of it as the large sculpture he intends it to become.

Carving is not easy. It takes skill and strong muscles. Once you break off a piece of wood or stone, it can never be replaced. One slip of the hand could ruin the whole idea. "If you're going to shape a piece into a sculpture, you must handle a hammer and chisel; you must be able to do it without knocking your hand," said Moore. He sometimes crawls over his sculptures, slowly hammering away at them until he is satisfied.

At the age of eighty-two, he spends his days at his country home not far from London making huge objects in stone, wood, and bronze. He once said that such great artists as Michelangelo and Rembrandt were better at the end of their careers than at the beginning. Someday people will probably add, "and don't forget Henry Moore."

Lesson 6

Following Directions

Directions are instructions for how to do something. Directions may be spoken or written. When directions are spoken, you must listen carefully. When directions are written, you must read carefully.

For example, here is a page from a student's book.

MATCH THEM UP!

Below are columns of opposites. Match the pairs. Write the letter from the right-hand column in the blank by the number it matches in the left-hand column.

_____ **1.** button   **a.** disappear
_____ **2.** appear   **b.** unhappy
_____ **3.** happy   **c.** unbutton
_____ **4.** obey   **d.** antiaircraft
_____ **5.** aircraft   **e.** disobey

This student did not read the directions carefully. The student drew lines to show which items match. The directions say to write the letter from the right-hand column in the blank by the number it matches in the left-hand column. If a teacher were using a grid, a piece of paper that covers everything but the answers, the teacher would think that the student hadn't filled in the answers. The student would get a zero even though the student knew all the answers.

Now look at the comic strip below. Marcie tries to give Patti Cake directions. (Notice that Marcie calls everyone, including Patti Cake, Sir.)

PEANUTS by Charles Schulz

Patti Cake didn't understand Marcie's directions. But she went ahead and tried to follow them, even though she thought the directions didn't make sense. If you don't understand the directions, ask questions.

Exercise. The selection below gives you directions for making an equatorial sundial. Read this selection carefully. Then read the directions that follow the selection.

How to Make an Equatorial Sundial
Marne Wilkins

Materials needed: board for the dial surface about 12 inches by 12 inches, pencil and string or drawing compass, broom handle or spike, protractor, road maps, level.

While sundials are not the very best method for telling time, they can teach us many things—not only about time, but also about how people can use their own ability to observe and see their world. For example, in order to make a sundial, the direction of north has to be found.

Can you imagine how early man found north in the daytime without a compass? One way to do this is to measure the shadows cast by the sun. Use a level surface and draw three circles on it, one inside the other, all having the same midpoint.

At the center mount a perfectly vertical upright, such as a tall spike or a cut-off broom handle. The shadows that the vertical makes can be used to measure both noon and north.

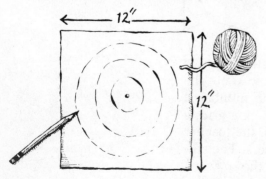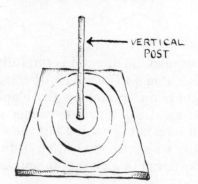

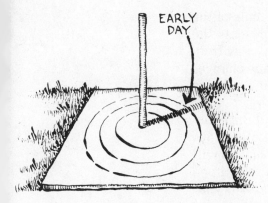

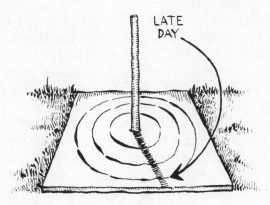

Early on a sunny morning, mark the place where the shadow of the upright stick crosses the biggest circle. Later, on the same day, watch and mark where the shadow falls across the circle in the late afternoon. Make a straight line connecting these two points.

Repeat the same process for the next two days on the two inner circles. Do this at the same times each day. Mark the center on each of the three connecting lines and draw a line along those three center points. They will line up perfectly if the vertical is true. This line should point to north and mark noon solar time.

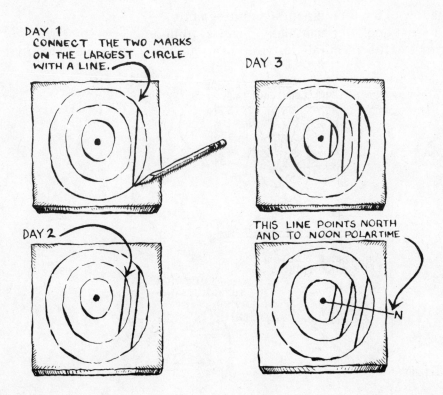

With the help of a watch, you can mark similar shadow points every 15 minutes. Or you may complete your sundial by using the degrees of latitude for your location and a protractor to measure them on your dial.

The latitude is important for measuring by the sun because our earth tips a little.

The *vertical* of your dial represents the tipping angle of the earth or *axis*. The level surface the dial is on represents the *plane* of the earth's surface. As such a plane moves away from the north or south poles toward the equator that plane changes its angle in relation to the equator from parallel at the poles to perpendicular at the equator itself.

If you are somewhere between the north pole and the equator, like I am, you must find out where! And that is called your angle of latitude. If you get out a road map of your area, you will find degrees (of angles) of latitude on the side edges of it, so check to see where your location is on the map, and run your finger across to the side margin and find the place that your degree of latitude is written. Subtract that degree from 90 degrees (the vertical degree the equator represents to the axis).

MAP OF THE
COUNTRY

YOUR
TOWN

Now, keeping the shadow of the broom handle pointing north, tilt the dial surface to that angle (or that many degrees) from horizontal and your dial will be accurate for your location.

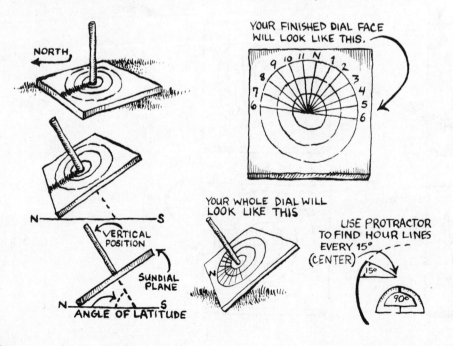

NORTH

N —————— S

VERTICAL
POSITION

SUNDIAL
PLANE

N —————— S
ANGLE OF LATITUDE

YOUR FINISHED DIAL FACE
WILL LOOK LIKE THIS.

YOUR WHOLE DIAL WILL
LOOK LIKE THIS

USE PROTRACTOR
TO FIND HOUR LINES
EVERY 15°
(CENTER)

15°

90°

290

Name _____

Of course there are many other ways to make sundials and through the years when they were used, they became mathematical feats. The same is true of hourglasses and water clocks. The basic principles were fairly obvious to any person who could observe, but the superb and really intricate refinements people made in time pieces, especially for royalty, were amazing.

A little pocket sundial, called a journey ring, was built and can still be purchased for use today. It can only have come about because people paid attention to the sun all year, and many people made many corrections. Like the spinning wheel, the real reason we gave up the old style ways was for speed and convenience, not because the old way was not good.

Where I live in the mountains, when someone asks how many miles it is to a distant place, we are apt to answer in hours instead of miles because that is really what matters here. Sometimes, no matter how convenient our new tools are, it is good to be in touch with nature's place in our plans: in this case, range after range of mountains.

An equatorial sundial can demonstrate well how our tipping earth is in very special relation and balance with our sun. Perhaps as you learn about that relationship, you will help us all to learn how we can find even more help from the sun in the future.

Directions. If the directions in the statement are correct, write C in the blank at the right. If the directions are wrong, write W in the blank at the right.

a. Draw three circles on a level surface.   _____

b. These circles should be one inside the other.   _____

c. Mount a horizontal pole in the middle of the circles.   _____

d. On a cloudy morning, mark the place where the shadow of the pole crosses the largest circle.   _____

e. Next, mark where the shadow crosses the largest circle in the late afternoon.   _____

f. Connect these marks.   _____

g. Repeat this procedure the next day, but draw your marks on the second largest circle.   _____

h. On the third day, draw your marks on the outside circle.   _____

i. Draw the line from the pole through the midpoint, or middle, of the three lines you have drawn.   _____

j. Mark shadow points every twenty minutes.   _____

Lesson 7

Taking Notes

When you take notes, you select important facts from what you read or hear and write these facts down. Taking notes has two advantages. First, the act of writing something down helps you to remember the information. Second, the notes themselves give you something to refer to, or study from, later.

Here are a few tips for taking notes from written material.

1. First skim the selection to get a general idea of what it is about.
2. Try to take notes in your own words. This takes practice. It helps to pretend that you are telling the facts to your best friend over the phone.
3. If you copy the exact words from the book, put quotation marks around them.
4. Keep a record of the source from which you are taking your notes.
5. After you read each paragraph, write a sentence summarizing the information in it. (When you summarize, you present all the information in a concise form.)

Exercise 1. Here is an article on "How Dictionaries Are Made," by S.I. Hayakawa. First skim the article. Then read each paragraph carefully. In the blank next to each paragraph, write a sentence summarizing it.

Summary Statement

(a) It is widely believed that every word has a correct meaning, that we learn these meanings principally from teachers and grammarians (except that most of the time we don't bother to, so that we ordinarily speak "sloppy English"), and that dictionaries and grammars are the supreme authority in matters of meaning and usage. Few people ask by what authority the writers of dictionaries and grammars say what they say. I once got into a dispute with an Englishwoman over the pronunciation of a word and offered to look it up in the dictionary. The English-woman said firmly, "What for? I am English. I was born and brought up in England. The way I speak *is* English." Such self-assurance about one's own language is not uncommon among the English. In the United States, however, anyone who is willing to quarrel with the dictionary is regarded as either eccentric [odd] or mad.

a. _____
_____
_____
_____
_____
_____
_____
_____
_____
_____
_____
_____
_____
_____

(b)   Let us see how dictionaries are made and how the editors arrive at definitions. What follows applies, incidentally, only to those dictionary offices where firsthand, original research goes on—not those in which editors simply copy existing dictionaries. The task of writing a dictionary begins with reading vast amounts of the literature of the period or subject that the dictionary is to cover. As the editors read, they copy on cards every interesting or rare word, every unusual or peculiar occurrence of a common word, a large number of common words in their ordinary uses, and also the sentences in which each of these words appears, thus:

> pail
> The dairy *pails* bring home increase of milk
> > Keats, *Endymion*
> > I, 44-45

b. _____

_____

_____

_____

_____

_____

_____

(c)   That is to say, the context of each word is collected, along with the word itself. For a really big job of dictionary writing, such as the *Oxford English Dictionary* (usually bound in about twenty-five volumes), millions of such cards are collected, and the task of editing occupies decades. As the cards are collected, they are alphabetized and sorted. When the sorting is completed, there will be for each word anywhere from two or three to several hundred illustrative quotations, each on its card.

c. _____

_____

_____

_____

_____

(d)   To define a word, then, the dictionary editor places before him the stack of cards illustrating that word; each of the cards represents an actual use of the word by a writer of some literary or historical importance. He reads the cards carefully, discards some, rereads the rest, and divides up the stack according to what he thinks are the several senses of the word. Finally, he writes his definitions, following the hard-and-fast rule that each definition *must* be based on what the quotations in front of him reveal about the meaning of the word. The editor cannot be influenced by what *he* thinks a given word *ought* to mean. He must work according to the cards or not at all.

d. _____

_____

_____

_____

(e) The writing of a dictionary, therefore, is not a task of setting up authoritative statements about the "true meanings" of words, but a task of *recording*, to the best of one's ability, what various words *have meant* to authors in the distant or immediate past. *The writer of a dictionary is a historian, not a lawgiver.* If, for example, we had been writing a dictionary in 1890, or even as late as 1919, we could have said that the word *broadcast* means "to scatter" (seed, for example), but we could not have decreed [ordered] that from 1921 on, the most common meaning of the word should become "to disseminate audible messages, etc., by radio transmission." To regard the dictionary as an "authority," therefore, is to credit the dictionary writer with gifts of prophecy which neither he nor anyone else possesses. In choosing our words when we speak or write, we can be *guided* by the historical record afforded [given] us by the dictionary, but we cannot be *bound* by it, because new situations, new experiences, new inventions, new feelings are always compelling us to give new uses to old words. Looking under a *hood*, we should ordinarily have found, five hundred years ago, a monk; today, we find a motorcar engine.

e. _____
_____
_____
_____
_____

(from *Language in Thought and Action*, S.I. Hayakawa, © 1972, Harcourt Brace Jovanovich)

Exercise 2. It is important to record the source of your notes. The source is where the information came from. Refer to the article in Exercise 1 to answer the questions below. Write your answers in the blanks provided.

a. What is the title of the article?

_____

b. Who wrote this article?

_____

c. What book did it come from?

_____

d. When was this book copyrighted? (You will find this information next to the symbol ©.)

_____

e. What is the name of the publisher of this book?

_____

Name _____

Lesson 8

Outlining

Outlining helps you to remember the information in a selection. Outlining is organizing a selection so that important information stands out from lesser details.

You can divide most selections containing factual information into several major parts or topics; for example, "Sleeping Bag." You can further divide these major topics into subtopics. For example, under the topic "Sleeping Bag" you might have the subtopic "Construction." Then, under the subtopic, you can list specific information found in this part.

The idea of outlining is to divide and organize. First, divide the article into major topics. Then, divide those topics into subtopics. Indicate the major topics by Roman numerals (I, II, III). Indicate the subtopics by capital letters (A, B, C). Indicate the divisions of the subtopics by Arabic numerals (1, 2, 3).

A typical outline looks like this:

I. First topic

  A. Subtopic
  B. Subtopic

    1. Detail
    2. Detail
    3. Detail
II. Second topic
  A. Subtopic
  B. Subtopic
III. Third topic
  A. Subtopic
    1. Detail
    2. Detail
  B. Subtopic
  C. Subtopic

Notice these features:

I, II, III, etc. These Roman numerals show you the main headings.

A, B, C, etc., indented. These capitals show you the less important ideas.

1, 2, 3, etc., indented again. These Arabic numerals list the details.

There are no complete sentences.

There will be an order to these parts. For example, biography, history, and fiction are usually told in time order—one thing happening after another.

Directions. Read the items in the box below. Then use these items to fill in the outline skeleton that follows the box.

Shape or size   Edge-stabilized
Comfort   Roominess
Down   Construction
Cotton   Tent
Double-quilted   Single wall

Camping Equipment

I. Sleeping bag
   A. Type and amount of insulation

      1. _____
      2. Synthetic

   B. _____

      1. Close fitting with hood

      2. Not much larger than user

   C. _____

      1. Baffled

      2. _____

      3. _____

II. *Tent* _____

   A. Type

      1. _____

      2. Nylon

   B. Construction

      1. _____

      2. Double wall

   C. Ease of pitching

III. Pack

   A. _____

   B. _____

   C. Durability (lasting quality)

Lesson 9

Understanding the Parts of a Book

Books contain two sections that you will find helpful. These sections are the frontmatter and the backmatter.

The frontmatter contains the *title page*, the *copyright page*, a *preface* or *foreword*, and the *table of contents*. The *title page* tells you the title of the book, the author, the publisher, and the place of publication. The *copyright page* appears on the reverse side of the title page. It tells when the book was copyrighted and by whom. If there are any *acknowledgments*, credit for material used from other books, these also would appear on the copyright page. The *preface* or *foreword* is a note to the reader by the author, editor, or another involved person. The *table of contents* lists the titles of each chapter and the page where each chapter begins. Often it also lists major sections within each chapter and the page where each section begins. If the book is divided into units or parts, the titles of these are listed too.

For example, look at the following section from a table of contents of *Warriner's English Grammar and Composition: First Course*.

Contents

Part One of the book is called *Grammar*. The title of the first chapter in Part One is *The Sentence*. Chapter 1 begins on page 3. There are thirteen sections in Chapter 1. The section called *Compound Verbs* begins on page 22.

The backmatter may include a *glossary*, a *bibliography*, and an *index*. The *glossary* is a dictionary of words in the book that the reader may not know. The *bibliography* is a list of other books about the topic that the reader might want to read. The *index* is an alphabetical listing of topics and subtopics and the pages on which they appear.

For example, look at part of the index from *Warriner's English Grammar and Composition: First Course.*

Information about the topic *Base of sentence* can be found on pages 98 and 101. The topic *Be* is divided into three subtopics. Information about the subtopic *as helping verb* can be found on page 59. Information about the topic *Biographical dictionaries* can be found on page 398.

Exercise 1. Part of the table of contents from *American History* by John A. Garraty is shown below. Study this table of contents. Then answer the questions that appear after it. Write your answers in the blanks provided.

CONTENTS

a. What is the title of Unit One?

_____

b. What is the title of Chapter 1 in Unit One?

_____

c. On what page does this chapter begin?

_____

d. In Chapter 1, on what page does the section _The Great Migration_ begin?

_____

e. In Chapter 1, on what page does the section _The Age of Discovery_ begin?

_____

f. What section begins on page 30?

_____

g. What is the title of Chapter 2?

_____

h. On what page does Chapter 2 begin?

_____

i. In Chapter 2, on what page does the section _False Starts in America_ begin?

_____

j. What section begins on page 45?

_____

Exercise 2. The section of the index below is from the book *General Mathematics* by William Gerardi, Wilmer L. Jones, and Thomas R. Foster. Study this index. Then answer the questions that appear after it. Write your answers in the blanks provided.

INDEX

Boldfaced numerals indicate the pages that
contain formal or informal definitions.

a. Look at the topic *Addition*. On what pages would you find information about addition of decimals?

_____

b. On what pages would you find information on addition of whole numbers?

_____

c. Look at the topic *Angles*. On what pages would you find information on measuring angles?

_____

d. On what page would you find information on right angles?

_____

e. Look at the topic *Applications*. On what page would you find information on addition and subtraction of fractions?

_____

f. On what page would you find information on using probability?

_____

g. Look at the topic *Area*. On what pages would you find information on the area of a circle?

_____

h. On what pages would you find information on the surface area of a rectangular prism?

_____

i. On what page would you find information about the topic *Automobile Repair*?

_____

j. On what page would you find information on the topic *Average*?

_____

Lesson 10

Using Reference Books

There are many kinds of reference books. Each kind contains different information. For example, if you want to find out how to spell *soccer*, you would look in a dictionary. If you wanted to know who invented soccer, you would go to an encyclopedia.

Here are descriptions of four main kinds of reference books.

Reference	What is in it?	Other facts
Almanac	Records, lists of facts like capitals, Presidents, and sports records.	New editions come out every year so the facts are up-to-date.
Atlas	Maps, tables, and charts.	
Dictionary	Words—their meanings, spellings, and pronunciations.	Some dictionaries also have the origins of words and place names. Special dictionaries contain words on only one subject, like sports.
Encyclopedia	Detailed information on a huge range of subjects. May be one book or a set of books.	Some encyclopedias cover only one subject, like sports or science.

Exercise 1. Use the table above to help you decide which kind of reference book would give the best and quickest answer to each question below. For example, you could find the spelling of *soccer* in an encyclopedia or an almanac. Using an almanac, though, would take longer than using a dictionary. Write the word *almanac, atlas, dictionary,* or *encyclopedia* in the blank next to the question.

a. How many people live in Australia? _____

b. How far is China from Australia? _____

c. When did the California Gold Rush occur? _____

d. How do you pronounce *tetrahedral*? _____

e. When did dinosaurs die out, or become extinct? _____

f. Who was Archimedes? _____

g. From what language did the word *macaroni* come into English? _____

h. Where is Viet Nam in relation to China? _____

i. What is the population of the United States? _____

j. What are five types of wind instruments? _____

Exercise 2. A set of encyclopedias sits on the shelf in alphabetical order. However, the set below got mixed up. It must be rearranged. In the circles on the spines below, write the numbers from 1-10 to show the correct alphabetical order.

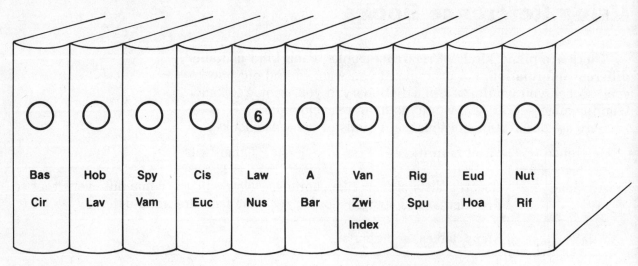

Bas	Hob	Spy	Cis	Law	A	Van	Rig	Eud	Nut
Cir	Lav	Vam	Euc	Nus	Bar	Zwi	Spu	Hoa	Rif
						Index			

(circle 5th from left shows **6**)

Exercise 3. Below is a list of writing topics. The key word in each topic is *italicized*. It is the word you would look up in the encyclopedia. Refer to the set of encyclopedias in Exercise 2. In the blanks at the right, put the number on the spine of the volume in which you would find the information.

a. A Short History of *Circuses* _____

b. The Truth About *Wolves* _____

c. How *Earthworms* Improve the Soil _____

d. How to Use an *Abacus* _____

e. The Invention of the *Telephone* _____

f. The Great White *Shark* _____

g. How *Lava* Is Formed _____

h. Poisonous *Mushrooms* _____

i. The Early Settlers of *Rhode Island* _____

j. *Christmas* Customs in the United States and Europe _____